UNDER BRIGGFLATTS

UNDER BRIGGFLATTS

A History of
Poetry in Great Britain
1960-1988

DONALD DAVIE

The University of Chicago Press

The University of Chicago Press, Chicago 60637
Carcanet Press Ltd.

© 1989 by Donald Davie
All rights reserved. Published 1989
Printed in Great Britain
98 97 96 95 94 93 92 91 90 89   5 4 3 2 1

Library of Congress Cataloging-in-Publication Data

Davie, Donald.
    Under Briggflatts : a history of poetry in Great Britain,
1960–1988 / Donald Davie.
        p.   cm
    Includes bibliographical references.
    Includes index.
    ISBN 0-226-13756-2 (alk. paper)
    1. English poetry—20th century—History and criticism.
I. Title.
PR611.D38   1990
821'.91409—dc20

This book is printed on acid-free paper.

Contents

PART THREE: The 1980s

Foreword

This is a book about the poetry of the British Isles since 1960. A narrow topic, it may be thought. But only when the field is thus narrowed can the achievements in the field be honoured as they deserve to be. And a main intention has been to give to certain men and women their just deserts: grateful recognition that up to now, in all too many cases, has been denied them. To do them that justice involves – so it has turned out – measuring them against past masters of poetry: against Byron and Shelley, John Dryden and Walt Whitman and others, who accordingly are found to be, and treated as, presences still living in the Britain of Elizabeth II, of Harold Macmillan and Harold Wilson, Edward Heath and Margaret Thatcher, of the Beatles and the Sex Pistols. These ghosts like Lord Byron still walk, not ghostly at all; though a more sweeping survey over a longer span of time would – we may suspect from past experience – have failed to detect them. Among them walk ghosts who speak other languages than English.

Accordingly, this is an essay in literary history rather than literary criticism. Each of these, to be sure, involves the other; and confounding or compounding the two kinds of attention can often be fruitful, though at other times obfuscating. Having in the past functioned as a critic, in this book I try to perform as a historian. And the difference between the two functions is clearer to me than it may be to my readers. Principally, literary history, like other sorts of history, is concerned to *commemorate*, to keep in memory – a concern that some literary critics may share, but to which criticism as such is not committed. Of its nature, therefore, literary history is more indulgent than criticism is. It is readier to suspend judgement, to give the benefit of the doubt. It is more anxious to ensure that no deserving name falls out of the historical record, than to make sure that undeserving ones do not creep in.

There are limits, however; and it is by not observing these limits that literary historians have brought their discipline into disrepute. The historical record cannot be comprehensive, in the sense of all-inclusive; and the literary historian presses it towards that unattainable condition only by being indiscriminate. There are books and authors that are eminently, properly, forgettable; and nothing is gained by rescuing these from the oblivion that they deserve. Accordingly, the literary historian makes value-judgements, just as the responsible critic does, though the historian makes them mostly by implication – by choosing to deal with certain works and authors rather than others. This makes him a principal architect of 'the canon' – an institution that some commentators ask us to see as of its nature sinister and oppressive, though it is hard to see how this can be, since every historian's canon can be revised by the next historian in line. If this book seems to promote certain British authors as, however modestly, canonical, it is on the understanding that these judgements are disputable and ought to be disputed. Nevertheless my judgements were not arrived at lightly; and so the reader may safely assume that I deal with no poet whom I do not consider as in some measure admirable.

History is narrative, and I conceive of my three chapters as chapters in one unfolding story. However, there is no strong and single story-line, no 'thesis'. If there were, this book would be a polemic; and that I very much did not want, because the poets among my contemporaries who matter to me have all suffered – some more, some less – from being treated as case-histories by commentators with axes to grind. (I am not without such axes myself; but in this book I have tried not to grind them.) Accordingly I have attempted to arrange my material in such a way that a reader with a special interest – for instance, in Irish poetry – can satisfy his or her curiosity without having to read the book from beginning to end. On the other hand, of course, I hope that many readers will read from first to last. That there is no *one* story-line does not mean that there are not any such; there are several, and they intertwine. Moreover, unless I am mistaken, they have to do with poetry in general, not just British poetry of the last thirty years.

PART ONE

The 1960s

A Religious Dimension – MacDiarmid and MacCaig – Remembering the Western Desert – Edwin Muir and Austin Clarke – Basil Bunting – The Gurus – Elaine Feinstein – 1968 – Sylvia Townsend Warner – Larkin's Politics, and Tomlinson's – Thomas Kinsella – 'Ferocious Banter': Clarke and Hughes.

A Religious Dimension

William Empson's *Milton's God* (1961, revised 1965, and still being amplified as late as 1981) may be thought to have inaugurated a new era not just in British poetry but in British culture generally, a period in which questions of religious belief would move back – uncertainly, and at first imperceptibly – towards occupying that central position from which, decades before, they had been dislodged, as it then seemed irreversibly. To those, Believers and Unbelievers alike, who understood that Empson had taken Milton's *Paradise Lost* as a text by which to inveigh against Christianity in all its forms through the ages, it may have seemed that this was a simple lapse of taste or else an amusing anachronism, breaking the unspoken compact of mutually contemptuous tolerance by which Believer and Unbeliever had long ago agreed to lie down together. But of course Empson, the author of *The Gathering Storm* (poems, 1940) and *Some Versions of Pastoral* (1935), meant to imply that the tacit compact must be abandoned because it was intellectually disgraceful: the issue as between Christian Belief and Unbelief was too important to be smuggled away under the facile though civilly serviceable formula, 'Live and let live'.

It would be some time before this challenge was taken up. Through the next several years it would continue to be supposed that social engineering, working through political and administrative or elsewhere, necessarily violent, action, could solve and heal social divisions. But subsequent public events, notably in Northern Ireland, seemed to vindicate Empson's undeclared assumption that social conflicts were on the contrary metaphysical, or at least were conceived to be so, very bitterly, by the parties in conflict; and that such antagonisms could be handled and contained only by recognizing the metaphysical dimension to the contending allegiances. Of such antagonisms, the one between Believer and Unbeliever, however it might be muffled by the amiability of English social life (itself a frail prophylactic, as subsequent developments would show), remained the most crucial, and potentially the most explosive, in a nation that now included Muslims, Hindus, Sikhs and Rastafarians as well as Christians and Jews, atheists and agnostics. Already when Empson's book appeared, the preoccupation with Christian belief and the Christian church in the poetry of David Jones and John Betjeman, R. S. Thomas and Geoffrey Hill and C. H. Sisson – very different poets, not all of them believers, but all on the way to being prominent and influential – chimed in with Empson's polemic, and vindicated it as timely. His book and theirs, taken together, helped to defuse the situation by at least assuming once again that religious experience of some kind was what British people of whatever colour had a right to get heated about, for or against.

In Ireland, in Scotland, in Wales, few citizens had ever doubted this. It was peculiarly English culture that had been secularized. And so as religious experiences very gradually moved back near the centre of English concerns, the English reader who cared could begin to bridge the gulfs that had yawned between him and Irish or Welsh or Scottish poets. This was particularly important in respect of two veteran poets who survived into the 1960s: Austin Clarke in Ireland, Hugh MacDiarmid in Scotland.

They had much in common. For MacDiarmid's quarrel with the culture of post-Reformation Scotland, his vehemently reiterated appeal over the head of John Knox to the pre-Reformation Scotland of James IV and William Dunbar, was in important respects very like Austin Clarke's appeal from the Jansenite Romanism of modern Ireland to the medieval Irish Catholicism of Cashel and Clonmacnoise. To the Scottish poet as to the Irish one, what had been cramped and thwarted by an arrogant and hysterical Church (Protestant in the one case, Roman in the other) was above all the capacity for joyous sexuality. And so they were both insistently erotic poets, defiantly obscene when they judged that was called for.

On the other hand they were also very different. The difference showed in verses that MacDiarmid contributed in 1966 to a 70th-birthday tribute to Clarke by several hands (assembled by John Montague and Liam Miller, Portlaoise):

> *Thinking of the corpus of Austin Clarke's work set against the entire production of contemporary English poetry known to me.*

> The Muse to whom his heart is given,
> Historia Abscondita,
> Is already working like a leaven
> To manifest her law.

> The Gaelic sun swings up again
> And to itself doth draw
> All kindling things, while all the rest
> Like fog is blown away.

This hectoring tone is quite foreign to Austin Clarke, as is the headlong improvisation which unaccountably has recourse in the sixth line to the archaic 'doth draw'. Moreover Clarke never had, as MacDiarmid implies, set up Gaelic poetry and culture in opposition to English; on the contrary, true to the precepts of his first teacher Thomas MacDonagh, martyr of the Easter 1916 rising, he had sought always to enrich the repertoire of English poetry by grafting on to it the assonantal and off-rhyming patterns of classical Gaelic (which Clarke knew, whereas the Lowlander MacDiarmid – born Christopher Grieve – never had more than a smattering). So too with their religious apprehensions. Like many relentless anti-clericals in Roman Catholic countries, Clarke was firmly a Christian Believer; whereas MacDiarmid, professing no Christian belief, satisfied his religious needs with an indefinite mysticism for which, maverick Stalinist that he was, he seems to have found hints in pre-Stalinist Russians like Leo Shestov and Vladimir Solovyev. In all these ways and others, pre-eminently for present purposes in the finesse of his verse-writing techniques, Clarke is infinitely the more scrupulous and subtle intelligence. What remains on MacDiarmid's side of the account is not just his courage (for Clarke showed plenty of that in flouting the unwritten laws of republican Ireland), but a *public* risk-taking that cannot be disentangled from his brazenness, his roughness in polemic, even his slipperiness in argument. By these means MacDiarmid became, and remained indisputably, the intransigent though not always consistent spokesman for cultural nationalism on behalf of the Welsh and the Irish as well as the Scots. And the same risk-taking is an exhilarating and distinctive element among all the imperfections of his poems.

MacDiarmid and MacCaig

MacDiarmid's poems had not always been imperfect. When his *Collected Poems* appeared in 1962 (revised 1967), no one suggested that the Lallans lyrics of *Sangschaw* (1925) and *Penny Wheep* (1926) could be much improved on. But the cultural nationalism of MacDiarmid and his more fervent Scottish admirers had for years back-fired, so as to validate the malicious lethargy of non-Scottish readers, who could always expostulate that they had to take these poems on trust, since they were written in a foreign tongue. Common sense with no axe to grind had always supposed, on the contrary, that MacDiarmid's Lallans or 'synthetic Scots' was a dialect of standard English, not different in principle from the Scottish English of Robert Burns, though certainly more forbidding when first encountered. English-speakers had not thought themselves definitively excluded by Burns's language; why should they think themselves shut out by MacDiarmid's? There were several reasons, and at least two pretexts: on the one hand Scottish nationalism, needing non-Scottish recognition yet resenting that need, had insisted that MacDiarmid's language in these lyrics was not a dialect of the colonialist oppressive language, English; on the other hand, on the poet's own admission, what he called Lallans was not a literary transcription of what was spoken in any region of twentieth-century Scotland, but represented an amalgamation of the spoken lexicon of several Scottish regions, crucially augmented by archaic usages retrieved from dictionaries. If Lallans was a dialect, it was an artificial dialect. But in Scandinavia and elsewhere there were precedents for such fabricated languages being successfully adopted as media of literature. What bypassed all such terminological quibbles, and the special interests of linguisticians and ideologues, was the experience of a few non-Scottish readers who delightedly encountered 'The Bonnie Broukit Bairn' and 'The Watergaw'. 'Crowdieknowe' and 'The Eemis Stane' and 'Wheesht, Wheesht', and were not to be bullied out of their possession of these poems, which characteristically delighted them as unprecedented orchestrations of sound before ever, by applying themselves to the glossaries, they construed them as lexically coherent also. There was and is considerable duplicity on the part of the metropolitan Englishman: two hours with his ears open in King's Cross or Euston railway stations would, as he overheard arriving Scottish travellers, give such a London reader quite enough access to the acoustic world that poetry in Lallans assumes, and reverberates in. A decisive landmark was reached in 1984 when, after decades of Scottish explanatory glosses and English bemused inattention to them, the American Harvey Oxenhorn showed that these poems were thoroughly accessible to non-Scottish readers with a little patience, and that such patience was amply rewarded.[1]

There was also to be, before Oxenhorn, John C. Weston's very careful American edition of *A Drunk Man Looks at the Thistle* (University of Massachusetts Press, 1971), a 'gallimaufry' of 1926 which it had become usual to consider MacDiarmid's masterpiece. Certainly it represents, thus early in the poet's career, a dissatisfaction with the constraints of the lyric, and a determination to move beyond them (even though the *Drunk Man* in fact incorporates lyrics of great beauty). However, MacDiarmid's strategy to this end was, even in 1926, strikingly old-fashioned, pre-modern. One critic in 1962 was reminded of Thomas Hardy's strategy when in *The Dynasts*, he too had wanted to find a form more ample and heterogeneous than the individual lyric. However that might be, one even older presence behind the poem was certainly Robert Browning.[2] The same critic, voicing what was plainly a minority view, spoke disparagingly and rashly of 'that awkward half-way house to drama, the Browningesque dramatic monologue'. This invited the obvious retort that Browning's achievement in the dramatic monologue could not be dismissed so loftily, and that if MacDiarmid seemed to ignore the more far-reaching structural innovations of Eliot's *The Waste Land* four years earlier, this was not necessarily a bad thing. But it was harder to set his objections aside when he quoted MacDiarmid's writing at its weakest:

> Eneuch? Then here you are. Here's the haill story.
> Life's connached shapes too'er up in crowns o' glory,
> Perpetuating natheless, in their gory
> Colour the endless sacrifice and pain
> That to their makin's gane . . .

Of these lines this captious reader commented severely: 'The ugliness of this writing is not the sometimes functional ugliness of

---

[1] Harvey Oxenhorn, *Elemental Things. The Poetry of Hugh MacDiarmid* (Edinburgh, 1984).

[2] See D. Davie, 'A'e Gowden Lyric', in *The Poet in the Imaginary Museum* (Manchester, 1977).

modernism: it is something inseparable from the dramatic mono-
logue, which fakes up by such uncouth gambols the liveliness of
those dramatic exchanges it cannot provide. The speaker gets more
and more embarrassed by his own garrulity, and the ugliness is how
his embarrassment shows up.'

John C. Weston's devoted labours showed clearly the inadequacy
of the *Collected Poems*, a volume in many ways even less reliable in
its 'revised' edition of 1967 than in its original version five years
earlier. Quite apart from the unreliability of the text and the way-
ward incompleteness of its Glossary, the *Collected Poems* did not, as
it claimed, include all the poems that MacDiarmid wanted to rescue
from oblivion. The poet, typically not apologizing but shifting the
blame on to other people, acknowledged this by publishing three
supplementary slim volumes, *A Lap of Honour* (1967), *A Clyack-
Sheaf* (1969) and *More Collected Poems* (1970). The upshot is that a
reader who has isolated certain poems that he particularly admires
(for instance the astonishing 'On a Raised Beach', 1934) is at a
loss where to locate it in what ought to be a definitive edition.
An authoritative canon and text was still to seek. And when, after
the poet's death, a selection of his letters appeared (edited by Alan
Bold, 1984), it became clear that this lack was the consequence of
MacDiarmid's always harried and opportunist habits: he did not keep
track of all the poems he had published, let alone those he had writ-
ten; and quite extended passages originally presented in the context
of certain poems would be without warning cannibalized by him and
wedged into quite different contexts. MacDiarmid in fact seems to
have been a publisher's and sub-editor's nightmare. This would not
matter so much if the same headlong and impetuous habits had not
made it inevitable that, at all stages of his career but increasingly after
1930, his admirable poems would have to be sorted out from much
disgraceful dross:

> The sin against the Holy Ghost is to fetter or clog
> The free impulse of life – to weaken or cloud
> The glad wells of being – to apply other tests,
> To say that these pure founts must be hampered, controlled,
> Denied, adulterated, diluted, cowed,
> The wave of omnipotence made recede, and all these lives, these
>   lovers
> Lapse into cannon-fodder, sub-humanity, the despised slum-crowd.

This is from a poem 'In the Slums of Glasgow', in *Second Hymn to
Lenin and other poems* (1935) and there is still a readiness to believe
that any objection to it has to do with hostility to its humanitarian

and politically inflammable content, not with the wretched fabric of its language, which reveals a writer too impatient to wait for *le mot juste*, instead offering for each ranging-shot at his meaning another at the other side of the target: 'to weaken *or cloud*', 'to fetter *or clog*, It is barely credible that a poet capable of this fustian should the year before in his 'Shetland Lyrics' have written 'Gruney', with its incomparable last line, hitting the bull of the target once and for all:

> You say there's naething here
>   But a bank o' snaw?
> But the sun whiles shows in't
>   Gleg een ana'.
>
> I'll be like these white birds
>   Sittin facin' the ocean
> Wi' here and there in their stillness
>   Vigil's pin-point motion.

Such are the labours of discrimination required of the reader of MacDiarmid: labours required also of the reader of Pound's *Cantos*, yet not to the same degree; for the monumental silliness of Pound at certain points is surpassed by the silliness of MacDiarmid – for instance in 'Direadh III' from *Lucky Poet* (1943), where appropriately he quotes Pound:

> And think of the Oriental provenance of the Scottish Gael,
> The Eastern affiliations of his poetry and his music,
> '. . . the subtler music, the clear light
> Where time burns back about th' eternal embers.'
> And the fact that he initiated the idea of civilization
> That to-day needs renewal at its native source
> Where, indeed, it is finding it, since Georgia,
> Stalin's native country, was also the first home of the Scots.

One sees how difficult discrimination is, when it is acknowledged that the poem which includes this intellectually contemptible and politically dangerous nonsense is, in its over-all structure as a Wordsworthian rambling meditation, by no means despicable.

MacDiarmid in any case will not go away. Alike when he is silly and when he is sage, when he writes badly and when he writes well, he has to be taken account of. He cannot for instance be shunted aside, as a problem only Scots need to cope with. How this can be, we see if we set beside him his fellow-Scot, a far more fastidious and accomplished writer, Norman MacCaig.

It is in MacCaig, not in the intransigent individualist MacDiarmid, that we can detect in the 1960s a momentous change of style, or perhaps only of stylistic fashion, which became ever more marked as the decade unrolled. MacCaig's collection of 1960, *A Common Grace* (his third), included several love-poems characterized by an elaborate baroque formality. These poems are epistemological at the same time as they are amorous; hence a title like 'Standing in My Ideas'. And the epistemology is one that it is easy to approve – which may be what is wrong with it:

> Even a leaf, its own shape in the air,
> Achieves its mystery not by being symbol
> Or ominous of anything but what is,
> Such is the decent clarity you bear
> For the world to be in. Everything is humble,
> Not humbled, in its own lucidities.

These lines are from a sumptuous love-compliment, 'Two Ways of It', a poem which, in the manner of some of George Herbert, even as it denounces the hyperbolical, achieves it. Such a sophisticated manoeuvre is highly rhetorical, but rhetorical in a sense that need not mean either 'dishonest' or 'academic'. 1960 was late for such elaborations; much practised in the early 1950s, though seldom or never so well as by MacCaig, the mode went decisively out of fashion when Robert Lowell, bell-wether of the Anglo-American flock, repudiated it for his *Life Studies* (1955). MacCaig, no doubt feeling which way the wind was blowing, dismantled the admittedly cumbrous machinery of such writing so as to fall into line with the more seemingly artless procedures that then came into vogue. But the virtues of such writing are undeniable and irreplaceable; and when the wheel of fashion has come full circle, they will surely be esteemed once again.

In any case, even as MacCaig wrestled into his verse such bold and abstruse conceptualizings, he never lost touch with sensuous perception. In 'Nude in a Fountain' we read:

> Light perches, preening, on the handle of a pram
> And gasps on paths and runs along a rail
> And whitely, brightly in a soft diffusion
> Veils and unveils the naked figure, pale
> As marble in her stone and stilled confusion.

In such lines, where the abstraction 'light' is made to perform such specific actions as perching, preening, gasping and running (not to speak of veiling and unveiling), we are offered a series of perceptions such as it is hard to find precedents for in English, though they can be found in foreign modernists such as the young Boris Pasternak. The rhetorical figures convey how light interacts with the metal of a rail or of a baby-carriage. The human sensibility, to be sure, is the irreplaceable medium by and through which such interactions can be registered; but the perceiving subject is in no way privileged, it is not for its benefit that light and metal interact as they do. The figures define how light interacts with metal, not how either of them, or the relation between them, feeds back to enhance 'the authoritative self'. That last phrase, together with others ('in no way privileged'), is taken over from the jargon of the criticism, mostly French-inspired, that would, after the 1960s revulsion against such a way of writing, be used to denigrate such styles in favour of another that then came into fashion.

In that more stripped and apparently casual style to which MacCaig switched, he may have reached his peak as early as *Measures* (1965), where occurs the uncompromising poem, 'Aspects':

> Clean in the light, with nothing to remember,
> The fox fur shrivels, the bone beak drops apart;
> Sludge on the ground, the dead deer drips his heart.
>
> Clean in the weather, trees crack and lean over;
> Mountain bows down and combs its scurfy head
> To make a meadow and its own deathbed.
>
> Clean in the moon, tides scrub away their islands,
> Unpicking gulls. Whales that have learned to drown,
> Ballooning up, meet navies circling down.
>
> Clean in the mind, a new mind creeps to being,
> Eating the old . . . Ancestors have no place
> In such clean qualities as time and space.

'Ancestors have no place . . .' Though MacCaig in later poems would sometimes offend against his own precepts, still that later writing in general would show that he meant what he said: the recorded human past is for him 'unclean', squalid and nonsensical; no patterns can be found in it such as might determine the present and point to a future, or a choice of futures. Thus he was to write how Clio, 'the Muse of history, yawning with boredom . . . has long since failed to be amused.' And of course it is just here, on this score, that a comparison with MacDiarmid becomes unavoidable.

If MacCaig feels like this about history, he has every right to say so. And it was refreshing to have it said in 1965, when poetry was becoming every day more politically inflamed. But if MacCaig's thoroughgoing scepticism about history has saved him from the self-contradictions, the absurdities and the duplicities that punctuated MacDiarmid's career, readers across the political spectrum may yet agree that MacDiarmid's engagement with history is one of the things we expect of a great poet, or of a poet ambitious to be great. And MacCaig's consistent refusal thus to engage himself cannot help but count against him.

It remains true that, because the climate for poetry remains politically inflamed (though less hectically than twenty years ago), MacCaig's achievement along his own lines is still underestimated. Reading something like 'Painting – "The Blue Jar" ' (from *Rings on a Tree*, 1968), one wonders if there is another modern poem from which the perceiving subject, the magisterial ego, has been more scrupulously eliminated. Though this is what some critics ask for, it seems they do not like it, nor even notice it, when they get it. To some readers, this scrupulous elimination of the poet from his poem will seem a small and perverse achievement; but of course it is neither.

As for MacDiarmid, there challengingly remains what Basil Bunting recorded in an obituary reminiscence (*Agenda*, 1978/9):

Driving home after a visit to Wylam we paused for a sandwich and something to wet it at Moffat, taking care to avoid the tourist traps with which Moffat abounds. The bar was long, dark and rather forbidding, a place for covenanters, it seemed, or equally contentious, stubborn people. A tableful of workmen eating their bait began to stir ominously as soon as we sat down, as though trouble might be brewing. While our sandwiches were cutting and the whisky barely tasted the largest workman rose frowning and came to our table; but what he said was: 'Is it no the great poet, Hugh MacDiarmid?'

Chris said nothing. I doubt if he heard. So I answered: 'It is.' On that all the workmen, six or seven of them, got up and stood around us. 'Ye'll drink on us,' they commanded, and drink on them we did until every man of them had paid a round, while they expressed their admiration, quoting his poems, asking his opinions on this and that, from whisky to Clydeside MPs. They would remember that day, they said, all their lives . . .

. . . What other poet is there, or has been these many, many years, who would be recognized and spontaneously honoured by men of no education and no pretension whatever? It was not

MacDiarmid's politics that attracted them; the poems they quoted were not political. It was not even the sound of their native dialect, for some of the poems they admired were in English. None of MacDiarmid's poems were simplified to aim at the poor, they were written for a hard intellectual audience. Their candour, their lack of side, the feeling that he meant what he said, with or without occasional stumblings of technique, these carried through the printed page to the least literary of men.

We had been recognized and stood drinks already once on that journey, but by middle-class reading men whose enthusiasm was real, no doubt, but not half so fully felt as that of the workmen at Moffat . . .

Remembering the Western Desert

Keith Douglas (1920–44) was killed in action in Normandy, but his good poetry came out of his earlier war service in North Africa and the Middle East. A book of journals, *Alamein to Zem Zem*, appeared in 1946, and in 1951 Douglas's *Collected Poems*, edited by John Waller and G. S. Fraser. His reputation however was firmly established only in the 1960s, with in the first place *Selected Poems* (1964), edited with an important introduction by Ted Hughes, and then with a revised *Collected Poems* (1966).

Hughes declared of Douglas: 'his temperament is so utterly modern he seems to have no difficulty with the terrible, suffocating, maternal octopus of ancient English poetic tradition.' But this comment has less to do with Douglas's poetry than with that of Ted Hughes, who was to build a great and continuing success, crowned at last with the Laureateship, on this conviction, eagerly embraced by others, that the English poet's inheritance from the English poetic past is a stifling encumbrance which he must learn to scotch and annul. Certainly the illustrious precedents do encumber and impede nearly every beginning poet, and we can see them doing so in the many poems that Douglas wrote as a precocious schoolboy and Oxford undergraduate, tutored by Edmund Blunden. Hughes's impression that Douglas had no such difficulties is obviously wide of the mark; the interesting question is whether Douglas learned to do better by scotching the inherited tradition, or by mastering as much of it as served his purposes.

Charles Tomlinson, discussing 'Some Aspects of Poetry since the War', remarked: 'it is no accident that Ted Hughes was a poet who recognized Douglas as potentially one of the most powerful writers of his generation.'[1] And he quoted in evidence the title-poem of Hughes's *The Hawk in the Rain* (1957):

> I drown in the drumming ploughland, I drag up
> Heel after heel from the swallowing of the earth's mouth,
> From clay that clutches my each step to the ankle
> With the habit of the dogged grave, but the hawk

[1] in *The New Pelican Guide to English Literature: 8. The Present*, ed. Boris Ford (1983).

Effortlessly at height hangs his still eye.
His wings hold all creation in a weightless quiet,
Steady as a hallucination in the streaming air.
While banging wind kills these stubborn hedges,

Thumbs my eyes, throws my breath, tackles my heart,
And rain hacks my head to the bone, the hawk hangs
The diamond point of will that polestars
The sea drowner's endurance: and I,

Bloodily grabbed dazed last-moment-counting
Morsel in the earth's mouth, strain towards the master-
Fulcrum of violence where the hawk hangs still.
That maybe in his own time meets the weather

Coming the wrong way, suffers the air, hurled upside down,
Fall from his eye, the ponderous shires crash on him,
The horizon trap him; the round angelic eye
Smashed, mix his heart's blood with the mire of the land.

But surely the congested strenuousness of Hughes's writing here – he
was to be much less turgid in *Lupercal* (1960) and *Wodwo* (1967) – is
precisely what we do *not* find in Keith Douglas, who must be saved
from the imputation that he was Ted Hughes born before his time.

Douglas's own account, in 'Words' (1943), may as well be trusted:

And the pockmarked house bleached by the glare
whose insides war has dried out like gourds
attracts words. There are those who capture them
in hundreds, keep them prisoners in black
bottles, release them at exercise and clap them back.
But I keep words only a breath of time
turning in the lightest of cages – uncover
and let them go: sometimes they escape for ever.

The levelness of the tone, and the poet's way of leaving each word a
space to breathe in, are surely very different from what we have seen
from 'The Hawk in the Rain'. And yet these lines might seem to give
warrant for Hughes's claim that in his best poems Douglas

has invented a style that seems able to deal poetically with what-
ever it comes up against. It is not an exalted verbal activity
to be attained for short periods, through abstinence, or a sub-
merged dream treasure to be fished up when the everyday brain

is half-drugged. It is a language for the whole mind, at its most wakeful, and in all situations. A utility general-purpose style, as, for instance, Shakespeare's was . . .

The Shakespearean comparison (typical of Hughes, who disdains to measure his protegé against any one less than 'the champ') dwarfs Douglas, as it would dwarf any one. There is a less presumptuous but still exalted comparison which surely defines Douglas's sparse achievement more exactly. The polemic against poetry as 'an exalted verbal activity', or as 'a submerged dream treasure to be fished up', surely – for those who have defied Ted Hughes so as to get a sense of past English poetry – recalls nothing so much as Byron's scoffings at the Lake Poets, his contemporaries:

> One hates an author that's *all author*, fellows
>   In foolscap uniforms turn'd up with ink,
> So very anxious, clever, fine and jealous,
>   One don't know what to say to them, or think,
> Unless to puff them with a pair of bellows;
>   Of coxcombry's worst coxcombs e'en the pink
> Are preferable to these shreds of paper,
> These unquench'd snuffings of the midnight taper.

Byron's stock stands so low in the 1980s, as it did in the 1960s when the bruited ideologies might have seemed to favour it, that to call Keith Douglas a Byronic poet may seem like a put-down. But Byron's foreign contemporaries, like Goethe and Pushkin, were not deceived when they extolled him. And among his great virtues surely is the one that Douglas claimed for himself when he remarked that 'I keep words only a breath of time/turning in the lightest of cages.' Byron was determined that the-man-as-poet should be seen as only one aspect of the man of action and of affairs, amorous and public; and it seems clear that Douglas, an ardent and proficient soldier, was equally concerned not to seem 'all author'. Hence both Byron and Douglas touch upon a word, an image or a trope, however felicitous, only to let it go as fast as it came. This is the secret of the effect of athletic speed and energy in both of them:

> Stop! – for thy tread is on an Empire's dust!
> An Earthquake's spoil is sepulchred below!
> Is the spot mark'd with no colossal bust?
> Nor column trophied for triumphal show?
> None; but the moral's truth tells simpler so.

As the ground was before, thus let it be; –
How that red rain has made the harvest grow!
And is this all the world has gain'd by thee,
Thou first and last of fields! king-making Victory?

Thus Byron on the field of Waterloo, inaugurating the masterly treatment of the great battle which travels from frivolity – 'There was a sound of revelry by night' – to carnage, just as Douglas in 'Cairo Jag' moves from frivolity – 'Shall I get drunk or cut myself a piece of cake . . .?' – to *his* battlefield:

But by a day's travelling you reach a new world
the vegetation is of iron
dead tanks, gun barrels split like celery
the metal brambles have no flowers or berries
and there are all sorts of manure, you can imagine
the dead themselves, their boots, clothes and possessions
clinging to the ground, a man with no head
has a packet of chocolate and a souvenir of Tripoli.

Douglas will not pause upon his gunbarrels, 'split like celery', any more than Byron will stop to elaborate his allusion to earthquake. Of 'Cairo Jag', as of several similar poems, we can say with Ted Hughes: 'Its air of improvisation is a vital part of its purity. It has the trenchancy of an inspired jotting, yet leaves no doubt about the completeness and subtlety of his impressions, or the thoroughness of his artistic conscience'. But Hughes cannot imply that this is 'utterly modern'; for we must say as much of passage after passage of *Childe Harold's Pilgrimage*.

Douglas left perhaps fifteen memorable poems, out of the hundred in the *Collected*. And these poems, again like Byron's best, describe rapid transits, they move a long way from first to last, they do not settle on a theme or an image-cluster and circle round it until they can move in and pin it down. (One sees the loss of pressure at once when Douglas does try to circle and effect a closure, as in 'Landscape with Figures', of which there are alternative versions, one in two sections, one in three, and neither satisfactory.) Byron's verses about a battle-field, and Douglas's, are poems about war but they have nothing to say about the 'problem' of warfare. No judgement is passed, there is no pretence that the poet is in possession of a scheme of values that can comprehend or justify the carnage. In this sense, as in more technical senses, Douglas's good poems are 'open-ended'.

It is interesting on this count as on others to set beside Douglas's poems of the Western Desert five poems by another survivor of the desert battles who, more luckily than Douglas, survived the War. These are little known, so two of them shall be given in full. The first is 'Going Westwards':

> I go westwards in the Desert
> with my shame on my shoulders,
> that I was made a laughing-stock
> since I was as my people were.
>
> Love and the greater error,
> deceiving honour spoiled me,
> with a film of weakness on my vision,
> squinting at mankind's extremity.
>
> Far from me the Island
> when the moon rises on Quattara,
> far from me the Pine Headland
> when the morning ruddiness is on the Desert.
>
> Camus Alba is far from me
> and so is the bondage of Europe,
> far from me in the North-West
> the most beautiful grey-blue eyes.
>
> Far from me the Island
> and every loved image in Scotland,
> there is a foreign sand in History
> spoiling the machines of the mind.
>
> Far from me Belsen and Dachau,
> Rotterdam, the Clyde and Prague,
> and Dimitrov before a court
> hitting fear with the thump of his laugh.
>
> Guernica itself is very far
> from the innocent corpses of the Nazis
> who are lying in the gravel
> and in the khaki sand of the Desert.
>
> There is no rancour in my heart
> against the hardy soldiers of the Enemy,
> but the kinship that there is among
> men in prison on a tidal rock

waiting for the sea flowing
and making cold the warm stone;
and the coldness of life
in the hot sun of the Desert.

But this is the struggle not to be avoided,
the sore extreme of human-kind,
and though I do not hate Rommel's army
the brain's eye is not squinting.

And be what was as it was,
I am of the big men of Braes,
of the heroic Raasay MacLeods,
of the sharp-sword Mathesons of Lochalsh;
and the men of my name – who were braver
when their ruinous pride was kindled?[1]

Here the poetic tradition that is called on to try to do justice to the
Desert battles is not the English, but another at least as ancient: the
Gaelic tradition in which the celebration of martial valour – some
may think it bloodthirsty, others will call it heroic – bulks larger
than in the English tradition, or at least has been regarded with
fewer misgivings in recent centuries. It is interesting to ask whether
the Gaelic poet (Sorley MacLean of Raasay, whose own translation
this is) finds his inherited tradition encumbering or enabling. And
the answer surely is: both. For the Hebridean soldier who speaks the
poem begins by confessing his shame at the eccentricity of the heroic
ethos he has inherited – 'deceiving honour spoiled me' – yet by the
end, as he girds himself for combat, has nothing but that dubious
or discredited ethos to fall back on. The effect is subtle, persua-
sive and affecting, even for those who read through the necessarily
distorting lens of translation. And though MacLean no more than
Douglas claims to be able to justify war, his poem can manage a
closure because it settles, though not without deliberate strain, into
a recognizable *genre* as Keith Douglas's poem does not.

One of Sorley MacLean's battlefield poems, 'Curaidhean' ('Heroes')
seems a companion-piece, and even a sort of rejoinder, to Douglas's
'Aristocrats'. And in the same way, Douglas's much-anthologized
'Vergissmeinicht' finds its counterpart in MacLean's 'Death Valley'.
But for another example of how the Gaelic tradition seems to command

[1] Sorley MacLean, *Reothairt is Contraigh/Spring tide and Neap tide. Selected Poems 1932-72*
(Edinburgh, 1977).

a harsh and terse heroic mode that seems to have been lost to English, we may take 'Move South'.

> South, south to Bir Hacheim,
> tanks and guns at high speed,
> there was a jump and kick in the heart
> and a kind of delight –
> it was the battle joy –
> as one heard in the tale,
> not knowing if it was a lie.
>
> Going South in the morning
> to meet the Africa Korps –
> we'll soon reach the French
> and put a stop to big Rommel!
>
> Before midday the shells,
> novel birds in the sky;
> we did not reach the French at all:
> a quick stop was put to our race.

For MacLean, even less than for Byron or Keith Douglas, war was a 'problem' that he must wrestle with. We know that of course he did recognize a problem there, and that he wrestled with it, but not in poems, or not in such poems as these. Whereas MacDiarmid on the one hand and Empson on the other valuably insisted that there was a place in poetry for what Empson called 'argufying', their contemporary MacLean, no less argumentative and combative, knew when to keep his argumentative opinions out of his poetry. Their practice does not invalidate his, nor vice versa; MacDiarmid and Empson are not 'intellectual' poets, nor MacLean 'anti-intellectual'. Rather, one may think, whereas they sought to over-ride the traditional distinctions between poetic genres, so as to assert and show how poetry was omnivorous and infinitely capacious, Sorley MacLean (and Keith Douglas) cherished the fact and idea of genre; that is to say, the commonsensical recognition that no one poem can, or should try to, take all of human experience for its province.

Edwin Muir and Austin Clarke

Edwin Muir died in 1958. Not a Scotsman but an Orkney Islander, Muir had nevertheless been prominent and influential in the efforts to bring about a cultural renaissance in Scotland. MacDiarmid had embraced him as a valuable comrade in that struggle, then broke with him violently when Muir declared himself for standard English rather than Lallans as the medium which, however regrettably, the ambitious Scottish writer must adopt.

Two of Muir's poems have virtually the same title: his 'Horses' of 1925, and 'The Horses' of 1956. Muir was a late starter in poetry, and 'Horses' is a touchingly incompetent poem, helplessly dependent at one point on Yeats ('Perhaps some childish hour has come again') and in another place on Keats ('Ah, now it fades! it fades! and I must pine'). The later poem, 'The Horses', is thoroughly achieved, a sustained and frightening vision:

> . . . That old bad world that swallowed its children quick
> At one great gulp. We would not have it again.
> Sometimes we think of the nations lying asleep,
> Curled blindly in impenetrable sorrow,
> And then the thought confounds us with its strangeness.
> The tractors lie about our fields; at evening
> They look like dank sea-monsters couched and waiting.
> We leave them where they are and let them rust:
> 'They'll moulder away and be like other loam.'
> We make our oxen drag our rusty ploughs,
> Long laid aside. We have gone back
> Far past our fathers' land.
>   And then, that evening
> Late in the summer the strange horses came.
> We heard a distant tapping on the road,
> A deepening drumming; it stopped, went on again
> And at the corner changed to hollow thunder.
> We saw the heads
> Like a wild wave charging and were afraid.
> We had sold our horses in our fathers' time
> To buy new tractors. Now they were strange to us

>As fabulous steeds set on an ancient shield
>Or illustrations in a book of knights.
>We did not dare go near them. Yet they waited,
>Stubborn and shy, as if they had been sent
>By an old command to find our whereabouts
>And that long-lost archaic companionship . . .

Different as this is from the technical gaucheries that Muir had perpetrated thirty years before, in other ways it is remarkable how alike they are, this late poem by Muir and that early one. For plainly, in the lines quoted above, Muir is not imagining (what is indeed unimaginable) the actual consequences of an atomic war. He is not looking into the future, any more than in the poem of 1925 he was looking into the past of his Orkney childhood when he wrote of the horses there:

>Their eyes as brilliant and as wide as night
>Gleamed with a cruel apocalyptic light.
>Their manes the leaping ire of the wind
>Lifted with rage invisible and blind.

Past, present and future are categories that do not apply; as in nearly every poem that Muir wrote, the action takes place in a visionary or fabulous time that clocks and calendars do not measure. Muir is a mythopoeic poet through and through.

In 1961 appeared another poem about horses: Austin Clarke's 'Forget Me Not'. And Muir's line about 'that long-lost archaic companionship' is glossed in Clarke's poem:

>Good company, up and down
>The ages, gone: the trick of knife left, horse cut
>To serve man. All the gentling, custom of mind
>And instinct, close affection, done with. The unemployed
>Must go. Dead or ghosted by froths, we ship them
>Abroad. Foal, filly, farm pony, bred for slaughter:
>What are they now but hundredweights of meat?

But Clarke's poem is as insistently *in* historical time as Muir's is out of it. For it was provoked by the revelation that the Irish were indeed raising their horses so as to slaughter them or have them slaughtered, and export them either on the hoof or as carcasses to feed the poor of the Continent. And it is as usual for Clarke's poems to be thus occasional and highly topical, as it is for Muir's poems to be nothing of the kind.

The contrast is even more striking if we look for the lines in 'Forget Me Not' which correspond to Muir's 'As fabulous steeds set on an ancient field/Or illustrations in a book of knights.'

To make the same point about the horse in the Age of Chivalry, Clarke treats us to a capsulated history of Western Europe:

> Yet all the world
> Was hackneyed once – those horses o' the sun,
> Apollo's car, centaurs in Thessaly.
> Too many staves have splintered the toy
> That captured Troy. The Hippocrene is stale.
> Dark ages: Latin rotted, came up from night-soil,
> New rush of words; thought mounted them. Trappings
> Of palfrey, sword-kiss of chivalry, high song
> Of grammar. Men pick the ribs of Rosinante
> In restaurants now. Horse-shoe weighs in with saddle
> Of meat.
>   Horseman, the pass-word, courage shared
> With lace, steel, buff.
>   Wars regimented
>
> Haunches together, cities move by in motor
> Cars, charging the will. I hear in the lateness of Empires,
> A neighing, man's cry in engines. No peace, yet,
> Poor draggers of artillery.

The comparison of the two poets could be extended. For instance Muir's 'Horses' corresponds to a passage in his *Autobiography* (1954), and in the same way passage after passage in 'Forget Me Not' can be matched in Clarke's autobiography, *Twice Round the Black Church* (1962). But it is better to pause here and to face the awkward fact that, given kinds of poetry as different as Muir's and Clarke's, no one's taste is, or can be expected to be, so catholic and unprejudiced as to respond to both kinds with equal ardour. We may *respect* both kinds; but we cannot be expected to love both equally.

Admirers of Edwin Muir can be left to make the case for their man. (They have powerful arguments, if they care to use them.) An admirer of Austin Clarke may say that Muir's poem, much as he respects its grave music, suffers from the lack of just that verbal energy and continual play of quick intelligence which throws up puns and allusions in 'Forget Me Not'. Once one has acquired a taste for the way language is used in 'Too many staves have splintered the toy/That captured Troy', the language of Edwin Muir is bound to seem, however worthy and responsible, undeniably *tame*. Clarke's word 'staves' means first the staves of the barrel-body of the wooden horse by which Troy was taken; but also, as a variant of 'staff', all the sticks that have thwacked horses' hides through the centuries when the horse was man's servant; and finally 'stave' in its technical sense in music delivers the message, 'Too many songs since Homer's have devoted themselves to the matter of the Trojan war; the theme has been done to death (splintered)'. If this is not to say much in a little space, it is hard to know what is. And so the initial impression that Muir is the more economical writer, saying in two lines what Clarke conveys in sixteen, is seen to be illusory.

There is in any case a sense in which a mythopoeic poem will always be shorter than a poem which, so far from rising into vision-ary timelessness, trusts the categories of past, present and future, and ranges to and fro among them. For in order that a myth may be made which will shape and encompass the multitudinous variety of histori-cal experience, that experience must be stripped of what is local and contingent; it is the rendering of the contingencies – of place as well as time – which in a non-mythopoeic poem takes up the space that the mythopoeic poem can do without. And Austin Clarke was an extreme case of the poet who trusts the local and contingent through thick and thin, who refuses to rise above the congested heterogeneity of the world as we experience it through our senses, enmeshed in particular circumstances, of *this* time in *this* place. What makes Clarke a specially troublesome case is that he lived his days in a place, the Irish Republic, which was in many ways anomalous, where social and political life had taken on forms hardly to be found in other English-speaking societies of the twentieth century. W. B. Yeats, surviving into this socio-political situation, exerted himself – like the mythopoeic poet he was, or always strove to be – to show that underneath the peculiarities of Irish life could be found the lineaments of myths which encompassed and made sense of the life of mankind, Irish and other. That was not Clarke's way; he immersed himself in the life of modern Ireland in all the eccentric particularity of that life. And so issues which bulk larger in Ireland than elsewhere in the English-speaking world – for example, the breeding of horses for slaughter, or again the non-availability of contraceptive devices inside the Republic – bulk disconcertingly large in Clarke's poems. This means that for the non-Irish reader, on top of the difficulties that come of Clarke's being unashamedly a *poeta doctus*, a proudly learned poet, there arises another set of difficulties: the need to know in con-siderable detail the history of modern Ireland, especially the history of public opinion inside the Republic, as well as Irish history through previous centuries. This makes Clarke sound like a very provincial, even a parochial poet. And in one sense he was so, quite consciously and defiantly. It means in any case that the non-Irish reader, and for that matter many Irish readers also, have to work much harder to get what Clarke has to offer them, than to get at Edwin Muir. And so Clarke will always be caviare to the general, as Muir is not.

When a poet so great as Yeats is born to a country so small as Ireland, this is a wonderful windfall for every one in that country *except the poets*. For them it is a disaster. For, if the young Edwin Muir could not prevent his own voice from being at times drowned out by the organ-voice sounding from across the Irish Sea, how much more difficult it must have been for a poet like the young Austin Clarke, moving about the very city where the master-poet was housed, where the ringing and imperious voice sounded in his ears, as it were, every hour of the day. In any case, for Irish poets as for others as far away as the Antipodes, Yeats must figure even today as the great ventriloquist; if they relax their concentration for a second, or become any more familiar than they must with the highly distinctive Yeatsian idiom and cadence, they find themselves transformed into puppets sitting on the great ventriloquist's knee, using not their own voices but his. Yeats in the 1920s and 1930s pointedly chose to place the laurel of his approval on other brows than Austin Clarke's, and undoubtedly this goes far to explain Clarke's mostly feline and mischievous comments on Yeats. But there were plenty of other reasons for mutual antipathy between Clarke, urban, petty bourgeois, and Roman Catholic; and Yeats, shabby-genteel, Protestant, admirer of rural peasantry and land-owners. Moreover a degree of antipathy to Yeats would have been inevitable for any ambitious and serious Irish poet of Clarke's generation; only by making himself deaf to Yeats's voice could any such poet save himself poetically and forge a style true to the integrity of his own different temperament and concerns.

This necessity for the young Clarke to keep his distance from Yeats should probably be borne in mind when we observe him between the wars choosing to exploit just those centuries of Irish history which Yeats least cultivated – the centuries of Celtic Romanesque, after the heroic age and before the Elizabethan plantations. The great symbol and metropolis of that Ireland is the Rock of Cashel, the hill in Tipperary still crowded with the ruins of Romanesque churches; and if Yeats at times invokes the Rock, Clarke has a better right to do so. He earned that right, or he proved it, by many poems in the two collections, *Pilgrimage* (1929) and *Night and Morning* (1938). It is in these books that, by no means coincidentally, Clarke displays the extraordinary technical innovation, or body of innovations, by which he made available to other poets writing in English a whole kit or cabinet of erstwhile undiscovered musical resources. As early as

1937, in a few crisply elegant and exact sentences, Clarke had isolated and defined these innovations:

> Assonance, more elaborate in Gaelic than in Spanish poetry, takes the clapper from the bell of rhyme. In simple patterns, the tonic word at the end of the line is supported by a vowel-rhyme in the middle of the next line . . .
>
> The natural lack of double rhymes in English leads to an avoidance of words of more than one syllable at the end of the lyric line, except in blank alternation with rhyme. A movement constant in Continental languages is absent. But by cross-rhymes or vowel-rhyming, separately, one or more of the syllables of longer words, on or off accent, the difficulty may be turned: lovely and neglected words are advanced to the tonic place and divide their echoes.

It is not fanciful, hearing the interlacement of sounds in a Clarke poem such as 'The Scholar', to think it an equivalent for the ear of what strikes the eye when we look at the interlaced curves and angles on the geometrically carved shaft of a Celtic cross, or at illuminated letters in the Book of Kells. The English liking for the insouciant and slapdash amateur, in the arts as in other fields, is affronted by the scrupulous professionalism of Clarke, alike in his poems and in the note just quoted. But this is typical, if not of Ireland (for the Irish produce their own brand of sometimes engaging, amateurish harum-scarums), at least of the Gaelic Ireland that produced the bardic schools. And Clarke is unashamedly *poeta doctus*, no less in the fashioning of his poems as artifacts than in the learnedness of his allusions and references. 'Irish poets, learn your trade.' Thus Yeats; and Clarke obeyed the injunction, having indeed schooled himself in a harder school than dreamed of by Yeats.

A poet like Clarke who abjures and distrusts mythopoeia is obviously going to have a difficult relationship with the Christian myth along with all the rest. To say so is not to impugn the sincerity of any profession he may make of belief in the Christian verities. But he is likely to be mutinous inside any church at all. And so it is not surprising that anti-clericalism, angry, needling and insistent, informed more and more of the poems that Clarke wrote after 1945. Clarke called such short and acrid poems 'satires', but this is misleading. In many cases, an apter description would be 'epigram' or 'lampoon'; and the names of Landor on the one hand, of Swift on the other, may remind us that there can be great writing in both these neglected *genres*. Because these poetic kinds are neglected, seldom practised and little considered, there is little awareness of the conventions that govern them. It is foolish to ask of a lampoon, or of any kind of invective, that it be fair-minded; giving both sides of the case is just not in the contract. (Which is not to deny that we may object to a lampoon that it is facile, *cheap*; 'Medical Missionary of Mary' is one of Clarke's lampoons that may be thought objectionable on these grounds.)

'Forget Me Not' is not a lampoon, nor an epigram either. Yet we may well detect such a blindness to the terms of the implicit contract when a reader of 'Forget me Not', W. J. Roscelli, protests: 'I have seen too many people dying of starvation in Shimbashi slums to become greatly exercised over man's inhumanity to horses. If an export horse trade can boost a nation's economy and help eliminate poverty, I find nothing short-sighted or stupid in it, Lemuel Gulliver and Austin Clarke notwithstanding.'[1] It is easy to feel that this bluff humanitarian good sense is somehow beside the point, and yet not be able to see or say why. The truth is, surely, that 'Forget Me Not' does not declare it to be wrong to raise horses for slaughter, to slaughter them, or to eat their meat. What it *does* say is that a decision to set this process in motion cannot be taken on merely quantitative computations ('the greatest good of the greatest number', boosting a national economy), but should take into account imponderable because qualitative considerations like 'All the gentling, custom of mind/And instinct, close affection, done with.' And the poem surely says or implies with justified indignation that this particular decision, like nearly all such decisions in modern societies, *was* taken after merely quantitative computations of short-term profit and loss.

One of the qualitative costs that must be counted in the disappearance of the horse as man's workmate – not one of the most grievous costs, but one of the most surprising – is counted sardonically at the end of Clarke's poem:

> Tipsters respect our grandsires,
> Thorough-breds, jumpers o' the best.
> Our grass still makes a noble show, and the roar
> Of money cheers us at the winning post.
> So pack tradition in the meat-sack, Boys,
> Write off the epitaph of Yeats.
>   I'll turn
> To jogtrot, pony bell, say my first lesson:
>   *Up the hill*
>   *Hurry me not;*
>   *Down the hill*
>   *Worry me not;*

[1] W. J. Roscelli in *The Celtic Cross* (Purdue University Studies, 1964), p. 69.

> *On the level,*
> *Spare me not,*
> *In the stable,*
> *Forget me not.*

> *Forget me not.*

The same artless lines, except for the repeated 'Forget me not', had opened the poem, which had then gone on:

> Trochaic dimeter, amphimacer
> And choriamb, with hyper catalexis,
> Grammatical inversion, spring of double
> Rhyme

– which is a prosodist's learnedly exact description of just those italicized verses. And these are (so the poem tells us a few lines later) the 'work-a-day, holiday jingle' which the poet as a child learned to say when riding in a neat pony-trap or horse-drawn cab with his Uncle John, who figures largely in *Twice Round the Black Church*. After the prosodist's analysis, we have:

> So we learned to scan all, analyse
> Lyric and ode, elegy, anonymous patter,
> For what is song itself but substitution?

And what this means to say is that some of the patterns of rhythm which sound, or used to sound, in the head of verse-making man were the several patterns of varied but regular occurrence beaten out by a horse's hooves as the horse trotted or walked, cantered or galloped. In fact Clarke is inverting and yet endorsing the point made by T. S. Eliot in a much quoted guess that man's sense of rhythm and measure may have been permanently altered by the internal combustion engine. The characteristic pun on 'substitution' makes the point for those who look: it is a technical term of prosody, but 'what is song itself but substitution?' means also that in poetry we substitute a pattern in the reality of language for patterns that we discern and want to express in reality outside of language. Among those linguistic patternings are those, peculiarly important to verse, which reveal themselves to the ear, and can be analysed by counting syllables, counting the beat, counting metrical feet. Yeats's epitaph – 'Horseman, pass by!' – we must indeed 'write off'; and with it we write off all the centuries in which no rhythms were so insistently present to man, from earliest childhood, as the rhythms beaten out by horses' hooves – rhythms so insistent that one may indeed wonder whether they were not imprinted on man's nervous system.

But this consideration, though it brilliantly and intriguingly frames Clarke's poem (and makes it a post-symbolist poem, inasmuch as we now see it describing itself), is far from accounting for the indignation and outrage which are at its heart. (These inform also his 'Knacker Rhymes' in a booklet of 1960 where the title, *The Horse-Eaters*, forces the theme on our attention.) Hasn't Clarke got the whole thing 'out of proportion'? Surely not. For what Clarke sees and protests against is *sacrilege*. And so it is just here that we find the grounds for saying, with Augustine Martin (the best of his Irish admirers), that Clarke is 'a deeply religious man'. 'Forget Me Not' reminds us that in the ancient world the horse was a sacred animal; for Clarke what is sacred is not the horse, but the relationship between horse and man. The sanctity of that tie is the non-quantifiable cost which is left out of account if with W. J. Roscelli we refuse 'to become greatly exercized over man's inhumanity to horses', because of 'too many people dying of starvation in Shimbashi slums'.

And so we come full circle to where we started, with *mythopoeia*. Clarke's poetry seems to make no new myths, and to celebrate no old ones. More often it exerts itself sardonically to puncture and explode myths, in the sense of dangerous fictions with which the Irishman deludes himself about his national identity and his supposedly peculiar virtues. And yet the poems about the horse-trade show that at the heart of Clarke's world, as in the strikingly different mythopoeic world of Edwin Muir, there *is* myth, since there is a belief in the sacred. To find this belief professed in a tone of voice that is still sardonic is especially arresting; it gives us pause, as Muir's voice cannot. On the other hand, the sardonic tone misleads all but the most careful reader; for the tone makes us look anywhere but where, since sacrilege is denounced, sacredness is affirmed. And so there is that much excuse for a misreading like W. J. Roscelli's. But if we are sure that none the less it is a misreading, we may hesitantly conclude that every poet's task is ultimately and essentially, if not mythopoeic, at any rate religious; and that it is dangerous for any poet to think otherwise.

Basil Bunting

In *Loquitur* (1965), Basil Bunting reprinted, as number 36 in a sequence of 'Odes', a poem that he dated as of 1948:

> See! Their verses are laid
> as mosaic gold to gold
> gold to lapis lazuli
> white marble to porphyry
> stone shouldering stone, the dice
> polished alike, there is
> no cement seen and no gap
> between stones as the frieze strides
> to the impending apse:
> the rays of many glories
> forced to its focus forming
> a glory neither of stone
> nor metal, neither of words
> nor verses, but of the light
> shining upon no substance;
> a glory not made
> for which all else was made.

The poem is untitled. A pedestrian title might be 'Of Conciseness'. This will not seem reductive if we attend to the note which Bunting, normally a niggard in such matters, supplied to the poem in *Loquitur* and subsequently in *Collected Poems* (1968-1978):

> A friend's misunderstanding obliges me to declare that the implausible optics of this poem are not intended as an argument for the existence of God, but only suggest that the result of a successful work of art is more than the sum of its meanings and differs from them in kind.

The echoes of the Nicene Creed and of the beginning of John's Gospel are prominent enough to make the friend's misunderstanding not implausible. And indeed Basil Bunting's Quakerism has generally been too little heeded. Though his whisky-drinking and richly vernacular and amorously wide-ranging *persona* may seem to set him outside the circuit of the Society of Friends, there is no evidence that he ever forswore the sectarian allegiance that caused him as an eighteen-year-old to register for military service, precisely to declare himself a conscientious objector and so to serve a prison-term, thereby earning the enduring respect of Ezra Pound. (That was in World War One; quixotically, he insisted on serving with zest and distinction in several theatres of World War Two.) It is not for nothing that Bunting named his masterpiece *Briggflatts* (1965) after an ancient Quaker meeting-house. And little as his fellow Free Churchmen have realized it, all of his poetry can be seen as a flower of dissenting Protestantism. As he would explain to Paul Johnstone in 1977,

> Quakerism is a form of mysticism no doubt, in that it doesn't put forward any logical justification whatever, only the justification of experience. It is comparable pretty easily with a pantheistic notion of the universe . . . What you believe is your own affair so long as you follow out the process of simply waiting quietly and emptying your mind of everything else to hear what they would call in their own language the voice of God in your inside. We don't use that kind of language nowadays, but it is a simpler one than the various psychological phrases which we would use.[1]

This suggests that all Bunting's poetry is, for good or ill, a poetry of what Dissenters have always called 'the inner voice'.

All the same, Ode 36 is certainly leached of its power, and sold short, if we see it as principally a theological or devotional utterance. For it *is* what it says: its assertion that good verse-writing is analogous to the setting flush of tesserae in a mosaic composition (for instance the mausoleum of Galla Placidia at Ravenna) is made good by the way the poem's own words, like the mosaicist's 'dice' of stone or glass, are set side by side in the verse-lines, with no connective, no 'cement', beyond the monosyllabic preposition, 'to'. Every one knows that conciseness is a rule of good writing, whether in verse or prose; but this writing, and the proposition that it makes, pushes that truism to and beyond its normal acceptable limits. Words (images, we might say, but only if we accept that anything named is by that token in some degree 'imaged') are set flush one by another, the syntactical connections between them elided or suppressed,

---

[1] *Meantime*, No. 1 (1977). See Carroll F. Terrell (ed.) *Basil Bunting. Man and Poet* (National Poetry Foundation, 1981), p. 81.

enriched if never quite supplanted by connectives of melody, of rhythm. This was Bunting's procedure always, and he held to it with a rigour beyond what British taste could stomach, in his own lifetime and since. For whereas *Briggflatts* was on its first appearance hailed somewhat uncertainly as a masterpiece, in the years since its mastery has been tacitly taken to be, if real, eccentric. British poetry looks very different if we take *Briggflatts* to be, on the contrary, central to it.

There are those who think that after 1945 the poetry of Bunting is manifestly better than any other poetry in English written in the same period. It is in a class of its own. But this was so far from received opinion that it could not be taken seriously. The trouble was that Bunting wrote always for the ear. And ever since, with the death of Robert Bridges in 1930, the science of English prosody had been generally and tacitly abandoned, writing with and for the ear had been not just disregarded but positively disapproved of. In Britain the only responsible voice raised in protest against this had been William Empson's, and Empson could recognize apparently only such auditory shapes as emerged from traditional metres like the iambic pentameter. Even as criticism vaunted itself on ever more refined techniques for defining the semantic dimension of poetry, understanding of poetry's auditory dimension was allowed to revert to a stage impressionistic and barbarous. Such a development cannot be understood as simply a frivolous change in taste, but rather must have testified to the general atrophy of a faculty: readers had ceased not just to listen, but positively to *hear*. And so in 1966, when Bunting's *Briggflatts* appeared, those who wanted to claim for the poem what it deserved were like music-critics addressing the tone-deaf. For a crude example, *Briggflatts* has for epigraph, 'The spuggies are fledged'; and there is a note to explain the Northumbrian word 'spuggies' (which is not in OED) as 'little sparrows'. So far, so good. But an American reader or say a New Zealander, or even a Home Counties Englishman, might still suppose that the desired and normal pronunciation of the word is *spudzhiz*. Only those who are intimate with Bunting's poetry can recognize that this is unthinkable: that the *dzh* sound, immediately picked up where it is inescapable in 'fledged', would produce an acoustic blur and sludge such as Bunting, even in this sentence that is not part of the poem, would never tolerate. The *g* in 'spuggies' has to be hard, as in 'rug'. The point is not to be easy on the ear, mellifluous; on the contrary, much of the time the intention is to be hard on the ear, to make the ear (and following it, the tongue) *work*; to prevent both ear and tongue from sliding all too easily from *dzh* to *dzh*, as also to prevent them melting all vowels into hazily approximate diphthongs. The sounds are to be exact, that is to say, distinct one from another; only in that way can the reader be made to dance, rather than slide or slur, from one sound to the next. Bunting's North Country pronunciation did indeed distinguish English vowels more sharply than standard pronunciation does. And Bunting was at pains to insist that his music would be heard only if his words were given that Northern pronunciation. This was especially in keeping with *Briggflatts*, which at the simplest, most accessible level is a poem in celebration of Northumbria, a region historically larger than, but centred on, the poet's native Northumberland to which he had returned after a nomadic life spent mostly in foreign parts, particularly in the Middle East. (Those foreign scenes get into the poem too, since they are among the speaker's memories.) But the Northernness of the poem, and particularly of its music, can be over-emphasized: though there are dialect words like 'spuggies', these are infrequent grace-notes, the poem is not written in dialect but in standard British English, that English however handled with an exceptionally tender care for its acoustic values. The deeply ingrained Englishness of *Briggflatts* has to be insisted on, because British insularity has sometimes tried to push Bunting into the margin by representing him as a rootless cosmopolitan. To such insular prejudice, none of Bunting's foreign attachments – not even his devotion to classical Persian poetry (from which he quarried much of the central and most difficult of the five sections of *Briggflatts*) – has given so much offence as his fellow feeling with certain Americans, particularly the two to whom he dedicated *Loquitur*, Ezra Pound and Louis Zukofsky. And Pound's name in particular bulks all too large whenever Bunting is spoken of. There is a disposition to regard him as a slavish disciple and imitator of that American poet. But if there was ever excuse for this, it disappeared in 1981 with the publication of an admirable and alas American symposium, *Basil Bunting. Man and Poet*, edited by Carroll F. Terrell. This showed clearly that Bunting had always been his own man, keeping his distance from Pound in the midst of his great affection for him. Notably he had always extolled Wordsworth, that great North Country poet, for whom in the Poundian Pantheon there seems to be no place at all.

Yet Bunting is undoubtedly a modernist, in the sense in which Pound is a modernist, though T. S. Eliot also. Historically this is Bunting's unique importance; for in the present century there is no British-English poet of whom as much can be said. And so Bunting's existence is an embarrassment to the numerous English historians who would have it that modernism in poetry was a temporary American-inspired distraction from a native tradition which persisted, undeterred though for a time invisible, behind the marches and counter-marches of modernist polemics.

Still, Bunting wore his modernism with a difference, an English or British difference. In the same year when *Briggflatts* appeared, Bunting's American contemporary George Oppen, who had appeared with him as long ago as 1932 in *An 'Objectivist's Anthology*, sneered at poems addressed to readers 'who may be imagined to admire the quaintness and ingenuity of the poet, but can scarcely have been part of the poet's attempt to find himself in the world – unless perhaps to find himself as a charming conversationalist.'[1] It is not hard to envisage some of the poems that Oppen may have had in mind, nor to share his impatient distaste for them. But it is surely rash to let Oppen hurry us into rejecting out of hand any notion that a poet's poems are parts of a conversation he conducts with his readers. It will certainly seem so to any one who finds validity in Wordsworth's description of the poet as 'a man speaking to men'. And Bunting in *Briggflatts* wrote:

> It is time to consider how Domenico Scarlatti
> condensed so much music into so few bars
> with never a crabbed turn or congested cadence,
> never a boast or a see-here; . . .

This is still a plea for conciseness; and if 'never a boast or a see-here' corresponds to 'no cement seen and no gap' in Ode 36, it can be seen to correspond also to Oppen's disgust with poetry that parades 'the quaintness and ingenuity of the poet'. All the same, 'It is time to consider . . .' The expression, the tone of it and the gesture it makes, are undoubtedly conversational. And the conversational quality of Bunting's verse in *Briggflatts*, though it is seldom so overt as here, in fact is constant. We are not overhearing the ruminations of a solitary speaking to himself, as we often are when reading Oppen or many pages of Pound's *Cantos*. For Bunting poetry, the writing and reading of it, is still a *sociable* affair, even if the society that it envisages is hard to find and may be thought ideal. For instance, the poet who conceives of himself as a man speaking to men will reflect that men normally expect to be addressed in sentences; and so Bunting, though he strenuously condenses his sentences, never abandons the subject-verb-object structure of the English sentence, whereas in Oppen and Pound what we read is quite often a series of disjunct phrases pulled free of any syntactical anchorage. This sets Bunting apart from other modernists to a degree that admiring chroniclers of

[1] See *Ironwood* 5 (1975), pp. 78–85.

modernism have yet to recognize. Instead, Bunting's reward was to see *Briggflatts* berated (by Peter Dale, in *Agenda*, Spring 1978) for 'the poverty of its use of syntax', for being 'tediously dominated by the simple sentence'!

The Gurus

The 1960s were the great years of the Western *guru*. The slangy appropriation of the term was itself typical of the decade, in its skin-deep orientalism but in other ways too. If 'guru' was an appellation partly deprecating and mocking, it was also more than half serious. To several generations of young intellectuals it became important to pretend that the teachers they were prepared to listen to – one was Herbert Marcuse (*Eros and Civilization*, 1955), another was Norman O. Brown (*Life against Death*, 1959) – were wandering sages and holy men, uncontaminated by any association with institutions like universities and university departments, or with the institutional authority these represented – an authority that the intellectuals in question wanted to think they had rejected. This was so much make-believe. Both Marcuse and Brown were securely and comfortably harboured by universities, as was Herbert Marshall McLuhan (*The Gutenberg Galaxy*, 1962, *Understanding Media*, 1964). As for the most eminent of all the gurus, Claude Lévi-Strauss, patentee of 'structuralism', it was hardly possible to think of an institutional niche safer or more resplendent than that of Professor of Social Anthropology in the Collège de France.

Lévi-Strauss's eminence is so conspicuous that it may seem McLuhan cannot be considered alongside him, as a figure of anything like equal weight. Literary people, however, consistently thus considered them, side by side, until well into the 1970s, when both of them in different ways suffered a sudden eclipse. Nor was this necessarily wrong. McLuhan is not such a light-weight thinker as he may seem to those who misconstrue his writing for preference in a discontinuous jokey or jaunty manner, lending itself to memorable wise-cracking slogans like 'the global village', or 'The medium is the message'. Those slogans have important meanings which the passage of years has not erased; and for McLuhan, writing like this was a deliberate strategy, a strategy moreover which came directly out of his deepest concerns. He was deliberately imitating the style of the tabloid newspaper; and that – the tabloid – was one of the 'media' which he was determined to study and analyse without prejudice. The tabloid newspaper, he pointed out, was essentially discontinuous – in its physical format (so many 'stories' on its front page, each in its panel, each with a headline in bolder type), even more than in its syntax and diction. Effectively, therefore, such a page of newsprint was composed on a principle of simple (but often striking and sometimes enigmatic) juxtaposition. And McLuhan boldly connected this with the poetics of juxtaposition-without-copula that Pound had argued for in his edition of Fenollosa's *Chinese Written Character as a Medium for Poetry* (1919), and had implemented in his *Cantos*. What made this more than an impressionistic bright idea was McLuhan's relating both phenomena to a datable technological innovation, the invention of the electric telegraph, without which, he pointed out, the tabloid lay-out would have been impossible.

This is typical of McLuhan's procedure, and it is what sets him apart from the other *gurus*, Lévi-Strauss among them: McLuhan's focus is historical or, as we learned to say in the 1960s, *diachronic*, whereas Lévi-Strauss's structuralism is, like the Saussurian linguistics which Lévi-Strauss took as his model, committedly *synchronic*. McLuhan took the invention of movable type by Gutenberg in the fifteenth century to have been a technical invention like that of the electric telegraph, with comparable or even greater consequences, not just for how we structure expression but how we structure experience. It is because we are all children of 'the age of print' that we fail to see how the printed page, continuous from left-hand to right-hand margin, is only one historically determined mode of conveying communications (and more than communications, experiences), though our knowledge of pre-print oral cultures surviving to our own day should have alerted us to this, and our experience of the television-screen, as the most recently invented alternative medium, should make the recognition inescapable. What made McLuhan notorious among conservative-minded literary people, and disliked by them, was the seemingly sanguine enthusiasm with which he regarded a late-come medium like television. And McLuhan, it is true, was temperamentally sanguine. Yet he always maintained that he was personally devoted to the print culture whose demise he was compelled to predict; and in fact the writings of his earlier years, when he was a thoroughly traditional literary historian, bear him out. His refusal to cry automatically 'Woe, woe!' was proof not of fatuous optimism but only of his determination to regard every medium *without prejudice*. If some of those influenced by him were thus fatuously optimistic – for instance, applauding the public poetry-reading as a happy reversion to a pre-print, oral culture – that was not McLuhan's fault.

A similarly unreflecting primitivism was read, with as little warrant, out of Lévi-Strauss's books on structuralism, though those books were even in translation (*Structural Anthropology*, 1963, *The*

Scope of Anthropology, 1967) too forbidding to win a popular fol-
lowing, and Lévi-Strauss's influence was disseminated through
popularizers. To this, however, there was one notable exception:
his *Tristes Tropiques* (1955), translated as *A World on the Wane* (1961).
This lovely and plangent, deeply personal and even 'confessional'
book revealed in the French *savant* a profoundly literary sensibil-
ity; and indeed his fellow-professionals in anthropology were to
complain, not without malice, that Claude Lévi-Strauss had the
sensibility of a poet. *Tristes Tropiques* tells how the then youthful
anthropologist found it intolerable to inspect the cultures he was
studying in the Amazon basin from the standpoint of an 'advanced'
European studying primitives. Instead he came to see, and to pro-
pose, that every culture, whether 'primitive' or 'advanced', achieved
an internally coherent structure so far as it managed to incorpo-
rate in its institutions and its rituals certain binary distinctions,
of which the most radical was probably that between male and
female. Given that they harmonized these binary oppositions, by
devices however bizarre and apparently unaccountable, no culture
was more 'advanced' than any other. And the devices in question,
though they might be as seemingly non-instrumental as rituals and
mythologies, or as pervasive as kinship-systems, might equally be as
seemingly utilitarian as customs of what to wear or how to prepare
food. Accordingly, we could be told in 1967 that 'clothing, cooking,
indeed all forms of social existence, are communication systems'.[1]
All these forms, we were invited to see, were 'languages'. This was
asserted by a critic of architecture, who certainly had learned to see
how architecture could 'communicate', by pursuing a route from
Saussure's and Jakobson's linguistics, through Norbert Weiner's
cybernetics, to Lévi-Strauss's anthropology. But literature is the
art whose artistic medium is language; and there is an obvious
difficulty in conceiving how something which *uses* language can at
the same time *be* a language. It was inevitable that linguisticians,
enjoying at this time unprecedented prestige, should want to cut out
the intermediate stages of the route, and should want to relate litera-
ture to language quite directly and therefore (however they might
declare otherwise) reductively. Many poets had recognized that all
the poems written or yet to be written in any given language are
potential in that language, which the poet therefore serves as merely
a conduit or at most an enabling agent. And literary theorists like
Northrop Frye (*Anatomy of Criticism*, 1957) had made the same point.
But this in no way opened a route to the promised land that some
ambitious linguisticians seemed to foresee, a future state of the art

[1] George Baird ' "La Dimension Amoureuse" in Architecture', *Arena* (June, 1967) p. 25.

(of *their* art) when it would be possible to enumerate exhaustively all the linguistic choices open to the poet, moment by moment, as he wrote his poem. (If it were possible to do this retrospectively, it would also be possible to do so in advance – one can see why poets were alarmed!) The most distinguished figure who could seem to lend colour to such aspirations was Roman Jakobson (*Fundamentals of Language*, 1971, but Jakobson's writings are innumerable and various). Under Jakobson's aegis came into being a sub-department of linguistics called balefully 'stylistics', and poets are probably too ready to believe that this science, born with Jakobson, also died with him, since no one since has combined his polyglot erudition with his literary sensitivity. Jakobson, a Russian who translated himself through Prague to Harvard, was a many-sided genius whose ideas, notably on the crucial distinction between metaphor and metonymy, continue to reverberate long after his death, not just in literary studies but in areas so apparently remote as Freudian psychoanalysis. Those of his writings which offer themselves as criticism of poetic texts are probably the least valuable, following procedures too cumbrous to be useful. Jakobson was never a guru, for he was too artless and selfless, also too dignified, to practise any technique of self-promotion.

The counter-attack upon linguistics from inside literary studies came only in 1975, with George Steiner's too little regarded *After Babel*. Expressions like 'the language of costume' or 'the language of gesture' are after all readily understood. All Lévi-Strauss's work proved was that such expressions are less metaphorical, more literal, than we had supposed. Costume and gesture were, we were invited to suppose, communication-systems just as language was. Steiner's momentous observation was that language itself is not exclusively, nor perhaps principally, a communication-system. Any given tongue, he proposed and showed, was at least as much *secretive*; its function, even as it facilitated communication inside the community of, say, English-speakers, was to bind that linguistic community against outsiders, speakers of another tongue. Steiner's argument thus had the effect of justifying hermetic and arcane poetic strategies, as no less faithful to the essential nature of language than strategies that were lucid and direct. No more in the 1970s than in the 1960s did the British public take kindly to such a justification for modernist (or non-modernist) 'obscurity'.

All in all, structuralism, though it served an illuminating and humanizing purpose in other fields of study (and in other areas of social life, which literary people like others could now observe through new eyes) transmitted to poetics only what students of poetics already knew. Such students had known for many years that a poem was a structure, mediating between stress and counter-stress, those stresses (so it was hoped and believed) mirroring in the microcosm of the poem oppositions in play in the societies that poems emerged from and were addressed to. Indeed structuralism, oddly enough, came into prominence at just the time when poets and their readers were beginning to wonder if poetic structures built out of self-cancelling ironies and ambiguities had not become inordinately sealed against direct traffic with the world of private and public affairs.

Elaine Feinstein

Through several years beginning in 1965 or 1966, the impressionable sections of British society were swept by recurrent tides of sympathy for the mostly young Americans who were protesting at their nation's warfare in Vietnam, and resisting being conscripted into a way which they disowned and condemned. There thus came into being a climate of sentiment which youthful anti-imperialists twenty years later might find it hard to credit: a historical moment, lasting for several years, in which the most exposed and valiant heroes of anti-imperialism in the West were thought to be Americans. Moreover, the struggle which these Americans maintained against the declared or undeclared but in any case overt strategies of the American state was by no means narrowly political. From the first in the USA and almost as soon among sympathizers in Britain and elsewhere, the protest against the Vietnam war ramified into espousing ethical and philosophical positions to which the American military involvement in South East Asia was almost incidental. What was generated was nothing less than what the spokesmen of the movement proclaimed: a 'counterculture', committed to overturning and reversing the accepted norms in areas so apparently remote from military operations as education and diet and self-employment, as well as drug-taking and sexual *mores*. American poets at the time declared themselves almost without exception on the side of those who repudiated the Vietnam war and, with only a few more exceptions, on the side of the counterculture. Accordingly, in the late 1960s there was in Britain an avid and responsive audience for American poets, and not just for such poets as had been screened first by the New York and subsequently by the London literary establishments. Gary Snyder, Charles Olson, Lorine Niedecker, Edward Dorn and Robert Creeley were among the American poets who, bypassing the New York clearing-house, were in those years excitingly available in British bookshops and in some cases on British platforms, even in British editions like those of the elegant and long-to-be-lamented Fulcrum Press.

It was in this climate of opinion and sentiment that Elaine Feinstein published in 1966 her first collection of poems, *In a Green Eye*. The poems were not overtly, nor even by implication, political. But this was one of the first of rather many books by young British poets which revealed how the poet had been to school to William Carlos Williams and to American disciples of Williams like Olson and Creeley, rather than to any of the approved canon of British poets. Feinstein had learned from these American models certain devices and certain mannerisms, notably an extremely sparse and idiosyncratic punctuation; and more valuably, she had learned to look for poems in the most workaday experiences, and to set down the resultant poems without worrying whether they were trivial. Trivial they often were, however, and lacking resonance. So *In a Green Eye* is important and intriguing, historically; but it is not intrinsically much more valuable than many collections which came out at the same time or soon after. It would appear in the event that this poet could grow out of this initial conditioning, as others could not.

1968

1968 was a year that, as it was experienced by many people and certainly by poets, had a character all its own. The date is still resonant among those old enough to remember. Only five years later John Berger acknowledged that resonance, and undertook to explain it:

> . . . In 1968, hopes, nurtured more or less underground for years, were born in several places in the world and given their names: and in the same year, these hopes were categorically defeated. This became clear in retrospect. At the time many of us tried to shield ourselves from the harshness of the truth. For instance, at the beginning of 1969, we still thought of a second 1968 possibly recurring.
>
> This is not the place for an analysis of what changed in the alignment of political forces on a world scale. Enough to say that the road was cleared for what, later, would be called *normalization*. Many thousands of lives were changed too. But this will not be read in the history books.

If in the aftermath of 1968 'many thousands of lives were changed', why should this not be 'read in the history books'? In fact, whereas these matters may have been passed over in books of political history, social historians – some of the best of them responsible journalists – have for some years now been putting the picture together. Berger goes on:

> When I look around at my friends – and particularly those who were (or still are) politically conscious – I see how the long-term direction of their lives was altered or deflected at that moment just it might have been by a private event: the onset of an illness, an unexpected recovery, a bankruptcy. I imagine that if they looked at me, they would see something similar.

[1] John Berger, 'Between Two Colmars' (*The Guardian*, 1973), reprinted in *About Looking* (London, 1980).

Normalization means that between the different political systems, which share the control of almost the entire world, anything can be exchanged under the single condition that nothing anywhere is radically changed. The present is assumed to be continuous, the continuity allowing for technological development.

This shows how determined John Berger is to find *political* meanings. And of course he might well contend that to people 'politically conscious' there is nothing in common life that is *not* political, if only we look at it hard enough; but it can also be thought that that way of hard looking is in some ways blinkered, and may even see what is not there. Certainly there are things to see that this way of looking will miss; as we recognize if we look at another account of 1968, written in the same year as John Berger's. The author is E. P. Thompson, writing an open letter to the distinguished Polish *emigré* Leszek Kolakowski:

> Your arrival in California coincided with a culture of 'radicalism', which had serious and courageous components, but which was surrounded by a halo of hysteria which – caught up and magnified in the lenses of the sensationalist media – reproduced itself across half the world as a 'youth culture' of self-indulgent emotionalism and of exhibitionist style. From Paris to Berkeley, from Munich to Oxford, the 'West' offered a supermarket of avant-garde products, some branded as 'Marxism', each cutting the price against the others. But how many of these products, when unpackaged, contained only old and discredited arguments under a new label, or a horrific make-up kit for the revolting young bourgeoisie (a fast sports-car, a villa in the Apennines, and the Thoughts of Mao-Tse–Tung) to act out their transient, fashionable pantomime? Posters of Che Guevara, juxtaposed against mini-skirts, 'Mao tunics', and military leather jackets, decorated the most modish swinging boutiques, in the King's Road and in Royal Leamington Spa; for a year or two, intoxicated by 'May 1968' in Paris – or, rather by this event as assimilated in instant myth – cohorts of leftist students imagined that, by some act of occupation of a few administrators' offices, they could announce in the heart of repressive capitalist society a 'red base' which would bring an instant voluntaristic proletarian revolution looming out of the streets.[1]

Between these two versions, both from the British political Left,

[1] 1973; reprinted in *The Poverty of Theory and other Essays* (London, 1978).

there is little doubt which has more to give to a history of these times which pays particular attention to how the times were seen through poetry. The pantomime, the dressing-up and make-believe, were indeed conspicuous in the events of 1968 and after, as others besides E. P. Thompson remember them; and to poetry, itself a play of fictions, such acted-out fictions are obviously relevant. The politically conscious, on the other hand, are not well placed to distinguish political action from political play-acting, to see the difference between radicalism and what came to be called, usefully and exactly, 'radical chic'.

This failure to distinguish must cast some doubt on John Berger's account or definition of the 'normalization' that according to him had already by 1973 decisively supervened. For if the hopes of 1968 were in this way theatrical, did not the same theatricality inform the dashing of those hopes? After all, when Berger says of normalization that it means that 'anything can be changed under the single condition that nothing anywhere is radically changed', does this not describe exactly the condition of the actor's life, or the theatrical producer's? John Gielgud or Humphrey Bogart or Peggy Ashcroft play many parts, wear many costumes, but 'nothing anywhere is radically changed'. At least with stars like these, the audience's response incorporates, and is meant to incorporate, the awareness that under all the disguises Gielgud remains Gielgud, Bogart is still delightfully Bogart, Ashcroft is still Ashcroft. Thus normalization may be as much play-acting as the specious abnormality that it is thought to have crushed or dragooned; there is as much theatrical fiction in the one dispensation as in the other. And of course there is abundant evidence that this is how public opinion, at least in the UK, perceives the political process, whether nationally or internationally. Brezhnev or whoever 'threatens'; Reagan or whoever 'stands firm'; Margaret Thatcher with a revealingly theatrical allusion declares 'The lady's not for turning'; and the Leader of the Opposition acts out in the House of Commons the condition of being choked with indignation. Not one of them escapes, in the eyes of the least sophisticated voter, the mordancy of Mandy Rice-Davies's retort: 'Well, he would, wouldn't he?'[1]

Belatedly Peter York for one, in his *Modern Times* (London, 1984), has penetrated to this consensus of theatricality which underlies and perhaps undermines all the sedulously touted antagonisms of British public life, though for that matter the professionally cynical breed of political commentator had taken it for granted long before. It

---

[1] Miss Rice-Davies, it may be necessary to explain, was a witness in an English political scandal of 1960, 'the Profumo case'.

might be argued that this was one area, perhaps the only one, in which post-1945 Britain had led the world. In the early 1950s it was possible to lament that, whatever else British life might have to its credit, it was 'drab', what it manifestly lacked was *style*. But that lack had certainly been made good by the time of 'Carnaby Street' – the internationally successful market of styles, of theatrical/non-theatrical costumes, which traded under the name of that particular West End alley. This phenomenon came well before 1968, and anticipated the street-theatre of that year. Indeed the development was abundantly predictable; one had only to take note of how successfully, for tourists both home-grown and foreign, the House of Lords and other institutions of the post-imperial power hung on to and profited by pomp and ceremony, imperial trappings and protocol. The Carnaby Street merchants recognized that the House of Lords and the Brigade of Guards could be brought as it were downmarket, so as to supply foreign visitors and the native populace with trappings and rituals just as gaudy and not a whit less satisfying for want of the archaic precedents which had given the original ceremonies a frozen and ghostly validity. And once the imperial insignia were thus in place, it became natural and indeed necessary to provide also the anti-imperialist costumes – hence the 'Mao tunics'.

It is not clear how far Peter York recognizes that London-as-a-market-of-styles was in being, and functioning, before 1960; at one point he speaks of today's marketers of design as 'a whole class of person that hardly existed before the Sixties'. What can be conceded to him is something that partly justifies John Berger in seeing 1968 as a turning-point; that is to say, the acceleration and proliferation of the tendency since that year. Particularly persuasive is York's treatment of the phenomenon called 'urban renewal':

> During the Sixties and Seventies, a new kind of theme park was emerging across the world: the gentrified change-of-use *quartier*, once plebeian or industrial in the real world, made over to the creative leisure life, the world of *taste*. In these places, a certain life is lived, a certain life *laid on*; bits of the past, of small plebeian businesses, of trades, of *characters* are retained to give atmosphere, while the essential class, ownership and occupational base changes out of sight.

This is admirably perceptive, though it may go wrong in laying stress on 'gentrification', since this may nourish a common enough nostalgia for the plebeian of yester year. Liverpool's Garden Centre, made over in the 1980s from an area of disused dockland ('once . . . industrial in the real world') into an area where one does nothing but stroll and watch the kiddies play ('the creative leisure life'), is thoroughly plebeian in the pleasures that it offers; yet it smells of grease-paint as pungently as gentrified Islington. The conversion of British social life into television documentary appears to be approved and enjoyed by all classes of society; there is no sign that it has been imposed by an influential minority.

Liverpool is one English city that in this perspective deserves at least equal billing with London. It is in the light cast up from the eerily unfrequented Mersey that we see most luridly the histrionics of much current sentiment. Liverpool is now, and has been ever since the blitz of World War II, a desolation. It was a desolation when it bred the Beatles, whose despairing bittersweet became in the 1960s a world-wide vogue which, the style having now achieved a nostalgic patina, the present city still attempts to batten on. The dishonesties necessarily practised, not only nor chiefly in Liverpool, in marketing a style that once proved a bonanza and still shows a profit, are glaring in the treatment customarily accorded to the wretched and pitiful life of the late John Lennon. His is, and always was, the very voice of desolation; yet it can be acclaimed as manifesting the sterling virtues of an invincible proletariat bending to its purposes both European existentialism and the inarticulate ideology of American blacks. 'In a curious way', writes one commentator, 'the experience of belonging to a subordinate culture was a common element' between the black American and the scouse. We learn from the same source that Lennon's adaptation of black musical styles 'was a statement of defiance – part of the process of putting imperialism into reverse which was later to produce the black-led uprisings in the great slave ports of Liverpool and Bristol in 1980 and 1981.'[1] Mindless and hopeless riots must become 'uprisings', and historical time must bring in its revenges with grotesque symmetry, if this is what it needs to keep the Lennon style, of life more than of music, still on the road as a business venture.

As English poets in the 1950s could be heard mourning that English life after 1945 'lacked style', so some of them were jubilant that in the heyday of the Beatles a style had been found. In both cases what we have is a sort of aestheticism. But in artists (poets) this is to be expected, and is not necessarily wrong. Where we may think they went wrong, and failed themselves as poets, was in running together the aesthetics of the creative and of the performing arts, or of the fine arts and the applied. If so, they were representative; for Britain since 1945 has given knighthoods to actors but not playwrights. An English poet in self-exile wrote of his country in 1969:

[1] David Widgery, 'Lennonism', *London Review of Books*, 21 February 1985.

> Beknighted actors, youth
> in tall hats, trailing feathers,
> society a congeries of roles . . .
> Napoleon was right;
> a nation of purveyors.
> Now we purvey ourselves.

And some years before the same poet had imagined a dialogue with a British diplomat long absent from the UK:

> 'What', said our diplomat,
> 'Sort of nation is
> This that I represent
> In South America?' I said:
>
> 'A nation of theatre-people,
> Purveyors, not creators,
> Adaptable cyphers, stylists,
> Educators, dandies.'

If this poet was talking politics, it was hardly party politics. The Britain he envisages in his poem, in both these poems, is a country where the performing arts are exalted above the creative, the middle-man above the producer, the transmitter or packager above the originator. In such a society histrionic make-believe is as much the habit of the political Right or Centre as of the Left. In what is an obviously immoderate vision, all British people of the 1960s are seen as chiefly occupied with posturing, striking attitudes; in the hope, so it seems, that their attitudes would be picturesque enough to attract the camera-crews or the Sunday journalists, equipped with fast-shutter lenses so as to feed the national self-regard week by week.

In 1985 Gavin Ewart, a London poet who had been popular for many years, looked back to the early 1960s when he had found it possible to write again after a long spell of sterility. This was in an epistle to his fellow poet, Peter Porter:

> Thirty years ago I first met you at a small party given by Charles Rycroft –
> but it wasn't until later that our paths became brothers, like Sherlock and Mycroft.
>
> At that time I had been more or less 'silent' for almost a quarter of a century
> (as they say of poets) and the likely lads, in Faber fable, tough and adventury,

were Gunn and Hughes with their loonies in leather, rampageous
    pigs, cats, hawks,
all ready to murder you quickly; from lad- and Nature-lovers there
    were few protesting squawks.

You on the other hand were into the serious satirical Colonial-in-
    London bit,
lighting Latimer candles to Culture – and a good many candles
    were lit . . .

Like any skilful writer of light verse, Gavin Ewart is careful to keep a
jump ahead of his readers. And so we can be sure that the vulgarity
here, both of language and ideas, is deliberate. Accordingly it may be
(though it seems unlikely) that Ewart is as scandalized as any one at the
way the poetic styles of Thom Gunn and Ted Hughes are defined in
terms of costume and accoutrements ('loonies in leather'), and in terms
of their themes, rather than for instance in their attitudes to the con-
ventions of metre or to how a poem can or should be structured. The
speaker of Ewart's poem, by ignoring such matters, plainly intends to
spurn style in that sense, in favour of the different style which has to
do with who is 'into' what in any given month or year. Accordingly:
'So we were into satire. Our London was brash, immoral, surprising
– 'What a city to sack!' – it was sacked by advertising.' Elsewhere in
the jaunty epistle it is made clear that Ewart and Porter and other
verse-writers were in the 1960s employed by advertising agencies, and
felt at home with them. And indeed the poem records a moment when
verse-writers came to the recognition that the making of poems could
be a natural extension of what they did when they made up advertising
captions: style as conceived of by advertisers – packagers *par excellence*
– could profitably be made the style also of poems.

    The information is invaluable, especially as the date of this recog-
nition can be fixed quite exactly. The recrudescence of Ewart's poetic
vocation – under as we have seen new auspices, and conceived in new
terms – came in 1962 or 1963. This is several years short of what John
Berger took to be the *annus mirabilis* 1968. It enables us to see that the
pantomimes of that year were by no means unheralded, all that was
new was for them to be politicized. Equally, 1968 was to cast a long
shadow forward, though not of the sort that John Berger looked for
and failed to find. Thereafter the poet would see himself as a *performing*
artist; and poetry would be thought of (we might say) as a service, not
a manufacturing, industry.

Sylvia Townsend Warner

In 1968 Sylvia Townsend Warner caused to be privately printed and privately distributed *King Duffus & Other Poems*. Every year sees many such productions, and there seems to be no machinery for keeping track of them. Doubtless most of them deserve to relapse unremarked into that obscurity from which they only half-heartedly seek to emerge. But undoubtedly there are exceptions; only a few years before, in Dublin, Austin Clarke in defiant dudgeon had brought out at his own expense, in editions of a couple of hundred copies, certain late collections that are among his finest. And in any case the author of *King Duffus* was not in any ordinary sense an obscure author. She had been famous ever since her earliest novels *Lolly Willowes* (1926) and *Mr Fortune's Maggot* (1927), her short stories had brought her an enthusiastic following on both sides of the ocean, and only the year before *King Duffus* there had appeared her remarkable biography of T. H. White. Her poetry, however, had undoubtedly been overshadowed and forgotten since her youthful collections *The Espalier* (1925), *Time Importuned* (1928) and *Opus 7* (1931). *King Duffus* seems to have been a demure or sardonic signal, to those few who cared, that as a poet she was still in business – as indeed she was, and to notable effect, though this would not emerge until her uncollected poems were published after her death.

These collections, up to and including *King Duffus*, pose in a very acute way a question that literary historians seldom address, though it is one that the serious reader is constantly bedevilled by: when is a style that is out of fashion also out of date? Do styles in poetry, or in any art, outlive their usefulness, or merely fall out of favour? To this question the shallow philistine and the camp-follower of the avant-garde have the same ready answer; for them, to be out of fashion is to be out of all reckoning. The sentimentalist and self-styled 'classicist' believe on the contrary that a style which once served well is serviceable for ever more, and hence that a change in fashion is never a change in taste or in sensibility. In the twentieth century, when changes whether of fashion or of taste have been radical and frequent, many readers have found themselves 'left behind', and have accepted that condition either shamefacedly or defiantly, according to temperament. 'Georgian' is one name for the style or range of styles that many such readers find themselves left behind with. The term has a clearly definable historical basis in the five *Georgian Poetry* anthologies that Edward Marsh edited between 1912 and 1922. But it has been, and still is, abused. In particular through several decades it was used widely as a term of blanket condemnation. In 1964 the New Zealander C. K. Stead, in his influential *The New Poetic*, undertook to vindicate at least some of 'the Georgians', and this initiative was cordially, perhaps too cordially, welcomed. It was seldom remarked or remembered that Stead's reclamation had been strictly limited: 'What my study of the period showed was that the early Georgians had themselves been something of a revolutionary force, and that the split between the later Georgians . . . on the one hand, and the Modernists . . . on the other, had given the Georgian movement as a whole a bad name which it scarcely deserved.'[1] There is nothing in this to bring comfort to admirers of for instance 'The Sailor' from *The Espalier*; it is accomplished certainly, as Townsend Warner was from the first, but the accomplishment is frigid – it spins out its narrow topic, and expresses no sentiment but what is time-honoured in the folk-song tradition rather than brought home to, or derived from, the experience of those to whom the folk-song situations are remote. ('Going to sea', after all, is hardly the same in the age of wireless-telegraphy as it was in the days of Boscawen.) *The Espalier* plainly belongs with 'the later Georgians', not with Rupert Brooke.

Time Importuned is only a little, and yet significantly, different. An opulent and elaborate poem, 'The Load of Fern' (opulent not just in its imagery but in its strophic structure) owes nothing to any Georgian but a great deal to Robert Bridges – who has been wrongly lumped in with the Georgians, as Walter de la Mare has been, and even Rudyard Kipling. Without doubt the poem has no point of contact with 'the Modernists' (not with Pound nor Eliot, but equally not with such dubious modernists as 'the Sitwells'). But a reader who resisted the tides of fashion so as to keep admiring 'The Load of Fern', or the Bridges poems that lie behind it (notably 'A Passer-by'), would surely be in the right. For such writing is out of fashion, but not necessarily out of date. Particularly at issue in such a case is the pastoralism, the assumption – common to Bridges, to Townsend Warner, and to the Georgians – that the English rural village was the social arena in which human dramas were enacted, human sentiments were honoured, in the only way that poets could deal with. It is easy, and moreover it is necessary, to point out that the urbanized Englishman of the twentieth century was ill-served by poets who seemed to tell him that his dilemmas, insofar as they had dignity,

---

[1] C. K. Stead, *Pound, Yeats, Eliot and the Modernist Movement* (London, 1986), p. 2.

were identical with those of his rustic forebears. But whereas Edward Thomas and even Thomas Hardy seem to have declared that rustic England would persist indefinitely *as a historical fact*, others – Robert Graves by implication, Edmund Blunden sometimes, Townsend Warner sometimes – seem to have suggested contrariwise that it would persist *ideally*, not as a fact but as a remembered paradigm by which quite different urban facts could be measured and set in order. That was how the pastoral convention had worked in the past; and at some points in *Time Importuned* that is how it seemed to work for Sylvia Townsend Warner, as it had for Bridges.

With *Opus* 7 these issues come to a head. Claire Harman calls it 'a little masterpiece'. And whereas this is surely extravagant, it is easy to agree with her that the poem deserves attention such as it has never yet received. A homely and far from idyllic narrative of village life, told in nearly 700 rhyming pentameter couplets, the precedent that it appeals to is obviously the poems of Crabbe. And George Crabbe is securely a classic or, as we would learn to say, canonical; admired by Ezra Pound and F. R. Leavis as by Benjamin Britten and E. M. Forster. Accordingly, by the lights of the academic classicist a modern poem in this mode, if it were well enough written, might well be as good as 'Peter Grimes'. More pertinently, though Crabbe's narrative poems are very different from Wordsworth's we do not have to approach the two poets in a wholly different frame of mind, with a quite different sort of attention; and yet this is how it is when we turn from *Opus* 7 to a modernist poem like Eliot's *The Waste Land*. Why this should be, is hard to make out, especially since Warner, already moving into her long dalliance with the Communist Party, had been at some pains to situate her narrative historically: her village is, as never before, firmly a post-1919 village. And yet this new found responsibility to the date on the calendar has the effect of high-lighting more than ever the incongruity between the matter and the manner, the impression of new wine in an old bottle. The interest of the case lies precisely in the fact that *Opus* 7 is from most points of view well-written; the author is in earnest and extremely intelligent, not just with the intelligence that sparkles in her story-telling but with the specifically *verbal* intelligence that distinguishes the poet. The conclusion seems inescapable: whereas the avant-gardistes are wrong to dismiss out of hand or with a condescending nod such unfashionable writers as Bridges or De la Mare, on the other hand it is surely true that some (perhaps all) poetic genres have a limited time-span, that they can outlive their usefulness – either when the socio-cultural context changes around them, or else when the masters of the genre have exhausted it simply by realizing every one of its potencies.

Larkin's Politics, and Tomlinson's

The pantomime make-believe of British public life in the 1960s (and since, for that matter) had been, in one of its aspects, derided by Philip Larkin in *The Whitsun Weddings* (1964):

> That day when Queen and Minister
> And Band of Guards and all
> Still act their solemn-sinister
> Wreath-rubbish in Whitehall.

However, it is not the poet who says this, but a hatefully distinct *persona* whose mode of being is epitomized in the title: 'Naturally the Foundation will Bear Your Expenses'. It is not Larkin but this person, flying off to Bombay to repeat a lecture he had given three weeks before in California, who reflects:

> It used to make me throw up,
> These mawkish nursery games:
> O when will England grow up?
> – But I outsoar the Thames . . .

Outsoaring the Thames (or the Humber) was what Philip Larkin notoriously would never do. This *persona* is not William Empson, but he sounds like a man who would willingly subscribe to, and take for granted, the socio-political as well as the religious sentiments of the author of *Milton's God*. And Larkin the poet hates him. Larkin's problem was, and would always be, that he had not, and would never trouble to construct, arguable grounds for the aversion that he rightly felt for such people; aversion to the academic profession as such – professed by Larkin, himself a university librarian! – was the laziest cop-out. If the speaker of this poem is detestable (as he is), the grounds for that detestation need to be spelled out. And in fact they are not hard to find; though Larkin could never be bothered to find them.

Another poem in *The Whitsun Weddings* deals with a very similar occasion, perhaps a Remembrance Day ceremony in Westminster Abbey or St Paul's. The poem is called, 'Broadcast':

Giant whispering and coughing from
Vast Sunday-full and organ-frowned-on spaces
Precede a sudden scuttle on the drum,
'The Queen', and huge resettling. Then begins
A snivel on the violins:
I think of your face among all those faces,

Beautiful and devout before
Cascades of monumental slithering,
One of your gloves unnoticed on the floor
Beside those new, slightly outmoded shoes.
Here it goes quickly dark. I lose
All but the outline of the still and withering

Leaves on half-emptied trees. Behind
The glowing wavebands, rabid storms of chording
By being distant overpower my mind
All the more shamelessly, their cut-off shout
Leaving me desperate to pick out
Your hands, tiny in all that air, applauding.

Despite its characteristic felicities (both the glove and the shoes are
beautifully managed, surely), this poem hardly lives up to the
promise of its first four lines: the image that bridges from the
second stanza to the third is all too dependent on the need to
find the rhyme, 'withering'; and in the last stanza the outlandish
rhyme-word, 'chording', is Hardyesque in the worst sense. And yet
the piece is very affecting. It is plain that the speaker, who may surely
be identified with the poet, is distraught at not being able to join
with the unidentified, tenderly evoked woman in her 'applauding'.
The emotion is not far from that of Hardy's 'The Oxen': 'Hoping it
might be so'.

A much more famous or notorious poem is 'Annus Mirabilis' from
Larkin's next and last collection, *High Windows*. It looks rather differ-
ent if we apprehend it, as the poem itself insists that we should, in the
context of the early 1960s – specifically, of 1963:

Sexual intercourse began
In nineteen sixty-three
(Which was rather late for me) –
Between the end of the *Chatterley* ban
And the Beatles' first LP.

The poem may be spoken either *in propria persona*, or from the mouth of an imagined character. (Much of the prurient interest it has attracted depends on the first alternative.) Either way, neither the raising of the ban on Lawrence's *Lady Chatterley's Lover*, nor the take-off of the Beatles into international fame, is seen as an unmitigated good. Because of these developments, we are told, the quarrel or wrangle between the sexes 'sank':

> Everyone felt the same,
> And every life became
> A brilliant breaking of the bank,
> A quite unlosable game.

It would be an exceptionally naïve reader, particularly of Larkin, who took these verses at their face value. No game, in Larkin's universe, is 'quite unlosable'. And the *persona*'s virginity, so jealously hoarded for so long, what is it traded for, 'Between the end of the Chatterley ban/And the Beatles' first LP'? Might it not have been expected to fetch a higher price? 'So life was never better than/In nineteen sixty-three' means that never before was life – and life's gifts, for instance of the person – held so cheap, traded at such cut-price rates.

This is to cast Philip Larkin as a bitterly recalcitrant though unreflecting and for the most part unconscious Tory. The signs of this were abundant, and should have pre-empted the surprise that greeted, in *High Windows* (1974), his threnody, 'Going, Going':

> And that will be England gone,
> The shadows, the meadows, the lanes,
> The guildhalls, the carved choirs.
> There'll be books; it will linger on
> In galleries; but all that remains
> For us will be concrete and tyres.

It is entirely appropriate that the most politically reactionary poem in *High Windows*, about the withdrawal of British troops from east of Suez, should be pointedly dated as early as 1969:

> Next year we shall be living in a country
> That brought its soldiers home for lack of money.
> The statues will be standing in the same
> Tree-muffled squares, and look nearly the same.
> Our children will not know it's a different country.
> All we can hope to leave them now is money.

* * *

Charles Tomlinson has said: 'There is no occasion too small for the poet's celebration.' But is this true? Commonsense, not without quite distinguished endorsement from past centuries, thinks that it is not true; that on the contrary there are occasions too trivial, too lacking in dignity or resonance, to deserve the ceremoniousness that, as Tomlinson rightly perceives, verse-writing always brings with it. The unfortunate effect in such cases is *portentousness*. 'The Red Wheelbarrow' by William Carlos Williams – it is the hackneyed instance, which Tomlinson does not fail to cite approvingly – is surely in this way portentous:

> so much depends
> upon
>
> a red wheel
> barrow
>
> glazed with rain
> water
>
> beside the white
> chickens.

'So much depends,' says the little squib (for it is nothing more), on the wheelbarrow, the glaze of rain, the chickens. But just how much *does* depend? The momentousness of the sparsely arranged scene is blankly asserted, not proved. Or rather it *is* proved – by sleight of hand; for if the little scene is not momentous, how did it come to be framed, in all its sparsity, by so much white paper? The reverential hush is thus not only demanded, but enforced. The poet cannot lose; whatever claims he makes for the momentousness of his subject-matter are vindicated simply by the way those claims are made.

Such poetry is invulnerable, existing in a self-sealed and self-justifying realm called 'aesthetic', from which no appeal is allowed, or can be made, to other realms like the ethical or the civic. The literary histories invite us to associate such a belief in the unbreachable autonomy of art with haughty and disdainful decadents of the 1880s and 1890s. The achievement of Williams, of his followers and admirers, has been to show that the most secure haven for such doctrines is on the contrary in an ideology that is aggressively egalitarian, and also secular. A moment's thought shows that this must be true. For the belief that 'there is no occasion too small' is naturally at home in a society that makes no distinction between small occasions and big ones, a society that resists any ranking of certain human and civic occasions below or above certain others. Thus it is social democracy that cossets and protects the aesthete, as no other form of society does. Williams's 'It all depends' asserts and takes for granted the absence of any agreed hierarchies, hence the freedom of any individual to establish and assert his own hierarchy, without fear of being challenged.

Tomlinson endorsed Williams, and asserted 'no occasion too small', in relation to his own poem, 'Swimming Chenango Lake'. This appeared in his ground-breaking 1969 collection, *The Way of a World*, but it had previously appeared on its own in the USA in a booklet where it was accompanied by a brief lecture, 'The Poem as Initiation'. This began: 'I would like to speak in defence of ceremony.' But if this seemed to promise a defence of hierarchy, the hearers were soon disabused; for what Tomlinson went on to say was that all occasions for poetry were equal, since none was too small to be made ceremonious. All the same, there was some fudging of the issue. For on the one hand, whereas indeed taking a swim in a lake seems a small occasion, when we read the poem we discover that this swim was undertaken just before the onset of winter, that it was perhaps the last swim that would be practicable that year; and this makes the occasion quite a large one, acquiescence in the turn of the season towards seeming death. This aspect of the poem as a seasonal rite is what saves it, so some may think, from being portentous. Moreover Tomlinson goes on: '. . . and I would like to speak also in defence of the poem as part of this particular ceremony'. For the poem was publicly read, it appears, on an American college campus as part of an initiation ceremony of the local chapter of the Phi Beta Kappa honour society. And this introduces ironies that Tomlinson might prefer we should not notice. For whereas non-Americans and also many Americans think of Dr Williams's America as, for good or ill, unceremonious and non-hierarchical compared with most European societies, the Phi Beta Kappa society, which is as old as the Republic, is both ceremonious and unashamedly élitist. What's more, as Tomlinson gracefully acknowledged in references to Phi Beta Kappa poems by W. H. Auden and Robert Frost, poetry has frequently been co-opted into the society's ceremonial. Accordingly, Tomlinson's argument seemed somewhat at odds with its occasion.

Some readers of this important poet have found him rather often in two minds on this matter. Repeatedly in Britain he has been called an aesthete; and although he can be shown to be nothing of the sort, he certainly has the aesthete's habit of displaying his own fastidiousness

– his is not the art that conceals itself. His tone accordingly has the aesthete's hauteur, it is not the tone of the social democrat. And sure enough, he has made it plain that he embraces social democracy only grudgingly and *faute de mieux*:

> Hard edges of the houses press
>   On the after-music senses, and refuse to burn,
> Where an ice-cream van circulates the estate
>   Playing Greensleeves, and at the city's
> Stale new frontier even ugliness
>   Rules with the cruel mercy of solidities.

In this rendering of a typical and commonplace scene from social-democratic England, the poet's distaste for the 'stale new frontier' is so evident that it is hard to believe he finds such scenes acceptable. (Should there not be legislation, he seems to protest, to prevent the archaic and lovely 'Greensleeves' being canned for dissemination by ice-cream vans?) And yet in its context as the last stanza of 'Prometheus', a poem about the Russian Revolution, the verses do assert that the architecturally squalid housing-estate, and the trader whose trademark is 'Greensleeves', must be tolerated. The oxymoron 'cruel mercy', taking up and intensifying the preceding oxymoron 'stale new', is meant in all earnest: if such inelegance and lack of refinement represent the price to be paid for avoiding the perfervid melodrama of revolutionary politics, then the bargain is a cruel one but the bargain must be struck, and we must be grateful that this option, in all its shabbiness, is mercifully open. For what is the alternative? It has been spelled out in previous stanzas, which have named Lenin and Trotsky, but also the musician Scriabin and the poet Blok. And it is the latter two, not the men of action but the men of art, who are held most responsible:

> Scriabin, Blok, men of extremes,
>   History treads out the music of your dreams
> Through blood . . .

One could hardly go further in denying the aesthete's (and the deconstructionist's) assumption that the artist is responsible to no one but himself. On the other hand, the claim that the artists of Revolution wield more influence than the political and military leaders flies in the face of the common assumption that the arts are a marginal luxury. And so it is no wonder that this profoundly political poem should have been disregarded by those who most vehemently insist that poetry and politics be brought together. Tomlinson's vision, unyieldingly secular, is of a sort that frequently falls for political utopias; but his poem says that all such utopias are murderous. It is what nobody wants to hear, not even the poet's admirers, who are happiest with his epistemology and have therefore missed the significance of *A Way of a World*, in which a poet who had seemed a-political revealed his deeply considered and disconcerting politics.[1] If Tomlinson, on 'ceremony' and related matters, seems at times to run with the hare and hunt with the hounds, it is in part because his view of politics and of public life is disenchanted beyond what either his British or his American readers are prepared to contemplate. The British reader should be able to guess the reservations that Tomlinson leaves civilly unspoken when he honours sanguine American democrats like W. C. Williams or George Oppen or (another sort of North American) the Mexican Octavio Paz. There is no evidence, however, that British readers have done this.

[1] See K. O'Gorman (ed.), *Charles Tomlinson. Man and Poet* (Columbia, Missouri, 1988).

Thomas Kinsella

It seems unlikely that Thomas Kinsella (b. 1928) has ever had as many readers as either John Montague (*Poisoned Lands*, 1961; *Tides*, 1970; *The Rough Field*, 1972), or Richard Murphy (*Sailing to an Island*, 1963; *The Battle of Aughrim*, 1968). To single him out is not to imply that he is the best of these Irish poets, nor that his rivals have played to the gallery whereas he has not. The interest of Kinsella's case is that he has chosen, or been impelled in, a direction that is open to all English-language poets, though nowadays taken by few. It is the direction that may be called allegorical.

The possibility of it was first intimated in the title-poem of Kinsella's 1958 collection, *Another September*, where the last of three decorously metred and rhyming stanzas reads:

> Wakeful moth-wings blunder near a chair,
> Toss their light shell at the glass, and go
> To inhabit the living starlight. Stranded hair
> Stirs on the still linen. It is as though
> The black breathing that billows her sleep, her name,
> Drugged under judgement, waned and – bearing daggers
> And balances – down the lampless darkness they came,
> Moving like women: Justice, Truth, such figures.

As a whole, the piece is a better-than-average specimen of the well-made poem of the 1950s, as produced in Britain and America and Australia rather more than in Ireland. One of the decorums observed by such poems is adhered to, smoothly and neatly, when the personified abstractions, 'Justice' and 'Truth', are by the nicely judged 'such figures' deflated without being disowned. Such a suave balancing act ('Paid on Both Sides', said Auden; and Kinsella started as a very Audenesque poet) was characteristic of the 1950s, and Kinsella was at one with his more ambitious peers at home and abroad in coming to think that the trick of it, so easily mastered, did not measure up to the intensities of the ensuing decade. Whereas most of his contemporaries drew the moral that personified abstractions should be expunged from their writing (despite the ease and urbanity with which Auden continued to deploy them), Kinsella chose to continue using them but to dispense with the protectively ironical deprecation that in the Audenesque models had always encased them.

Kinsella's earliest poems had been elegantly constructed echo-chambers, in which the most audible voices were those of Auden and Yeats. In his 1962 collection *Downstream*, Auden is still very much in evidence: not only the Auden of jokey personifications ('The bloodshot bulk of Laziness/Obscures the vision; Discipline/Limps after them with jutting chin,/Bleeding badly from the calf:/Old Jaws-of-Death gives laugh for laugh'): but also the greater poet who could sing in lyric stanzas:

> Her chair drawn to the door,
> A basket at her feet,
> She sat against the sun
> And stitched a linen sheet.
> Over harrowed Flanders
> August moved the wheat.
>
> Poplars sharing the wind
> With Saxony and France
> Dreamed at her gate,
> Soared in a Summer trance.
> A cluck in the cobbled yard:
> A shadow changed its stance.

These are the first two stanzas of 'The Laundress', a haunting poem which teases however by leaving it unclear whether the allusion to World War One ('Flanders . . . Saxony . . . France') is intended or inadvertent. Not much else in the collection is at this level. One longer poem, 'A Country Walk', is in blank verse of a sort but departs from that metre whenever keeping to it gets too difficult. It achieves distinction only at points where it echoes Yeats. Elsewhere it ekes out its metre with adjectival and adverbial 'fillers', and it makes nothing of the great virtue of the metre – its capacity for playing off, through sliding *caesurae*, syntactical shapes against metrical. In the title-poem the demands and opportunities of *terza rima* are as little apprehended as, in 'A Country Walk', those of blank verse; and the faults are even more glaring, if only because of the presumptousness of seeming to emulate Dante:

> Nerveless by the European pit
> – Ourselves through seven hundred years accurst –

We saw the barren world obscurely lit
By tall chimneys flickering in their pall,
The haunt of swinish man – each day a spit

That, turning, sweated war, each night a fall
Back to the evil dream where rodents ply,
Man-rumped, sow-headed, busy with whip and maul . . .

The point of recovering such verses from merciful oblivion is to show how hard it was for Kinsella to shed the precocious accomplishment that he had while working his earliest vein, and to admire him the more for taking that plunge. All the same, not all the defects of 'Downstream' are technical merely. For in the lines quoted the historical allusion is unmistakable: 'the European pit' with its 'tall chimneys' must refer to the Nazi Final Solution, and the line about 'seven hundred years accurst' is obtrusively Yeatsian not only in its diction but also, deplorably, in the tactlessness or worse that cannot mourn the fate of European Jewry without reminding us of the woes of Erin.

Six years later, *Nightwalker and Other Poems* was a great deal more assured. And the greater assurance came with the discovery of allegory, or with the decision that an allegorizing habit of mind might be trusted, not provisionally as by Auden but absolutely. In a poem called 'Ballydavid Pier' the poet claims or protests, 'Allegory forms of itself'; and we are persuaded that for a cast of mind like Kinsella's, so it does. For 'allegorical', we might substitute 'emblematic' or even 'heraldic'. Thus, in a poem about the old age of the seventeenth-century master poet Egan O'Rahilly we read:

Iris leaves bent on the ditch, unbent,
Shivering in the wind: leaf-like spirits
Chattered at his death-mark as he passed.

He pressed red eyelids; aliens crawled
Breaking princely houses in their jaws;
Their metal faces reared up, chewing at light.

And clearly there is as little attempt to render what O'Rahilly physically *saw* as to render the actual landscapes and seascapes round Ballydavid Pier. When the Cromwellian or other English colonizers of Ireland are seen as 'metal faces reared up, chewing at light' this seems to be genuinely Dantesque, from that Gothic side of Dante which particularly appealed to the English Romantics.

Such grotesquely heraldic effects are deployed most exuberantly in a section of the long title-poem, 'Nightwalker':

> Look! The Wedding Group:
> The Groom, the Best Man, the Fox, and their three ladies
> – A tragic tale: soon, the story tells,
> Enmity sprang up between them, and the Fox
> Took to the wilds. Then, to the Groom's sorrow,
> His dear friend left him also, vowing hatred.
> So they began destroying the Groom's substance
> And he sent out to hunt the Fox, but trapped
> His friend instead; mourning, he slaughtered him.
> Shortly, in his turn, the Groom was savaged
> On a Sunday morning, no one knows by whom.
> And look, over here, in the same quarter,
> The Two Executioners – Groom and Weasel –
> '77' burning into each brow;
> And look, the vivid Weasel there again,
> Dancing crookbacked under the Player King . . .

To make sense of this, the Irish reader is as dependent as any other on the good offices of Maurice Harmon who, enjoying the confidences of the poet, reveals that the wedding in question was that of Kevin O'Higgins in 1921, when his Best Man was Rory O'Connor; that the Fox who stands beside them in the wedding photograph was Eamon De Valera; that in the Civil War O'Connor was killed in a planned reprisal sanctioned by O'Higgins; that seventy-seven was the number of Republicans executed on the joint orders of O'Higgins and Ernest Blythe ('Weasel'), Minister for Finance in the Free State Government; and that O'Higgins himself, as Yeats's readers may remember, was in 1927 assassinated on his way to Mass. Long after the war was over, De Valera appointed his old enemy Blythe to be 'Player King', i.e. Director of the Abbey Theatre. Other parts of 'Nightwalker' are not much more penetrable, and without the help of Maurice Harmon we are left in the dark.

There is not much point in asking indignantly if the reader has no rights, or how Kinsella could have expected his readers to have the out-of-the-way information needed to unlock this puzzle. Kinsella, it seems clear, thinks such questions illegitimate, or at least will not pause to answer them. He might vindicate his practice from quite a different angle, by arguing that only his bestiary-*fabliau* tapestry would serve to convey his sentiments about the internecine violence which erupted in Ireland as soon as the British had been expelled; for the sequence of events, though they are despicable and indeed bestial in themselves, is yet seen by him as 'mythological'. It is hard to say whether the artless staccato of the narrative, with its oddly stereo-typed and faded diction ('Enmity sprang up', 'vowing hatred'), is in keeping with the medieval flavour of the device, or not.

Certainly, if we cudgel our brains to find precedents for such writing, it is hard to think of any later than the Middle Ages. Yet at least one later name suggests itself, a name that is conspicuous by its absence when Maurice Harmon includes in a list of Kinsella's youthful reading 'the romantics, Keats and Wordsworth'.[1] Neither Keats nor Wordsworth is readily detectable in Kinsella's poetry, but one of their contemporaries is; he who wrote '*The Mask of Anarchy*':

> I met Murder on the way –
> He had a mask like Castlereagh.

It is in Shelley surely that we find effects of Dantesque Gothic, in whom we find also an allegorizing habit; and sure enough when Kinsella surprisingly lunged into an overtly political lampoon,[2] what came out was in its explicit anger not unlike '*The Mask of Anarchy*', written about the Peterloo massacre. To think of Shelley moreover helps with Kinsella's mixed metaphors. Some of these we have seen already. Others are more startling:

> The night she drank the furnace of the Lamb,
> Draining one image of its faint *I am* . . .

> . . . and then the great ease
> when something that was stalking us
> is taken – the head cut off
> held by the fur
> the blood dropping hot
> the eye-muscles star-bright to my jaws! . . .

The use of imagery here may well recall Shelley's 'I see the waves upon the shore,/Like light dissolved in star-showers, thrown . . .' of which Denis Donoghue has remarked: 'the removing simile doesn't intend making the waves more fully known but giving them a fur-ther imaginative relation to the speaker'.[3] In the same way Kinsella's

---

[1] See Maurice Harmon, *The Poetry of Thomas Kinsella* (Dublin, 1974), p. 64.
[2] *Butcher's Dozen: A Lesson for the Octave of Widgery* (Dublin, 1972), published eight days after the report of the Widgery Tribunal investigating thirteen deaths at the hands of British paratroopers in Derry on 30 January 1972.
[3] *London Review of Books*, 19 September 1985, p. 12.

'star-bright' does not intend to tell us anything about 'eye-muscles'. And if Kinsella's practice can be justified, it will have to be on the lines of Donoghue's argument that Shelley knew of finer relations among things than those of plausible similarity on the one hand, contrast on the other. Undoubtedly Kinsella can sometimes by such strangely abstract imagery create a milky or opaline beauty peculiarly his, as in 'The Dispossessed' (from *New Poems 1973*), a poem which treats of Christianity in a way characteristically sombre, not to say morose. The poem is set on a lakeside, but the lake is not that of Galilee nor is it any Irish lough. Like the lakes of Shelley, it is nearer to a Platonic Idea of 'lake': which is to say (so the empirically minded will think), more like a state of mind. This Shelleyan alternative, much as we may distrust it, remained open in the 1970s and the 1980s, particularly of course for those whose cast of mind was Utopian.

'Ferocious Banter': Clarke and Hughes

'Ferocious banter' is a category we may gratefully steal from an unusually lively book of 1984, David Trotter's *The Making of the Reader*. Trotter has another name for it: 'anti-pathos', a less felicitous expression, but one that has the merit of defining the quality by its opposite. Trotter isolates and circumscribes the quality by, in the first place, connecting with sparkling audacity Bertold Brecht, Gramsci, Percy Wyndham Lewis, and the Wallace Stevens who wrote 'The Comedian as the Letter C'. Elsewhere he finds it, among Stevens's American successors, in Frank O'Hara and Ed Dorn. And he puts the concept to work most strenuously when he applauds three English poets who normally trade in 'pathos' for departing, each in 1971, into 'anti-pathos': Ted Hughes in *Crow*, Geoffrey Hill in *Mercian Hymns*, and J. H. Prynne in *Brass*.

The category is more ancient, and the quality or effect in question is more traditional in literature, than David Trotter cares to bring out. It is the harshly comic; and a learned commentator might trace it all the way back to Aristophanes, might find it in Petronius and at moments in Juvenal, more certainly in Marlowe's *Jew of Malta* (where T. S. Eliot called it 'tragic farce'), in Dryden's *MacFlecknoe*, from time to time in Pope, insistently in Swift, and also perhaps in Byron's *Vision of Judgement*. The advantage of calling it 'ferocious banter' is that this isolates the comic from light verse on the one hand, from satire on the other – two quite distinct though neighbouring categories with which the comic is frequently confounded.

Trotter is surely right to isolate, as the master of this kind in the modernist generations, that least regarded of the Anglo–American modernists, Wyndham Lewis, though it crops up also in Lewis's co-evals, in the Eliot of 'Sweeney Agonistes' and the Pound of Canto 12. But among British poets of later generations it is to be found more frequently than is suggested by Trotter's singling out of Hughes and Hill and Prynne. Certainly the key is struck time and again by Austin Clarke, and not just where we might expect to find it, in his *A Sermon on Swift* (1968):

> In prose, plain as pike, pillory,
> In octosyllabic verse turning the two-way

Corner of rhyme, Swift wrote of privy matters
That have to be my text. The Lilliputian
March-by of the crack regiments saluting
On high the double pendulosity
Of Gulliver, glimpsed through a rent in his breeches;
The city square in admiration below. But who
Could blame the Queen when that almighty
Man hosed the private apartments of her palace,
Hissed down the flames of carelessness, leaving
The royal stables unfit for Houyhnhnms, or tell (in
A coarse aside) what the gigantic maidens
Of Brobdingnab did in their playfulness with
The tiny Lemuel when they put him astride
A pap, broader then the mizzen mast of his
Wrecked ship, or hid him in the tangle below?

This scabrous comedy of plain speaking which at the same time feasts
on *double entendre* serves in the poem as a whole what is for Clarke a
very serious purpose: a plea for the rightful necessity of the obscene
(as distinct, no doubt, from the pornographic). So earlier, in 'Beyond
the Pale' (from *Flight to Africa and other poems*, 1963), Clarke had
dwelt at length and with relish on the legendary perverse coupling
of Dame Kyttler (or Kyteler, as Yeats had it) with the Devil, a union
that engendered the fabulous black cats of Kilkenny; moving from
that without transition to a leeringly comic treatment of matrimony:

Only one poet, Coventry
Patmore, who wived three times, has written of love
In matrimony, pulled the curtain back, showed
From post to post, the hush of featherbed,
Lace counterpane, mahogany commode;
And here from hoop and bustle, petticoats, pleating,
Long drawers, to eiderdown, our Fanny glowed; . . .

And yet the same imagery is turned to a beautifully tender eroticism
in 'Mabel Kelly', the next poem in the collection:

Lucky the husband
Who puts his hand beneath her head.
They kiss without scandal
Happiest two near feather-bed.
He sees the tumble of brown hair
Unplait, the breasts, pointed and bare
When nightdress shows

    From dimple to toe-nail,
  All Mabel glowing in it, here, there, everywhere.

Plainly, the tone makes all the difference.[1]

   Moreover 'ferocious banter' does not have to be bawdy. It is
not sexual at all in the third of 'Three Poems about Children'
(from *Ancient Lights*, 1955), which Charles Tomlinson in a too
little regarded comment judged plainly superior to the 'Refusal to
Mourn the Death by Fire of a Child in London', Dylan Thomas's
more famous and popular poem on the same theme of children
done to death by adult aggression and selfishness.[2] The occasion of
Clarke's poem is a fire which consumed a church-run orphanage in
rural Ireland, and the attempt by church dignitaries to put a consoling
gloss on that horror:

          Martyr and heretic
          Have been the shrieking wick!
          But smoke of faith on fire
          Can hide us from enquiry
          And trust in Providence
          Rid us of vain expense.
          So why should pity uncage
          A burning orphanage,
          Bar flight to little souls
          That set no churchbell tolling?
          Cast-iron step and rail
          Could but prolong the wailing.
          Has not a Bishop declared
          That flame-wrapped babes are spared
          Our life-time of temptation?
          Leap, mind, in consolation
          For heart can only lodge
          Itself, plucked out by logic.
          Those children, charred in Cavan,
          Passed straight through Hell to Heaven.

The tender-minded reader may be outraged by any suggestion that
Clarke's treatment of his atrocious subject can be called in any sense
'banter', or that this poem can be said to be comic. But that is to
miss the force of 'ferocious'. Comedy of this sort is neither unfeeling

---

[1] 'Mabel Kelly' is one of five 'Eighteenth Century Harp Songs', freely adapted from
Gaelic songs by Turlough O'Carolan (1670-1738), poet, harpist and composer.
[2] See *Pelican Guide to English Literature 8: The Modern Age*, ed. Boris Ford (1983).

nor light-hearted. It is the poet's indignation at the blandness of the
Bishop that drives him to a terse rendition of the Bishop's impu-
dence and cruelty. The jarring offence to decent feeling is enacted
in the jarringly raucous rhymes, so thickly sown and all but two
wrenched off the beat: 'heretic'/'wick', 'lodge'/'logic'. If, as some
have taught, comedy is rooted in a perception of the incongru-
ous, the poem is profoundly and savagely comical. For whereas
its subject is the shameful incongruity between the event and the
ecclesiastical comment on it, its form mirrors this in the forced
and deliberate incongruity of the rhyming words in each rhyming
pair.

Clarke or another Irishman might think that comedy of this sort
– *black* comedy, as the 1960s began to call it – was an Irish or
Anglo-Irish speciality. For not only is it the distinctively Swiftian
note, in prose (*A Modest Proposal*) as well as in verse, but it has
been a staple of the modern Irish theatre, from Synge's *Playboy of
the Western World* through even such a mild-mannered playwright
as Lennox Robinson to the Samuel Beckett of *Waiting for Godot,
Endgame* and *Krapp's Last Tape*. In the 1960s it was indeed theatre-
critics, playwrights, and theatre historians who forced it upon theatre
audiences, promulgating and explaining not just black comedy but
related concepts like the Theatre of Cruelty and the Theatre of the
Absurd. Poetry-readers, enamoured of the lyric, resisted longer than
playgoers, and this showed in their mixed and baffled response to
Ted Hughes's *Crow*.

Certainly in *Crow* Hughes banters his readers, and certainly the
banter is ferocious, if only in its remorseless picking away at Chris-
tian consolations. Several commentators noticed how 'Crow', the
central figure in the sequence, has much in common with the
protagonists of some comic-strips. Moreover, jeering laughter is
commonly, though not invariably, the way in which Crow expresses
himself. And sometimes laughter, his own laughter, is in the uni-
verse the only principle that Crow finds constant and inconsumable.
This happens in 'Crow Hears Fate Knock on the Door':

> Yet the prophecy inside him, like a grimace,
> Was I WILL MEASURE IT ALL AND OWN IT ALL
> AND I WILL BE INSIDE IT
> AS INSIDE MY OWN LAUGHTER
> AND NOT STARING OUT AT IT THROUGH WALLS
> OF MY EYE'S COLD QUARANTINE
> FROM A BURIED CELL OF BLOODY BLACKNESS –
>
> This prophecy was inside him, like a steel spring

Slowly rending the vital fibres.

And yet in the last line the whole poem is reversed, its anti-pathos suddenly reversed into pathos, and pathos of a very ordinary and demanding kind: 'Slowly rending the vital fibres.' Such last-minute reversals – from anti-pathos to pathos, or more often the other way round – are very common in *Crow*. Very often Hughes's bantering consists in his setting us up for, and then delivering, a stagey punch line:

> 'Beat the hell out of it, and ate it . . .'

> 'And everything goes to hell . . .'

> 'In the morning they wore each other's face . . .'

> 'Where his wife and children lie in their blood . . .'

> 'Till he began to laugh.'

In the worst cases, the meaning or message is so entirely reserved for the last punch-line that the items which make up the body of the poem can be randomly chosen and proffered in random sequence. This seems to happen with 'Crow and the Birds':

> When the eagle soared clear through a dawn distilling of
>   emerald
> When the curlew trawled in seadusk through a chime of
>   wineglasses
> When the swallow swooped through a woman's song in a
>   cavern
> And the swift flicked through the breath of a violet
>
> When the owl sailed clear of tomorrow's conscience
> And the sparrow preened himself of yesterday's promise
> And the heron laboured clear of the Bessemer upglare
> And the bluetit zipped clear of lace panties
> And the woodpecker drummed clear of the rotovator and the
>   rose-farm
> And the peewit tumbled clear of the laundromat
>
> While the bullfinch plumped in the apple bud
> And the goldfinch bulbed in the sun
> And the wryneck crooked in the moon
> And the dipper peered from the dewball

Crow spraddled head-down in the beach-garbage, guzzling a
dropped ice-cream.

Co-operating rather strenuously, one can with more than a little dif-
ficulty identify the eagle with heroic poetry, the curlew with elegiac,
the swallow and the swift with kinds of lyric, the owl with gnomic
poetry. But after that the association is so free as to be meaningless.
'Of yesterday's promise' chimes with 'of tomorrow's conscience' in
a rhetorical parallel that has no substance beyond the rhetorical; and
one is plainly missing the point, or rather missing the point that no
point is being made, if one asks why the bluetit should be linked with
lace panties, the woodpecker with the rotovator, the peewit with the
laundromat, the goldfinch with the sun but the bullfinch with the
apple bud, and so on.

In 'Crow Hears Fate Knock on the Door', the prophecy inside
Crow – his destiny, we may suppose – is said to be 'like a grimace'.
In many other places, for instance six times over in 'The Contender',
the word is not 'grimace' but 'grin'. And grin is an appropriate facial
expression for the delivering of ferocious banter. Yet in the poem
called 'A Grin', the grin is rather the *rictus* which afflicts the face in
extreme moments of pain, ecstasy or horror. In these poems the grin,
even at its most jeeringly composed and cruel, is never far from the
grimace of suffering. And it seems we are meant to notice that, to
pity Crow as well as fear him. But this means that pathos is never
far away, that the banter in all its ferocity is masking a bleeding heart.
So we must feel if we compare it with the far more unsettling banter
of a truly ferocious comedian like Austin Clarke.

PART TWO
The 1970s

Thom Gunn – Elaine Feinstein and Women's Poetry – The Waste Land Drafts and Transcripts – C. H. Sisson's Politics – Sisson's Poetry – Philip Larkin and John Betjeman – Prosody – Bunting, Tomlinson and Hughes – Translations, and Competitions – Poetic Theory – R. S. Thomas – Jack Clemo – Anglo Welsh Poets – Poets' Prose – The Edward Thomas Centenary – Thom Gunn

Thom Gunn

Thom Gunn, greatly to his credit, was one British poet who recognized Bunting's achievement in *Briggflatts*, though his momentous essay, 'What the Slowworm Said', which in astonishingly brief compass shows how Bunting's poem can more than hold its own with Eliot's *Waste Land* and Pound's Canto 37, did not appear until 1982 in the Manchester magazine *PN Review*, where even so late it attracted little attention. In the same year, Gunn had told the American public that *Briggflatts* represented 'perhaps the richest and most alive twenty pages of poetry written in the language this century'. There had been graceful notices also from Tomlinson and Davie. And to be sure Bunting had as early as 1970 acquired on both sides of the Atlantic a certain following. But a following is what a writer has when he has not attained a public. And in the 1970s a following is all that twenty or thirty years of devoted and distinguished work had brought to Geoffrey Hill and W. S. Graham, Roy Fisher and Charles Tomlinson, C. H. Sisson and Jack Clemo. Others, like Robert Conquest and Norman Nicholson, had not achieved even that much. Leaving aside short-lived *furores* such as flared up around the Merseyside poets (Adrian Henri, Roger McGough and others), leaving aside also the special cases of the Poet Laureate John Betjeman and the returned veteran W. H. Auden, whose last collections appeared in the 1970s (*Academic Graffiti*, 1971, *Epistle to a Godson*, 1972, *Thankyou, Fog,* 1974), only three poets can be thought to have reached a public: Ted Hughes and Philip Larkin, along with the newcomer Seamus Heaney, who rose meteor-like from his first collection, *Death of a Naturalist* (1968) and was fixed in the firmament three collections later, with *North* (1975). What it is in these three very different poets which has recommended them to a public rather than a following is a problem that has puzzled and exercised commentators and other poets over the years, not always without some spiteful envy in their puzzlement.

Particularly odd in this connection is the case of Gunn himself, who once had a British public but seemed later to have only a following. His being a long-time expatriate in San Francisco may have had something to do with this, though it is hard to see why or how. The period when he achieved and held a public was the late 1950s;

so that it seems perverse to take him as in any way representative of the 1970s. Yet there are good reasons for doing so. Not only was Gunn in the 1970s writing as intelligently as ever (*Moly* 1971, *Touch* and *To the Air*, both 1974), but more pertinently he was, among British poets with an established and deserved reputation, the one who endorsed most enthusiastically the 'revolutions' of the 1960s, political but also and more notably social and sexual. The entire collection called *Moly*, for instance, endorsed and explored the new social situation that came into being when drug-taking was not indeed legitimized but in wide circles practised and condoned. It may seem that poems which hit so neatly the new climate of liberation or libertinism would have enjoyed a considerable success. Not so, however; and the objections to the book had overtly nothing to do with moral disapproval or civic concern, but turned on features of Gunn's style:

> Oh a man's flesh already is in mine.
> Hand and foot poised for risk. Buried in swine.
> I root and root, you think that it is greed,
> It is, but I seek out a plant I need.
> Direct me gods, whose changes are all holy,
> To where it flickers deep in grass, the moly: . . .

More than any avant-garde tersenesses or discontinuities, Gunn's metre here and his rhymes, so determined to draw attention to themselves, deter the reader who wants poetry to spur him into feeling. And the cries of injured frustration which greeted *Moly* showed that in the short run Gunn had succeeded in alienating the public. 'Without exception,' declared one reviewer, 'the *Moly* poems are dead' – dead, that is (so we infer) to the presence of this reader, who was waiting to be 'moved'. Trying again, the reviewer (it was Michael Fried) expostulated: 'Their failure is not essentially a feature of tone. They do not *smell*.' But did Philip Sidney's poetry 'smell'? Did Shakespeare's, in those scenes of *A Midsummer Night's Dream* where the rhymes are as clangorously obtrusive as Gunn's rhyme of 'holy' with 'moly'? The art that refuses to conceal itself runs an insurmountable wire fence between itself and the reader; the reader may look through the wire mesh, but he cannot join in, except by the exercise of a sympathetic imagination. He cannot smell what is going on; he can only see it. And that is an affront that the reader finds too gross to stomach, if he has been schooled in a rhetorical theory of literature so as to think that the writer's prime duty is to him, the reader, rather than to the writer's own experience, his own subject. Conceiving of poetry as a service industry, such a reader expects *service*; he expects the experience to be brought all the way over to him, not left halfway where his own sympathies must go out to meet it.

Thom Gunn gave particular offence because the subjects that he treated with this aggravating coolness were precisely those which the modern reader supposed he had a special right to feel tempestuously or intensely about. When Gunn in another poem in *Moly* presented the spiel of a San Francisco drug-pusher in a form strikingly reminiscent of Herrick's 'Cherry Ripe' or Dowland's 'Fine Knacks for Ladies', what could he have been implying, if not that this traffic, which has called up so much agitated emotion for and against, is no more sensational than the trade that was plied by many a Jacobean Autolycus? On grounds of private morality, or personal hygiene and civic order, we may or may not agree with him; but that is another question. By purely formal means, in particular by highly conscious use of the pentameter couplet, one of those ready-made forms which vulgar modernism had declared illegitimate and exploded, Gunn had presented one 'burning topic', and one possible attitude to it. And in doing so, *in order to do so,* he had avoided both rhetoric and the anti-rhetoric that is merely rhetoric inverted.

In Gunn's development this represented a penetration, behind the ambiguous and magnetic figure of John Donne who had fascinated him from the start, into the Renaissance poetic out of which Donne sprang, and from which he diverged. In particular it represented a creative penetration of Shakespeare. Does Shakespeare cue the reader or the playgoer how to feel about the spectacles he presents in *A Midsummer Night's Dream*, in *As You Like It*, in *Much Ado About Nothing*? Surely, after all that the commentators have pretended to the contrary, the very titles – together with many internal features – show that Shakespeare did no such thing; that with a smiling arrogance he refused to cue our emotions, and threw his refusal in the playgoers' faces. Samuel Johnson, who preferred Shakespeare's comedies to his tragedies, did not feel affronted; but it seems that we do. Yet Johnson, we are taught to think, held to an inadequate because rhetorical theory of literature; the truth is surely that an age which thinks poetry not essentially different from advertisers' copy is far more rhetorical in its expectations of poetry than Johnson's ever was.

In 1979, when Gunn published his *Selected Poems*, it seemed clearer than ever that his great distinction was to have dug back further than any of his contemporaries into the English of earlier centuries, so as to recover that phase of English – Donne's, Marlowe's, above all Shakespeare's – in which the language could register without embarrassment on the one hand the sleazy and squalid, on the other hand the affirmative, the frankly heroic. In some early poems that Gunn sensibly left out of his *Selected Poems*, this had been overt in subject matter and hints of fustian rhetoric. It had been part of the young Gunn before he went to the United States and studied with Yvor Winters. Winters demanded emulation of the great Renaissance masters, and Gunn had kept faith with that Stanford tradition by producing admiring selections from Jonson and Fulke Greville. But his style assimilated those Renaissance precedents in a way quite different from Winters or any other American. His poem to Winters, included in the *Selected*, was a homage appropriately couched in Winters's own manner; and so it reads as affectionate pastiche, ventriloquial, not really in Gunn's voice at all. In his mature work the Renaissance presence is not narrowly stylistic but rather, one is tempted to say, ideological. For instance he believes, though in a very sophisticated way, in destiny:

> I have been always most close
> when you had least resistance,
> falling asleep, or in bars;
> during the unscheduled hours,
> though strangely without substance,
> I hang, there and ominous,
>
> Aha, sooner or later
> you will have to name me, and,
> as you name, I shall focus.
> I shall become more precise.
> O Master (for you command
> in naming me, you prefer)!
>
> I was, for Alexander,
> the certain victory; I
> was hemlock for Socrates;
> and in the dry night, Brutus
> waking before Philippi
> stopped me, crying out, 'Caesar!'

(Winters would never have risked that 'Aha', nor perhaps would he have approved it.) The Renaissance styles – of life as much as of writing – were invoked by Gunn not to judge the tawdry present, nor to keep it at arm's length, but on the contrary so as to comprehend it in a way that extended to it not just compassion but dignity:

What he did is, now,
immaterial. It is the
execution that matters, or,

rather, it is his conduct
as he rests there, while
he is still a human.

Similarly, though readers of the *Selected* were denied 'Street Song',
about the San Francisco drug-pusher, they had the young wino in a
poem called 'Sparrow', which takes as epigraph the quatrain: 'Chill
to the marrow/pity poor Sparrow/got any change Sir/Sparrow needs
change Sir':

I stand here in the cold
in a loose old suit bruised and dirty
I may look fifty years old
but I'm only thirty

My feet smell bad and they ache
the wine's gone sour and stale in my pores
my throat is sand I shake
and I live out of doors

I shelter from the rain
in a leaky doorway in leaky shoes
and there is only pain
I've got left to lose

I need some change for a drink
of sweet wine Sir a bottle of sherry
it's the sugar in it I think
will make me merry

I'll be a daredevil then
millionaire stud in my right mind
a jewel among men
if you'll be so kind

The bastard passed me by
fuck you asshole that's what I say
I hope I see you cry
like Sparrow one day

This is anything but a slice of life. Gunn manages to express compassion while avoiding the self-serving and self-congratulating, ultimately patronizing rhetoric of the 'caring' parties or the 'caring' services; and he does by alluding to kinds of poetry from before services in that sense, or service industries, were thought of. The allusion to pitiful songs in Shakespeare's plays isn't anywhere in the diction but all in the metre and rhyme, and in the delicate way in which the status of the poem as 'song' is indicated, for instance, by the suppression of punctuation. It must have been this far from obvious sense of the matter that Colin Falck had in mind when he credited Gunn with 'the lines of most near-to-Shakespearian power in twentieth-century English or American verse'. It is an astonishing claim to make for any one; and yet we may think it no more than just. In the event we were to see, as Gunn turned from the 1970s into the 1980s, that this precarious balance between Shakespearean precedents and libertine morality could not be sustained for long.

Another thing that Gunn's *Selected Poems* showed, at least to a British reader, was how indelibly Gunn remained a British writer, despite his long residence in the USA and his hospitality to American influences and precedents. When Gunn's *Selected* appeared, an earnest and gifted young American had lately ended a poem:

> Reflection in the living room window glass
> has put the potted ivy and geranium out in the street.
> A man strolls through them with his dog.
>
> His chest is in flames.
> What a relief to see the fires of loneliness
> there too, breaking
>
> from another man's heart![1]

How unthinkable it would be, in any Gunn poem, to read: 'What a relief to see the fire of loneliness/there too, breaking . . .' It is not that Gunn has contempt for such vulnerably open sentiments. On the contrary, he can be seen time and again manoeuvring to say such things. But manoeuvring is what he does; and after all his manoeuvres, the best he can manage is something terse and bitten-off, the generosity of his fellow-feeling only a hovering implication over his verse-lines. It is just this ultimate constriction in Gunn's poetry – not anything in his psyche but we may think inherent in the British English which is his medium – that moves the British

[1] Reginald Gibbons, in *Roofs Voices Roads*.

reader most deeply. So in his poem called 'Autobiography', it is not the London references that move us, so much as the enormous difficulty that British English has – having, as it were, suffered and been tarnished so much – in registering *inclusiveness*:

> A green dry prospect
> distant babble of children
> and beyond, distinct at
> the end of the glow
> St Paul's like a stone thimble
>
> longing so hard to make
> inclusions that the longing
> has become   in memory
> an inclusion

The difference between that and the young American poet's 'fire of loneliness' may strike us as the real gulf between British English in poetry and American English. At all events, whenever traffic between British poets and American poetry is in question, we encounter this notion that British English is more 'experienced', more *knowing* (for good and ill) than American English is, whether in poetry or politics or anything else.

Elaine Feinstein and Women's Poetry

One did not need to have shared many of the hopes nursed by the counter-culture of the 1960s, to sympathize with some of the people left high and dry when the tide of hope receded, as it seemed to do very rapidly once the Americans had extricated themselves without dignity from their defeat in Vietnam. The ebb-tide melancholy was beautifully caught in a poem as early as 1971. Called 'In the Matter of Miracles', and tenderly dedicated 'For Jimmy: nabbed again at the Elephant' (the unspecific and colloquial 'nabbed' is wonderfully well chosen), the poem appeared in Elaine Feinstein's second collection, *The Magic Apple Tree*:

> Toothless at twenty-three, fine
> hair on your grey chin:
> you were sitting on a
> railway bench, drawn in, as
> though you feared the touch of
> a shoulder would scorch you
>
> and were setting out to
> London, Ireland, who
> knows where
> alone after a year in
> the breakage and hash of
> a fairy-tale revolution
>
> at 5 a.m. that morning you were
> humping our stuff out of a lorry
> cheerfully, but you wondered then
> and over coffee and bread afterwards
> when did we think the revolution would happen?
>
> and so as the horn sounds to vigil
> this New Year we must
> remember the miracles that
> are daily and wholly refused,
> the orbits that simply continue
> perhaps for all of us?

But in fact not all the hopes had been dashed, not all the liberations aimed at and half achieved had been rescinded. This poem's diction is itself 'liberated'; for it must have been the best of the American 'Black Mountain' poets, perhaps Ed Dorn, who showed Feinstein how to combine the throw-away colloquialism of 'humping our stuff' with the elevation of 'the horn sounds to vigil', both strains sounding together in 'the breakage and hash'. Among the other liberations that were irreversible was the liberation, psychologically at least, of Woman. Militant feminism, not indeed a product of the counter-culture but accelerated and strengthened by it, was – so the 1970s had to recognize – here to stay. A lot of it was, and would increasingly become, strident and desperate. Elaine Feinstein was too serious about her calling to use her poems as vehicles for polemic; but by the time of *The Magic Apple Tree* it was borne in on her readers, perhaps even on the author herself, that her theme was and had to be the barely reconcilable tension between herself as wife and mother, and herself as independent person, in her case as artist.

What distinguished Feinstein from many other women poets was the fervour with which she recognized the claims justly made upon her, as wife even more than mother. In *The Magic Apple Tree* poems like 'Anniversary', 'Birthday/a Dark Morning', 'Happiness', and 'Marriage' seem to be without parallel as expressions of the passion and concern with which a wife regards her husband. (Astonishing, when one thinks about it, how seldom such a surely common complex of feelings has found expression in literature. Doubtless their expression was itself a product of women's liberation – if so, a consequence of that liberation which the more intransigent liberators took little notice of, and set no store by.) But the male reader, in his gratitude for such pieces and the lovely phrasing of them, runs the risk of not noticing the counter-stress that is insistently present in the collection as a whole. This counter-stress often turns on the concepts 'abandon' and 'abandonment'; it is the wish to escape, to be wholly individual, to identify therefore (across the gender difference) with such as 'Jimmy, nabbed again at the Elephant', who is 'setting out to/London, Ireland, who/knows where'. The poet is, she confesses defiantly, what some of her child's schoolfellows have called her, a witch – with a witch's privileges, and a witch's freedoms. The doubleness of her attitude is in several poems mirrored in her being at once irritated and entranced by the low-key subdued landscape she inhabits: Cambridgeshire, and more generally East Anglia.

A decisive development in her poetry was announced in *The Magic Apple Tree* by 'Offering: for Marina Tsvetayeva'. This poem is itself unsatisfactory, ending on a windy exclamation, 'O black icon'. But it signalled what was revealed in that same year (1971) in *Marina*

Tsvetayeva: Selected Poems, translated by Feinstein with the indis-
pensable help of Angela Livingstone who had been, as Ed Dorn
had been, Elaine Feinstein's colleague at the University of Essex. A
poet who had forged her British idiom largely on American models
now turned that idiom to serve a Russian poet: it was hard to think
of a precedent. But the affinity between the Russian poet and her
Anglo-Jewish translator was not in the first place any matter of
idiom or style. Tsvetayeva seems to be – more than Sylvia Plath,
for instance – the undeniable instance in our century of a woman
poet who embraced the lyrical abandon, abandonment in life as
well as writing. All the horrifying mischances which culminated
in Tsvetayeva's suicide in 1941 at the age of forty-eight seem to
have been invited by her. Max Hayward, introducing the Feinstein
translations, surprisingly compared Tsvetayeva with another famous
Russian suicide, Vladimir Mayakovsky, finding in both poets *le goût
de l'absolu,* a temperament which 'forced both of them to seek in
public causes the abnegation of self demanded by their unfulfillable
natures.' And Feinstein says of Tsvetayeva: 'She must have been
an eccentric, impractical, and probably an over-demanding per-
son; many speak of the antagonism she roused in them . . .' Yet
Tsvetayeva had a husband and children, and recognized her obli-
gations to them; it was in search of them that in 1939 she, once the
impassioned celebrator of Czarist resistance to Red Revolution, made
her fateful decision to return to Russia after twenty years in exile.
What impelled Elaine Feinstein to serve this formidably uncompro-
mising woman was surely not simple curiosity, nor scholarly duty,
nor yet any cool appraisal of how her own verse-style might profit
by the exercise, but because in Tsvetayeva's life and writings she
saw her own predicament writ horrifyingly large. It may be that
memorable translations come about only when the tie between poet
and translator is thus intimate and urgent.

   Tsvetayeva, as we know her through Feinstein's versions but from
other testimonies also, was always inordinate. Excitable, exclam-
atory, self-destructive, she wrenched Russian, and domineered over
it. Diction, versification, syntax – none of these, as she inherited
them, were good enough. The hysterical harridan over-rode them
all. We know the type, or we may think we do. But in fact no doubt
what we shudder at is not Tsvetayeva but her Anglo-American ana-
logues, as we conceive of them, and conceive that we have met them,
in person or on the pages of their books. Whatever she may have
been as a person, as a force working in and upon Russian language
Tsvetayeva is defined by that language – at which point any analogy
between her and poets in English breaks down. For Russian is a rock-
ribbed language, compared with English; it can submit to violences

which would batter English into incomprehensibility, whereas Russian, elaborately inflected, survives them with its expressive capacity not just unimpaired but enhanced. Suppressing verbs for instance, as Tsvetayeva does continually, makes English invertebrate, whereas in Russian the burden of meaning and structure is merely shifted on to the dative and instrumental cases of attendant nouns. Differences of this order between languages expose as foolish the common notion that a translator can choose between conveying the letter of the original, and its spirit.

There are strident exclamatory styles in modern English. And those who recognized Elaine Feinstein in the 'E. B. Feinstein' to whom Charles Olson had addressed one of his manifestos might well have expected with foreboding a translation into Olson's kind of discontinuous and exclamatory English. Not at all! Foreseeing and guarding against the misconception that would come of rendering turbulence by turbulence, Feinstein chose instead to stress the formality which paradoxically co-exists in the Russian poet with the violence. Tsvetayeva wrote for instance, she thought and felt, in stanzas – and very often in modest and traditional ones, like the quatrain. And Elaine Feinstein, subduing her own proclivities to Tsvetayeva's, preserved this stanzaic patterning – only for a reviewer to object that whereas the Russian quatrains rhymed, the English ones didn't! (As if the effect of rhyme in the two languages were not different.) On the other hand Feinstein, finding an unexpected resource in the odd punctuation she had picked up from the Americans, very boldly and happily abjured Tsvetayeva's idiosyncratic punctuation, on the correct assumption that Tsvetayeva's dashes and exclamation-marks, if reproduced in English, would have tipped over what is loud and vibrant in Russian into what in English is bullying and shrill. What emerged from this delicate negotiation between poet and translator was, for example, the astonishing nakedness of Tsvetayeva's quatrain to a much younger lover, untimely dead:

> And because you met the status of my
> first grey hairs like a son   with pride
> greeting their terror with a child's joy:
> I shall not let you go grey into men's hearts.

Introducing these translations, Feinstein, after confessing to a doubt 'how far a discussion of methods of translation attracts much useful reflection', remarked that 'with a poet such as Tsvetayeva, whose movement extends through many stanzas, the process was often a matter of reading towards every problematic line again and again from the opening of the English version, to be sure the total movement had been sustained.' And such 'total movement', or a strenuous pursuit of it, was conspicuous in her own next collection, *The Celebrants, and other poems* (1973). 'Celebrant', says the shorter OED: 'One who celebrates; esp. the priest who officiates at the Eucharist.' Thus the word is ambiguous: it can mean on the one hand every worshipper at a sacred rite (which may be orgiastic), on the other hand a member of a special caste trained and appointed to direct such rites. And the ambiguity is held to, rather than resolved, through the nine sections of the title-poem. By the end the poet's allegiance is declared – to that God who shall 'free us from the/black drama/of the magician.' But it has not been made clear how, nor at what stage, this sane wisdom has been attained to, from what the sequence celebrates at its setting out: the heretical Magus and his significantly female celebrants or hierophants:

> Bitten with toxic spiders, women
> dance themselves into exhaustion knowing
> the spirits that they bear are hostile
>
> and yet are proud to be a hostage to them,
> as if their hallucinations could be
> a last weapon against humiliation:
>
> Listen to their song: as
> servants of the tribe they now
> enter the crisis of their terror
>
> willing to free us from the same service,
> but their song draws us after them and
> some will follow   into their own unreason

Here it may be thought Elaine Feinstein in 1973 foresaw the women of Greenham Common, who would protest the siting of nuclear weapons on English soil, their protest manifestly and avowedly irrational yet possessed of a moral authority that every one had uneasily to acknowledge. For the poem to stop short of explicitly either condemning them or siding with them was its virtue as a poem: such are (it seemed to say) the characteristic movements and habits of a woman's mind, and how are such powerful impulsions to be handled and contained by men in charge of public affairs? All the same, the woman's vision is declared to be in the last resort 'unreason', as such corrigible by the reason of the male; and one may feel that this judgement has been arrived at too easily for comfort. Particularly admirable in this poem, in a way that affords no purchase to either side in the gender debate, is section seven, about Michelangelo.

As *The Magic Apple Tree* had signalled what was to come with a poem offered to Tsvetayeva, so *The Celebrants* announced a commitment for the future with 'Fever', a version from the Russian of Bella Akhmadulina. In the event this and other translations of Akhmadulina were not to appear until 1979 in the Carcanet Press collection, *Three Russian Poets*, where they found their place along with versions from Margarita Aliger and Yunna Moritz. Aliger and Moritz may be in different ways fine poets; but they do not seem so in Feinstein's conscientiously wooden English. Akhmadulina (born 1937) is a different matter. For she has explicitly – too explicitly, so some may think – appointed herself Tsvetayeva's heir. (She has claimed also the mantle of Anna Akhmatova, but rather plainly she wears it with less ease.) The explicit avowal is in 'I swear', which Feinstein translates – the poem which, according to Yevtushenko, marks Akhmadulina's breakthrough into poetic maturity. But she addresses Tsvetayeva just as fervently in 'Music Lessons' which ends, in Feinstein's English: 'I am like you! like you! I wanted to/shout that out with joy – but instead, I weep.' To the British reader this must seem inordinate, especially if he or she takes note of Yevtushenko declaring that after writing 'I swear' Akhmadulina 'felt herself nervously responsible for everything that was, is and shall be.' 'Was, is and shall be' – it is a tall order! Such tall talk is normal with Russian poets, as is a peremptory summoning into their poetic presence of the ghosts of their predecessors and co-evals. Thus Tsvetayeva had written 'Poems for Akhmatova' in 1916 and, between 1916 and 1927, 'Poems for Blok' – both sequences represented among Feinstein's versions; and so too had Akhmatova in old age (1961) written 'There are four of us', explicitly gathering Tsvetayeva into company with herself, Pasternak and Mandelstam. Yet Akhmadulina, who summons into the poems that Feinstein translates not just Akhmatova and Tsvetayeva but also Pushkin, also Pasternak, has surely indulged this habit to and over the limit. She addresses us in a tone that is hortatory and presumptuous, rather than poetic; if she is truly Tsvetayeva's heir, let her prove it rather than proclaim it.

Her poems read very well, suspiciously well, in Feinstein's English. Certainly Feinstein's idiom was not stretched to accommodate Akhmadulina, as it had been stretched to encompass Tsvetayeva. Gone are the hesitant or distraught lacunae with which Feinstein punctuated her Tsvetayeva versions; instead solid blocks of verse-lines, solid syntactically and in a modest way metrically also. This came about, so these translations suggest, because the tone of voice in which Akhmadulina addresses her readers is far more consistent than Tsvetayeva's. Tsvetayeva's voice sometimes mutters, sometimes whispers, even gibbers; whereas Akhmadulina's voice is always firm and ringing. (It is often, to be sure, engagingly humorous; but the humour is bluff and hearty.) Moreover, if Akhmadulina has written poems about specifically the woman's problem – how to reconcile her familial and domestic responsibilities with her need to be an individual – Feinstein chose not to translate them. The drama in the poems that she does translate is quite other. And it is stark: the confrontation between the poet, possessed yet responsible (and whether male or female), and the philistine public. This is a public issue (heaven knows, no new one); and Akhmadulina's voice, when she addresses the issue, is accordingly a public voice. She is at her best – and her best is good enough to deserve Feinstein's exertions on her behalf – when she broods on the duplicity involved in making the poet's private voice public:

> This generation demands performance. The guilt of that
> I take on without the gift or desire for it.
> For your sake I take on the shame of pretence
> so that in me may be seen some hint of the past,
> of how it might be with Marina and Anna alive
> when poetry and conscience could live together.
> So now in my throat, which is clean and clumsy,
> an echo sounds of the ancient Russian word.
> I have become an ambiguous, homely ghost
> of two poets whose lives can never return.

Faced with this account of how Akhmadulina considers herself the legatee of Marina Tsvetayeva and Anna Akhmatova, we can be moved and persuaded – chiefly because she acknowledges the impassable gulf between her generation and theirs. Neither of them ever had a public; and such following as they from time to time achieved was promptly alienated, either by their own perversity (Tsvetayeva among the *emigrés*), or else by bureaucratic fiat (Akhmatova under Zhdanov). In any case they are divided from Akhmadulina, who aspires to prolong their witness, by what she declares flatly: 'This generation demands performance.' The sort of performance that a Russian public demands differs in detail from what a British or an American public demands; but the demand is the same – that what is private and intimate be made public, not just in print but by way of the ever more sophisticated and intrusive techniques of the communications media, East and West. Caught in the bind, and recognizing it is irreversible, Akhmadulina concludes: 'So I burn to speak truth, and

I serve deceit/and must while I have life and energy.' The medium is the message: the message is true, but it is inevitably adulterated and perverted by the media through which it is transmitted. The predicament is British and American as much as it is Russian. And Akhmadulina's frankness about it is honourable.

When Elaine Feinstein in 1980 published *The Feast of Eurydice*, it seemed she had learned from Akhmadulina. Instead of the plot of Woman-in-a-world-of-men, she had switched to the more manageable because time-honoured fable of Poet-in-a-world-of-philistines, True, the ancient myth was told from the standpoint of the female partner, Eurydice rather than Orpheus; but not much was made of that. Moreover in the myth, the bacchantes who tear Orpheus limb from limb are female; but the poem made little of that either. One took the point when some readers complained that a poetic career which began among the feelingful intricacies of Anglo-American speech had come to rest, fourteen years later, in marmoreal neo-classicism.

The Waste Land *Drafts and Transcripts*

1972 was recognized, dutifully but without much enthusiasm, as the fiftieth anniversary of the publication of T. S. Eliot's *The Waste Land*. Every one knew that *The Waste Land* had been the most successful twentieth-century poem in English, influential and esteemed far outside the English-speaking world. Here was a poem that had certainly reached a public. Yet how? What in this poem had 'appealed'? No obvious answer was forthcoming. Small wonder if many suspected, and a few asserted, that there had been a confidence-trick; that the élite (a new élite in which professors of English figured largely) had foisted the poem on a public long cowed and compliant, but deferential no longer. This was no new thing: the attitude had been common in the 1950s, and indeed not unknown before 1939. But in 1972, when the populist ardours of 1968's 'participatory democracy' were by no means spent, there were many readers prepared to rebel against Eliot's authority. Thus the anniversary of *The Waste Land* came at a very awkward time, just when more readers than ever before were having rancorous second thoughts about a poet who in his lifetime had been idolized certainly to excess. And for younger generations of readers, those who had had little or no opportunity of responding to Eliot while he was alive (he had died in 1965), a great obstacle was the social and political attitudes which the poet had espoused. How explain to a British person born since 1945 (especially if that person was not white) that in 1930 one did not have to be either crassly stupid or cynically self-interested to take seriously, as Eliot undoubtedly did, the authoritarian royalism of Charles Maurras?

It was not only people on the political Left who were alienated. There were intelligent people of the Left who professed and felt far more sympathy for Eliot's explicitly and at times malevolently Rightist *confrère* Ezra Pound than they could feel for Eliot. For Pound had pushed his political sympathies and loyalties to an extreme, to the point where his sympathy with Fascist Italy had brought him within a hair's breadth of standing trial as a traitor to the United States, and earned him in any case eleven years incarceration in a mental hospital. By contrast, Eliot's carefully qualified and camouflaged expression of similarly authoritarian and at times anti-semitic sentiments had not prevented his being accorded the Order of Merit by a grateful sovereign, nor his being commemorated in Westminster Abbey, the national mausoleum of his adopted country.

This comparison is unfair to Eliot, who had shown himself, notably in an Introduction to his *Choice of Kipling's Verse* (1941), much more aware than Pound (or for that matter, Yeats) of the gulf that in principle should yawn between Toryism, however authoritarian, and Fascism. But comparisons between him and Pound were in 1972 stimulated, and exacerbated, by the publication that year of what were called the 'drafts and transcripts' of *The Waste Land*; that is to say, the heterogeneous packet of typescripts and manuscripts which Eliot dumped on Pound in Paris, out of which Pound had helped Eliot to extricate the poem that for fifty years had been known as *The Waste Land*. Sumptuously produced in facsimile by the London publishing house in which Eliot had been a partner, the volume had been scrupulously edited by the poet's widow so as to show at a glance how generously the one poet had acted as midwife to the other, how firm and trenchant his judgements were, and with what humility Eliot for the most part had followed the sometimes peremptory advice of his mentor. In most ways the book reflected great credit on both poets, and was affecting evidence of their mutual trust, of how their common dedication to the poetic calling precluded any taint of rivalry, of jealousy or envy or wounded *amour-propre*. On the other hand, the material which Eliot had put in Pound's hands turned out to be so inchoate that many readers were led to wonder how far the poem as they had had it all these years was in any authentic sense Eliot's at all. To be fair to him, he had repeatedly hinted that, when the evidence was in, it would show that Pound's contribution went far beyond the mere passing of judgement on particular passages; and indeed it turned out that the very structure of the poem had been extricated by Pound, rather than conceived and composed by the poet whose name appeared on the title-page. This was disconcerting, to say the least. It was not easy to think of a precedent, and one might be forgiven for concluding that the notorious obscurity of the poem came about not by the author's design but accidentally, because the work was the product not of one mind but of two. The poem, we might say, is in two minds about itself and its own meaning. The effect was inevitably to further discredit the modernism represented by Eliot and Pound, and so to push still further into the margin Bunting, who had schooled himself first with Eliot and then with Pound; a schooling that was evident in his belatedly modernist masterpiece *Briggflatts*.

Eliot and Pound, however, were very different, though the extent of the difference was only now, in the 1970s, becoming clear. Pound's disastrous interventions in active politics were possible only for a poet who was a realist in a very old-fashioned sense, who was concerned for public life, and thought (like activists of the Left) that a poet had the right and the duty to act in and upon that life quite directly; whereas the oddly distant weariness of Eliot's political pronouncements, even when he had been most *engagé* as the editor of *The Criterion* in the 1930s, had revealed a man never far from the solipsism that lay behind the *symboliste* endeavour, one for whom the psychological reality of private torments took priority over any reality which announced itself as social and public. This difference between the two poets showed up in *The Waste Land* drafts. For among the rather few objections by Pound that Eliot paid no attention to were one or two which required him to make consistent, in terms of locality and historical period, some of his references to London life. Eliot seems to have ignored these suggestions because for him the physical and social landscape of London was no more than a screen on which to project a phantasmagoria that expressed his own personal disorders and desperations (largely sexual, as one might expect, and as the drafts make clear); whereas Pound seems to have supposed that the subject of the poem was London in all its historical and geographical actuality, much as the city of Dublin had been the true subject of James Joyce's *Ulysses*. Quite independent of Pound, most of the myriad admiring commentators on *The Waste Land* had read the poem as Pound read it, seeing it as a judgement on twentieth-century urban life as exemplified in one representative metropolis – a reading of the poem which, it now appeared, the author of the poem had disowned. So many critical and even pedagogical reputations had been built on this reading that the reinterpretation which now seemed called for was not to be effected soon, nor without much resistance and some rancour. And this was only one of the ways in which the shade of Eliot in 1972 seemed to be the prisoner and the victim of the astonishing fame he had achieved in his lifetime. Eliot's ways of structuring poems – not just *The Waste Land* but also others he had written both earlier and later – were not emulated by any of the poets of note then writing in English unless by C. H. Sisson. Among Americans the admired figure was on the contrary Pound, as seen (not without serious distortions) down a perspective which comprehended also the figures of William Carlos Williams and, less universally, Charles Olson; in Britain the corresponding figure was Thomas Hardy, a poet seemingly untouched by the modernism which Pound and Eliot promulgated, whom Pound none the less had applauded, as Eliot conspicuously had not.

Partly because Robert Lowell at the height of his fame was in these years resident in England, British poets were keenly aware of the American poetic scene, if not always well informed about it.

Many had been persuaded by A. Alvarez or some other anthologist and commentator that the present century had reaped a richer poetic harvest in the United States than in the United Kingdom. Inevitably this bore harder on English poets than on the Welsh, the Scots, the Irish. For those other nations of the United Kingdom, the cultural oppressor could still be identified with the traditional bogey, the Englishman, whereas the Englishman in his turn now felt oppressed – by the Yankee. However, the bloody guerilla warfare already raging in Northern Ireland was a potentially tragic experience outside the range of American comprehension, if only because some of the causes of it reached back to an age before North America was colonised. And Irish poets of the Republic like Thomas Kinsella, or of the North like Heaney and James Simmons and Derek Mahon, responded to it. Meanwhile the English poet typically exploited further the anti-hero as lyrical *persona*, as displayed in the variously acrid and melancholy comedy of the poems of Philip Larkin; or else he might be impelled into exploring extreme situations as they presented themselves shorn of social implications or civic resonance – which is to say, on the psychoanalyst's couch. In any case his situation was complicated by the fact that London and some other English cities (notably Liverpool), until lately the administrative or commercial centres of an Empire, had transformed themselves – surprisingly, yet with a certain strict logic – into centres of the entertainment industry, particularly of popular song profitably directed at adolescence across the world. There were, as there still are, ineffective and undignified attempts by poets to buy into this 'pop' scene – ineffective because the products of the entertainment industry, as of any service industry, are ephemeral and self-consuming.

Also demoralising to the English poet was what he learned or heard about the poetry of other English-speaking nations overseas. It seemed that such nations were more drawn to American than to British models. Though by 1972 virtually every American poet of note was disenchanted, not to say disgusted, by the role that his nation had played in Vietnam, and in international politics generally, this did not affect his conviction that the American destiny was a serious, a momentous affair. The United States as Antichrist were as much the focus of poetry and prophecy as when they were the Messianic hope of the dispossessed of mankind. Indeed it sometimes seemed that the American poet was more chauvinistically exclusive when his nation had to be agent and vehicle of all the world's ills than yesterday when she was the ordained target of all its aspirations. Certainly the transformed and darkened sense of the nation's destiny had done nothing to displace that understanding of his own vocation which the American poet typically inherited from Whitman, an understanding which distinguishes him from every European, and from the English-speaking European most of all. He still felt called upon through his poetry to utter his land and his people, as certainly when he feared their destiny was diabolical as yesterday when he was sure it was redemptive. It is not hard to see, when the issue is posed in these terms, why other English-speaking nations should find themselves better able to learn from the American experience than from the British experience, to which they had been too long tied in relations of colonial and post-colonial dependence. The Australian poet, though he might take a proper pride in the Australian achievements of Judith Wright or James McAuley, could be forgiven for thinking that the essential poetic task – the forging of his nation's sense of itself as a distinct cultural identity – remained to be done; and that the pattern for that endeavour was to be found, not in any of the British poets whom he had studied in school, but somewhere within the circuit of that Whitmanesque *afflatus* with which American poets celebrated American land and the ambiguous exploits of the American white man. But it did nothing for the morale of the English poet to find that his Antipodean visitors, even if they were semi-permanent residents, looked on England as a remarkably well-organized museum adjoining a dress-designer's showroom.

The interesting question – indeed the compelling question for an English poet still looking for a poetic vocation in tune with his own sense of his Englishness – was how far that earlier generation of 'ex-colonials', represented by Eliot and Pound, had shared the detached and predatory attitude to England that he detected in American and Antipodean visitors about 1972. Certainly those earlier visitors – Pound, when one looked, no less than Eliot – had been more obsequious towards the traditional monuments than later visitors were. And Eliot's Anglicization had been so thorough, and so well-publicized, that there was and would continue to be a disposition to regard him as not just thoroughly Anglicized, but as in his generation the English poet *par excellence*. (Had he not later set up in business as an apologist for the Church of England? What more could one demand?) And yet sneaking suspicions could not fail to arise from the revelation of how dependent Eliot had been on the offices of a fellow-American, for extricating into publishable form his most famous poem. Was not Walt Whitman a figure in Eliot's background, as in Pound's? Both, for tactical reasons, concealed the Whitmanesque commitment. But it was there, for both of them: an extra-European commitment and aspiration which set them outside of, or at any rate oblique to, the English tradition. At least the publication of *The Waste Land* drafts made it harder to maintain the position: Eliot, yes; Pound, no – a position still upheld, even so.

C. H. Sisson's Politics

The eclipse of Eliot's authority was short-lived. It turned out that at least one earnest and accomplished English poet had been working what was in many ways a very Eliotic vein; and in a few years admirers of Geoffrey Hill had recovered for Eliot something like classic status. Theirs was a different Eliot, however; a Tennysonian poet – an Eliot who was certainly there, waiting to be uncovered, but very different from T. S. Eliot the modernist, who almost disappeared from sight.

However, this transformation took several years. And the Eliot who after 1972 first re-emerged from the time-shadow was (one might have thought) the figure least likely to make a come-back: the political thinker, the admirer of Charles Maurras:

> The Latin light
> Showed on the Mediterranean hills
> A frugal culture of wine and oil,
> Unobserved in their fog the British
> *toto divisos orbe*
> Propounded a mystery of steam
> In France they corrected the menus
> Writing for *biftec*: beef steak.
> Monsieur Maurras noted the linguistic symptoms
> He noted, beyond the Drachenfels
> The armies gathering . . .

> A Latin scorn
> For all that is not indelibly Latin
> *A fortiori* for the Teutonic captain
> Passing him on the terrace of the Chemin de Paradis
> Enemy and barbarian.
> *Inutile, Monsieur, de me saluer*
> His eyes looked out towards the middle sea
> He heard not even that murmur
> But an interior music.

These are stanzas from C. H. Sisson's 'Maurras Young and Old', a poem that had been in print since 1961, which however attracted no attention until the newly formed Carcanet Press selected from Sisson's three fugitive and unnoticed collections, *The London Zoo* (1961), *Numbers* (1965), and *Metamorphoses* (1968), augmenting that narrow and unrepresentative selection with some new poems so as to put together *In the Trojan Ditch* (1974). Only then did Sisson (born 1914) acquire the never very large nor very assured following which has precariously sustained him since. Such belated recognitions are not uncommon; when they happen, the serious reader is compelled to recover those earlier phases of the poet's development which, though available for study, had gone unremarked. And so it was in Sisson's case.

Such an investigation revealed in Sisson a poet who had, uniquely among his contemporaries and juniors, *a politics*: meaning by that something more substantial and respectable than the class-determined or vocationally determined prejudices which pass muster as the politics of most writers. Sisson had made this point obliquely in an essay, 'The Politics of Wyndham Lewis' (*Agenda*, VIII, I, Winter 1969-70): 'If he had re-written his political writings at the end, Lewis would, I think, have escaped from Manicheeism and from the indifference to the affairs of power which lay so uneasily upon him. He would have been driven from a politics designed to defend "the intellectual" (that abstraction of liberal democracy) to one of profounder attachments.' For Sisson a politics that was worth anything had to rest on profounder attachments than any which liberal democracy recognized – profounder than any allegiance to class, including the class of the labouring and exploited poor; and also more profound than an allegiance to those principles that the intellectual holds dear and holds pre-eminent – 'free spirit of enquiry', or 'the free play of mind'. The profounder attachment that Sisson would press on us is an allegiance to the nation, and to the Crown as embodying the nation.

We cannot confidently nor alarmedly dismiss this as the cloak-and-dagger rodomontade of an uncommitted man of letters. It turned out that Sisson, unlike any other poet of his or of immediately preceding and succeeding generations (Charles Olson was the nearest American analogue), had behind him twenty years experience of just what political administration means, year by year, day in and day out. It was an Under Secretary to the Minister of Labour, responsible for the organization and staffing of a government department numbering some twenty thousand people (including the employment exchanges), who had declared, in *The Spirit of British Administration* (1959, pp. 150-51):

The singularity of British government, in these days, rests as much in the conception of the Crown as in the conception of Parliament. The Mother of Parliaments basks in her reputation as a progenitor and model, and because democracy is what people now generally talk of, when they talk of government, no one seeks to deny her a certain importance. It is otherwise with the Crown. The monarch enjoys a world-wide publicity, but no one claims to copy us in the matter of the monarchy. Many pity us, and some of us even pity ourselves, for having retained this merely residual thing. For so the monarchy is generally regarded. Yet no student of government, or even of public administration, can afford to pass lightly over the notion of the Crown, nor to take it too readily for granted that the smooth-worn phrase, that Civil Servants are servants of the Crown, has no meaning that has any practical significance.

Again, it was no literary dilettante but a senior and seasoned civil servant who had remarked (*ibid.* pp. 156-7):

The maxim that the Queen's service must be carried on means, among other things, that it is of greatly more importance that there should be a government in Britain than that its complexion should be that of one or another party. It is of the nature of party politics to exaggerate and exacerbate differences and to represent policies, which are merely an aspect of things, as the thing itself. The thing itself is the great *res publica* whose continuance the Queen wills. She wills, all the time, all those laws which, by and with the advice of the Lords Spiritual and Temporal, and the Commons, she or her predecessors have enacted and have not repealed. She wills the continuance of all those rights she has protected without enact-ment. While she broods over this body of laws and institutions, and her servants daily perform the acts which constitute the life and continuance of that corpus, the party managers come along with their medicines and their scalpels to purge or trim some corner of it. The activity of the most fevered session of the House amounts to no more than that. Much is made of these adjustments, and much ought to be made; but more ought always to be made of the great work of time which is the subject of these meddlesome but necessary treatments.

And yet it was after all a poet who wrote this, no less a poet (rather more, indeed) for being a professional administrator. So much is clear from the crisp phrasing of this elegant prose, and the resonance of its metaphors ('she broods over this body of laws'). But also that phrase, 'the great work of time', is meant to send us to Andrew

Marvell's 'Horatian Ode on Cromwell's Return from Ireland', a pregnantly and designedly ambivalent tribute to Cromwell, the individual who 'Did by industrious Valour climbe/To ruin the great Work of Time.' The evidence, if it were needed, was in two essays in Sisson's *Art and Action* (1965): 'Reflections on Marvell's Ode'; and 'Second Thoughts on Marvell'. But we hardly needed this corroboration. For to what should a devoted and thoughtful monarchist have directed us, in 1959 or 1974, if not to the classic confrontation in English literature with the one and only regicide in English history, the executioner of Charles the First in 1649?

But this was, not indeed to the common Englishman in 1974 but to the English intellectual, unthinkable. That an Under Secretary at the Ministry of Labour should in the years after 1945, have thought Robert Filmer's *Patriarcha* better politics than the treatises of John Locke or the *Discourses* of Algernon Sidney – it was past belief! Only six years after the pseudo-revolutionary excitement of 1968, to have 'the realm' offered as a significant, indeed crucial concept in politics was not to be stomached. It had happened, however; and C. H. Sisson's writings in prose and verse were there to prove it.

To make the point once more, these seemingly outlandish convictions were grounded not in any high-flying theory or fantasy but in the actuality of what it meant to be an administrator in post-1945 Britain:

> For a man who is trying to make a trade agreement, or doing certain sorts of work in relation to foreign affairs or finance, there may be certain parliamentary points to watch but, on the whole, his attention will be fixed on the foreign competitor, on the potential enemy, or on mere figures. The game for him may be the classic game of Richelieu or Macchiavelli, though played in the context so different from theirs. It is the game in which the basic assumption is the existence of the realm as a separate entity, and the official is bent above all on keeping it afloat among its neighbours. This, however, is the ultimate assumption too of the administrator whose work is more closely tied to parliamentary affairs. The parliamentary end-game is not an end-game after all, but is important only because it is the index of forces on whose balance the coherence of the realm depends. The administrator, whatever his immediate task, is playing for the survival of the realm. (*op. cit.* pp. 152-3)

It was this hard-nosed awareness of what day-to-day administration is, that produced such unfamiliar but constitutionally irrefutable apophthegms as (p. 159) 'Elections, and an elected House of Commons, do not produce a government. They merely modify it . . .'; and (p. 158): 'It would be perfectly possible to govern England without Parliament or elections though it would certainly not be possible to govern it in this way for long with any efficiency.'

Some who were affronted or outraged by these sentiments began to gabble of private armies, of crypto-fascism, of 'the reactionary right'. Others more understandably alarmed, and expressing themselves more temperately, provoked a short flurry of literary/political debate in which royalism was usefully distinguished from monarchism, and in which the lacklustre but indispensable word 'constitutional' was once again given an airing. Few noticed that, from where Sisson stood, the British political right was if anything more culpable than the left. Walter Bagehot for instance, Victorian publicist and constitutional theorist, was in those days more of a hero for the Tories than for the Labour party; yet when Sisson came to deal with him in *The Case of Walter Bagehot* (1972), Bagehot, because he placed the apex of the British Constitution in Parliament and not in the Crown, got no mercy. In this small book Sisson was less temperate than in *The Spirit of British Administration*, and there were comments in passing, for instance about the allegedly dubious civil rights of British Roman Catholics, which seemed bizarre. What was entertaining and yet deeply serious was Sisson's avowing frankly that his animus against the unitarian Bagehot had much to do with the fact that Bagehot was a native of the same Somersetshire town, Langport, where Sisson had made his home since returning to his native West Country after years in the London computer belt. This showed the difference between Sisson and the déraciné Anglo-American Eliot, whose social and political views he often seemed to echo; those 'profounder attachments' that Sisson asked for certainly included – quite centrally indeed, as later poems were to show – attachments to region and locality.

All the same, Eliot and Sisson have much in common. Eliot for instance, as early as *After Strange Gods* (1934) and again in *Notes Towards the Definition of Culture* (1948) had elevated, over 'social consciousness', one sort of social *unconsciousness*: and Sisson seemed to say much the same, when he wrote in *The Case of Walter Bagehot* (pp. 127-8):

The final point in the State must rest on a certain incomprehension, and incomprehension is the beginning of theology. Few people now would imagine that they knew what was meant by the Divine Right of Kings, but any one might reach the point of mystification as to the coherence and persistence of national entities, which the hereditary monarchy so well expresses.

But we must note that, whereas in Eliot's thinking political obtuseness and inattention seems to be *required* of the majority (perhaps so that a privileged minority may the better lead them by the nose), Sisson's 'incomprehension' is seen as not required but inevitable, with an inevitability that only the more thoughtful and devout citizens would recognize. Sisson after all seemed to be saying only that nationhood is a *poetic* matter, something that mechanical or rationalist diagrams ('checks and balances', 'division of powers') must always falsify. If so, then it became permissible to wonder if in 1974 (or 1985) this was not what the bulk of the British nation still believed, though mostly it was unaware of believing it.

These were matters which, through several centuries, students of English literature had been used to having raised for them by that literature, in just these or very similar terms. In 1974 Sisson was, if not the only writer, certainly the only *poet*, to raise them. It seemed he was writing for those who, when in *The Times* or elsewhere they saw a plea for national unity translated immediately into a plea for coalition government, would think instead of stanzas from Sisson's noble adaptation of Horace's 'Carmen Saeculare' from *In the Trojan Ditch*):

> We have been through it all, victory on land and sea,
> These things were necessary for your assurance.
> The King of France. Once there was even India.
>
> Can you remember the expression 'Honour'?
> There was, at one time, even Modesty.
> Nothing is so dead it does not come back.
>
> There is God. There are no Muses without him.
> He it is who raises the drug-laden limbs
> Which were too heavy until he stood at Saint Martin's.
>
> It is he who holds London from Wapping to Richmond,
> May he hold it a little longer, Saint George's flag
> Flap strenuously in the wind from the west country.
>
> Have you heard the phrase: 'the only ruler of princes'?
> Along the Thames, in the Tower, there is the crown.
> I only wish God may hear my children's prayers.
>
> He bends now over Trafalgar Square.
> If there should be a whisper he would hear it.
> Are not these drifting figures the chorus?

C. H. Sisson's Poetry

It was in 1943, when he was nearly thirty and a soldier in India, that Charles Sisson wrote his first poem and his first translations. The translations were of Heine. In his own words, 'the Heine who was the Sword and the Flame of the German revolutionary struggles of the first half of the nineteenth century became the companion of the British Other Rank in his oppressive situation in the last decade of the British Raj.' Several years later, he was still not sure that verse was his vocation, and for him the question turned on whether he could master in verse what he called 'plainness'. This led him to translate Catullus: 'The exercise in plainness was what I wanted when I did the Catullus.' But if we ask ourselves what we understand by 'the plain', and how it consorts with such related notions as the lucid and the limpid, the simple and the bald, we recognize that plainness in poetry is itself something far from plain, certainly not self-evident. And scholars can narrate how much ink has been spilt on the matter of 'the plain style', from the Ancient World into the European Renaissance and since. One thing that Sisson meant by plainness' is presumably what we find in his 'Nude Studies':

> They are separate as to arms and legs
> Though occasionally joined in one place.
> As to what identity that gives
> You may question the opacity of the face.
>
> Either man is made in the image of God
> Or there is no such creature, only a cluster of cells.
> Which of these improbabilities is the less
> You cannot, by the study of nudity, tell.

Certainly this is plain, in one obvious sense; too much so, for some tastes. And the man who wrote thus had, we may well believe, learned to do so by translating Catullus:

> Ameana, the worn-out bitch,
> Is asking for a whole ten thousand,
> That girl with the flattened nose
> That used to go with the Formian bankrupt.

> Her family, or whoever looks after the girl,
> Had better call in her friends and doctors:
> The girl is mad, she has never enquired
> What a mirror would have to say about her.

Sisson was not the first modern poet to recognize that on the features of Catullus, *this* Catullus, could be superimposed those of the famous Jacobean divine John Donne, whose concerns – with Christian revealed truth, and carnality, and the relation between them – are more urgent to modern man than the ancient Roman's. (See Sisson's 'Letter to John Donne'.)

It was not Donne, however, to whom Sisson appealed as an English precedent and master; not Donne, but (insistently) Dryden. And that name is our warrant for supposing that Sisson's translations are, for him and for us, as important as his poems. After Heine and Catullus, it was Virgil who engaged Sisson's energies. And in undertaking, of all unlikely things, a complete version of Virgil's Eclogues, he was keenly aware of Dryden's versions as a standard he could not measure up to: 'Dryden wrote in the superb verse he was master of in his 'great climacteric'. For the Eclogues I wrote what I could manage at the age of fifty-three . . .' It was wonderful to hear, in the second half of the twentieth century, this proudly humble voice of the honest artificer; it was the voice of Dryden himself! But it spoke all too true. Dryden's version of the Eclogues is so good that it is hard to see any reason for making, or publishing, another; and Sisson's version may be thought a wooden curiosity. Far more startling and intriguing was his reduction of much of Aeneid VI to a sort of stenographic summary. But in any case he knew what he was up to, with Virgil: 'There is a certain elaboration, very unfashionable in our time and perhaps of little use for contemporary literary purposes. There is also something which we ought to value. This is a deep movement of feeling, below the surface of our exacerbated daily life, and which has greater significance than any "frankness" for those who want to understand the human brute'. This is not a Virgil that is prominent in Dryden's versions of him, splendid though they are. But it is a Virgil acknowledged to exist, and one that the plain style will not encompass. Sisson undoubtedly realized this. For *In the Trojan Ditch* presented along with the 'plain' poems, a lengthy and mysteriously resonant piece, 'In Insula Avalonia', where Sisson's patriotic and religious concerns came together in the legend of Arthur sleeping through the centuries in the Isle of Avalon near Glastonbury (a stone's throw from Sisson's home), and these concerns were interwoven in a verse which as it were went nowhere and said nothing, which was Shakespearean and at times Eliotic to just the degree that it was Virgilian – a style as far from 'plainness' as could be conceived:

> Dark wind, dark wind that makes the river black
> – Two swans upon it are the serpent's eyes –
> Wind through the meadows as you twist your heart.
>
> Twisted are trees, especially this oak
> Which stands with all its leaves throughout the year;
> There is no Autumn for its golden boughs
>
> But winter always and the lowering sky
> That hangs its blanket lower than the earth
> Which we are under in this Advent-tide.
>
> Not even ghosts. The banks are desolate
> With shallow snow between the matted grass
> Home of the dead but there is no one here.
>
> What is a church-bell in this empty time?
> The geese come honking in a careless skein
> Sliding between the mort plain and the sky.
>
> What augury? Or is there any such?
> They pass over the oak and leave me there
> Not even choosing, by the serpent's head.

Had Sisson written more verse like this – in years to come he would often express sentiments of similarly indefinite melancholy, but seldom in these throbbing or sobbing pentameters – he might have had a wider appeal. His more discriminating and refractory, perhaps simply his more *protestant* admirers continued to prefer the places where he still tussled with the manifold ambiguities of plain speaking, In *In the Trojan Ditch* the masterpiece of this kind was undoubtedly 'The Usk', which begins:

> Such a fool as I am you had better ignore
> Tongue twist, malevolent, fat mouthed
> I have no language but that other one
> His the Devil's . . .

The poem goes on, in angry self-reproach:

> Where in all this
> Is calm, measure,
> Exactness,
> The Lord's peace?

And the poet reveals that what he had hoped for was a style limpid enough to bear comparison with the clear running of the river Usk; but what he achieved, he goes on to say, was not that hoped-for limpidity, but something else – plainness:

> I speak too plain
> Yet not so plain as to be understood
> It is confusion and a madman's tongue . . .

'The Usk' is an extraordinary triumph of the plain style in poetry precisely because, even as it deploys that style, it convicts it of dishonesty. The writing rises to its greatest intensity at a point where the poet, through tormented puns on the Eucharist, vows himself to silence and, by so doing, out of the depths of his self-accusation, earns the right to figure as himself the Christ-figure, *Ecce homo*:

> Lies on my tongue. Get up and bolt the door
> For I am coming not to be believed
> The messenger of anything I say.
> So I am come, stand in the cold tonight
> The servant of the grain upon my tongue,
> Beware, I am the man, and let me in.

It is a deeply religious poem, and deeply blasphemous; the combination is only apparently incongruous. Its sixty lines end with the poet vowing himself, not just to silence, but to sleep and dream; and so it falls in with 'In Insula Avalonia', where the millennial sleep of Arthur in his unreal island calls for a style not plain at all but Virgilian. Fortunately neither promise – not of silence thereafter, nor of Virgilian dream – was kept: Sisson in subsequent years would continue from time to time to misjudge his own talent rather drastically, but there were to be sufficient poems to vindicate one's first incredulous impression that here was a poet who – not just in matters of translation nourishing composition, but in the situation of the devout Christian constantly battling his own instructed scepticism – could be mentioned in the same breath with Dryden, could sustain that awesome comparison at least for a while.

Philip Larkin and John Betjeman

Philip Larkin was also a plain-speaker in his way:

> Groping back to bed after a piss
> I part thick curtains, and am startled by
> The rapid clouds, the moon's cleanliness . . .

> When I see a couple of kids
> And guess he's fucking her and she's
> Taking pills or wearing a diaphragm . . .

These less than pungent colloquialisms come from Larkin's collec-
tion of 1974, *High Windows*; and there can be little doubt that they
were relished by many readers as indeed plain language, though it is
easy to see that on the contrary this is a very self-conscious and self-
advertising diction, an anti-rhetoric in fact, and of a very unsubtle
kind. To be sure there were in the poems other sorts of diction,
and the first snatch of lines for instance makes an immediate and
calculated collision with the poem's elevated and allusive title, 'Sad
Steps'. But then, the collisions themselves are unsubtle, and could
hardly be anything else.

The previous year Larkin had brought out *The Oxford Book of
Twentieth-Century English Verse*. It had been billed in advance as
'this successor to W. B. Yeats's *Oxford Book of Modern Verse*.' But
that was never on the cards. Larkin was nothing if not self-effacing,
though from motives perhaps as haughty as Yeats's. Not from him
any pugnaciously wrong-headed introductory essay, such as Yeats
had written in 1937. Instead, the briefest of prefaces: 'I found that
my material fell into three groups: poems representing aspects of the
talents of poets judged either by the age or myself to be worthy of
inclusion, poems judged by me to be worthy of inclusion without
reference to their authors, and poems judged by me to carry with
them something of the century in which they were written.' As one
reviewer exclaimed in exasperation, 'How many escape-clauses does
one need?' It was clear after this profession of intent that there was
no way of pinning Larkin down to endorsement of any one poem
he had printed. For either the poem had been judged by Larkin to

carry with it something of the century it was written in (and in any century, it might be argued, the bad poems carry more of that than the good ones), or else it was not Larkin but 'the age' that had decided the poem was 'worthy of inclusion'. But in that case, who was the familiar toad in All Souls who had spat into Larkin's ear the voice of 'the age'? It was a voice that could not bring itself to utter the names of Ford Madox Ford, David Jones, I. A. Richards, Roy Fisher, John Holloway or Elaine Feinstein, though it was ready with Elizabeth Wordsworth (1840-1932), Moira O'Neill, Herbert Asquith, Gilbert Frankau, Francis Brett Young, F. W. Harvey (1888-1957), G. D. H. Cole, Stella Benson, J. B. S. Haldane, Colin Ellis (1895-1969), Robert Rendall (1898-1967), and Sir Noel Coward. On to this anonymous authority Larkin could shuffle the responsibility for rescuing any number of bad poems from merciful oblivion. Did Larkin trust his own judgement, or did he not? Yeats did; but then Yeats took poetry seriously, as it really seemed that Larkin did not.

This was a grievous misfortune. To be, as Larkin was, the author of many poems generally esteemed and loved brings with it certain responsibilities. But the poems that we had loved, that we love and cherish still, turned out to have been written by a man who thought that poetry was a conjuror's trick or a professional entertainer's patter or at most a symptom for social historians to brood upon.

If there was any principle at all behind the selection, names like Gilbert Frankau and G. D. H. Cole seemed to point to it: writing poems was an amateur's activity. Novelists and economists, biologists and university librarians, could turn their hands to it when they had nothing better to do. This principle seemed to operate in the choice not only of poets but of poems. From Alex Comfort for instance Larkin had taken, rather than any example of Comfort's admirably elegant erotic poems (*Haste to the Wedding*, 1962), a piece of polemical doggerel contributed under a pseudonym to the newspaper, *Tribune*; and this, apparently, so as to print a similarly doggerel rejoinder by George Orwell. Thus the professional poet, Comfort, was sacrificed to the amateur, Orwell. And thus conclusively – so some angrily thought and said – was the clock put back to the languid and all too English amateurishness which two Americans and an Irishman had bullied us out of sixty years before. To such observers, it seemed that the volume was a monument to our insular complacency, and a device for perpetuating it. Commonwealth poets were excluded as well as Americans, so were translations, and so were 'poems requiring a glossary' that was to say, poems in Lallans. (Both rules were broken in special cases, as Larkin wearily acknowledged.) With all those troublesome Scots and Australians out of the way, and with thirty years of the century still to run, Larkin could still fill more than six hundred pages. He noticed that his anthology 'represents a much greater number of poets than are to be found in the volumes corresponding to this one for the nineteenth and eighteenth centuries'; but he did not let that worry him.

'Professional' and 'amateur' will be misunderstood. And indeed they are not quite the right words. Alex Comfort did not of course make his living by writing verse, and in that sense his poetry could be for him only an avocation. But vocation or avocation, writing poems was for some poets (including, we may suppose, Comfort) a *calling*; their commitment to it, however far they might be from practising it full-time, was not wholly unlike a religious vocation, or the vocation as we like to suppose of nurses – such poets think they have heard a call, to which they try to respond. It is obvious on the other hand that if Orwell and Haldane each heard a call (and doubtless both did), it was not a call to make poems. It was in this sense that they could be called 'amateurs'; and for them to bulk so large in a collection from which David Jones was excluded was something for which 'cynical' seemed not too harsh a word.

It could be thought that Larkin and his publishers had safeguarded themselves by offering this as an anthology of verse rather than poetry. And indeed, over long stretches one felt that the description might as well have been: *light* verse. But the volume necessarily gave us writing – T. S. Eliot's for instance or A. E. Housman's – which offered itself as *poetry*; that is to say, writing in which language was for good or ill lovingly explored as a medium, not rapidly marsllhaed to serve merely as an expedient vehicle. Two writers of the past who were primarily novelist – John Meade Faulkner, who was well represented, and Ford Madox Ford, who was conspicuous by his absence – both showed that they knew when they wrote poems they were exploring a medium; and so they could be called 'professionals'. Another novelist Gilbert Frankau, in his Kiplingesque rant, 'Gun Teams', was by contrast hammering together a mere verse-vehicle as heartlessly as G. D. H. Cole or A. P. Herbert or 'Sagittarius' or George Orwell; and so all these could be called 'amateurs'. Haldane's was a particularly interesting case because, in his 'Cancer's a Funny Thing', his attitude to his readers was no doubt as heartfelt as his attitude to his language was the opposite. The two sorts of writing, the two attitudes to language, are so different that to have them thrown together indiscriminately could only bewilder the well-intentioned reader.

There was no need to question Philip Larkin's good faith. There was plenty of evidence that any talk of poetry as a calling (some had thought it a sacred one) distressed and infuriated him, as a sentiment possible only to those who could not sympathize with common human suffering; and there was little doubt that Larkin's consistent suspicions on this score had been shared by many who loved him for exploding such aesthetes' pretensions. For that matter, it was obvious that pompous hypocrisy no less than sincerity and good sense had in the pre-war and wartime past traded on the notion of the poetic calling. No one who had read Larkin's poetry attentively could be surprised to learn that he was as sceptical about poetry as about most other values. If this was his considered attitude, he had every right to express it; yet not, it might be thought, obliquely, in an anthology backed by the authority of a famous publishing house and by his own authority as undoubtedly the best-loved poet of his generation. The pity was that the anthologist who thus scouted the idea of poetry as an exploration of language had time and again, and once again in *High Windows* in such an exploratory poem as 'The Explosion', demonstrated that in the act of writing he knew the experience of such exploring perfectly well, and had trusted it.

The best-loved poet of the generation before Larkin's was just as unmistakable; he was John Betjeman, whom accordingly Larkin had constantly applauded through years when in some influential quarters there had been a foolish disposition to regard Betjeman as only a quaint and comical rhymester. But Betjeman's love-affair with his public had been conducted quite differently from Larkin's. Betjeman's, one might almost say, had been a multi-media success. Musicians had helped him, notably Jim Parker with some very stylish and witty settings. But ironically Betjeman, who affected to be and perhaps really was a sort of nostalgic Tory, completed his conquest of the public by making more successful use than any other poet of the newest medium, television. Larkin, it was notorious, would have nothing to do with the television screen, though his refusal of it was so well publicized that, as an endearing and identifying quirk, it became in the end a way of backing into the limelight. By a similar strategy, Larkin so seldom promoted himself or agreed to explain his purposes, for instance to interviewers, that the occasions when he did so attracted special attention. In time it appeared that these self-revelations were always partial and some-times downright misleading. Some careful readers would shortly begin to notice for instance that, despite Larkin's having put it abroad that he would read no poems not written by Englishmen, he had in fact attended to certain Frenchmen rather closely, and at times had emulated them. Similarly with his claim that after his first collection, *The North Ship*, he had decisively and of set purpose switched from Yeats to Thomas Hardy as his English-language master; when one looked, this was not borne out by the internal evidence. Such laying of false or misleading trails was not complained of, for it was thought reasonably enough that Larkin only demonstrated his affirmed distrust of 'the media' when he refused to trust them with the truth. In this cat-and-mouse game with the public, Larkin was indeed like Hardy, who had similarly helped to spread misleading accounts of himself, his tastes, and his aspirations. This meant in Larkin's case that, since his own asseverations must be discounted, readers who were devoted to him were able to put him in whatever company they pleased; so that in a few years the poet who had expressed his vehement distaste for 'modernism' could be applauded as a poet of a kind with the modernist master Eliot. As Eliot was made to seem like Tennyson, Larkin could be made into a latterday John Keats; and the author of acrid and brutal poems like 'Sad Steps' (and many more) could be presented as a poet of wistful yearning.[1] True to his habit, Larkin never let on whether he liked this transformation.

He had in any case always been lucky enough to have or to make friends who would promote and explain him as he would not do for himself. One of these long-standing and conspicuously loyal friends was John Wain, who from 1973 to 1978 served as Professor of Poetry at Oxford and devoted an adulatory lecture to his friend's work. This lecture, subsequently reprinted (in *Professing Poetry*, 1977), may represent the high-water mark in Larkin's reputation. Wain made an interesting observation about Larkin's political sympathies when he pointed out that *High Windows* included for the first time in Larkin's career two 'straight satiric pieces', and that both were 'aimed at opinions and attitudes associated with trendy academia and the *New Statesman* left'. Larkin indeed had always been a populist; as Wain noted with enthusiasm, what the poet applauds in the end is ordinariness, 'the ordinary' – surely a populist attitude, designed to confirm and comfort the unambitious many against the thrusting and aspiring few. But there can be populists of the Right as well as of the Left, and indeed the right-wing variety was to become bolder and more assertive in the next few years. For when John Wain calls those whom Larkin assailed in these two poems 'a powerful in-group', though this was an understandable opinion still in 1975, election returns were to show that the disappointment of the pantomime revolutionists in 1968 had irreversibly weakened the British Leftist intelligentsia. The antagonists or vested interests that Larkin was tilting at were not so formidable any longer, though perhaps he no more than John Wain recognized this.

A Nip in the Air (1974) was Betjeman's last collection. It is not so good as his best, but is nothing to be ashamed of, except for a couple of commissioned or semi-commissioned pieces written in

---

[1] See John Bayley, 'The Last Romantic', *London Review of Books*, 5-18 May 1983.

his capacity as Laureate. Betjeman's unhandiness in that role was widely acknowledged, but counted unto him for virtue because of the widespread assumption – among people who could never have read Dryden – that good art can never be produced to order. It is another of the many paradoxes about Betjeman that, although he became a very public figure ('the most popular poet of the century', a more than usually insular book-cover was to proclaim him) he was, as he testified himself, a tormentedly private individual in the act of composition, and incapable of being anything else. Hence his tenure of the Laureateship can be thought to have been a great success, but not because of the poems that came out of it. To re-read *A Nip in the Air* ten years later, when the emollient and ingratiating figure had vanished from the television screen – the ingratiation, it must be said, less Betjeman's doing than that of his 'handlers', his producers and interlocutors – was to get a surprise. To begin with, the air that blows is indeed nipping: a lot of the poems are malevolent. And yet this too was nothing new: although Betjeman like Larkin was compassionate towards people who lived lives constricted by codes and limited expectations that they were unaware of, there had always been those whom in their public capacities he pilloried with scathing anger. In particular the real-estate speculator or 'property developer' had always been the villain of Betjeman's piece, and in *A Nip in the Air* a poem called 'Executive' is executed with particular venom to make such a one betray himself. An amalgam of comedy and pathos is often taken to be Betjeman's hall-mark, but that is to overlook the many pieces like this, for which the appropriate term is not 'satire' but 'invective'. Betjeman was often angry, and even before this last collection the anger had taken on a special edge from knowing itself to be unavailing, knowing that the desecration of the British scene could not be stopped. For such anger and desperation to appeal to so many, must mean something: either the public thought that such sentiments when articulated by a poet in the medium of verse could be enjoyed because they need not be taken seriously, or else – the more sanguine and after all more probable explanation – members of the public were grateful to Betjeman for articulating what they inarticulately but quite passionately felt; that the ugly transformation of British civic and rural landscapes affronted something deeper and more momentous than any easy sentiment about 'scenery' or 'the countryside'. The possibility has not been taken account of. To Betjeman's constituency, on this showing, the politically inflammable question whether the disfigurings are publicly or privately funded is secondary, indeed irrelevant. The most popular British poet of our time was angrily and explicitly opposed to what British governments of whatever political complexion would foist upon us:

it seems a matter that might have exercised some minds around Westminster.

It is the same, or not very different, with Betjeman's poems about mortality; poems which must, because of their subject, be called 'religious'. There had been such poems in every one of Betjeman's collections, and in *A Nip in the Air* there was for instance 'Aldershot Crematorium':

> Between the swimming-pool and cricket ground
> How straight the crematorium driveway lies,
> And little puffs of smoke without a sound
> Show what we loved dissolving in the skies,
> Dear hands and feet and laughter-lighted face
> And silk that hinted at the body's grace.
>
> But no-one seems to know quite what to say
> (Friends are so altered by the passing years):
> 'Well, anyhow, it's not so cold today' –
> And thus we try to dissipate our fears.
> '*I am the Resurrection and the Life*':
> Strong, deep and painful, doubt inserts the knife.

The sentiment here – 'Lord, I believe; help thou mine unbelief' – is not miles away from Sisson's in 'The Usk'. And the difference between this poem and Sisson's is the difference between a poem that aims at a public and one that can hope only for a following. Undoubtedly Betjeman had to forgo certain refinements; a more fastidious writer would have found some way to make 'deep' go with the insertion (or the incision), rather than with 'doubt'. All the same, the poem articulates memorably what most people feel in a crematorium or a graveyard; and it is intolerably high-hat to suppose that Betjeman's select audience does not include such readers, but is limited to those who can appreciate the delicious double-take (of comedy with pathos) that he wrings out of such placenames as 'Ruislip' or 'Lambourne' or 'Aldershot'. In this way too the phenomenon of Betjeman's appeal deserves far more consideration than any one has yet been prepared to give it.

Prosody

Another challenge that Betjeman throws down to us (or would, if we took him as seriously as we should) concerns his metres, or more comprehensively, his prosody. On these far from marginal matters, whether in Betjeman or in any one else, British critics in the 1970s maintained the deafening silence that they and their like had mostly kept for fifty years. Whenever disagreements about scansion, itself a disputable term, surfaced in letters to the *Times Literary Supplement* and other journals, the lack of agreement about even such basic terms as 'rhythm' and 'metre' was embarrassingly obvious. It was left to a few brave Americans to try now and then to rescue English prosody from a morass of sloppy thinking and *ad hoc* terminology. The American who emerged in 1980 to toil in this Augean stable was Charles O. Hartman, whose elegantly brief but dense 'essay in prosody' appeared from joint American university presses under the title, *Free Verse*. Hartman's principal purpose was neither historical nor polemical, but he uncovered many examples of scandalous muzziness perpetrated over the years not only by such as Amy Lowell, but by others like T. S. Eliot who should have known better.

None of these would-be clarifiers (so Hartman argued) had done more damage than those who showed for instance, in a passage of blank verse, how one line after another had four heavy stresses, and assured us on this showing that 'what really happens' is not pentameters at all but 'the old four-stress line', surviving from pre-Renaissance English in a thin post-Renaissance disguise. Hartman's way with these 'nativists' was admirably crisp and conclusive:

> If generations of poets have thought they were writing accentual-syllabic metre, not accentual or quantitative, and generations of readers have agreed, they were right by definition. To deny this is to pretend that verse exhibits factual characteristics independent of convention, and that these facts outweigh conventions in a reader's experience.

Readers who were uncertain about 'accentual-syllabic' and 'accentual' and 'quantitative' (technical terms, but readily explained in many a handbook or encyclopaedia) could still appreciate the drive of Hartman's argument: a prosody, he was saying, was not anything that 'really happens', but something that poet and reader agree to hear as happening. In a pentameter line one or more of the five stresses theoretically required might be 'notional'. But this did not mean that they 'weren't there,' nor that the line had less than five feet. For a prosody was precisely a set of notions shared by poet and reader in a tacit compact.

When we call it 'tacit', however, we mean that this too is notional. And so it is, of course: the poet signs a contract with his publisher, who counter-signs it; but no poet ever signed such a contract with his reader, and if he ever did no reader nor reader's representative could be found to counter-sign it. Thus we conceive of a prosody as a set of agreed notions, that agreement embodied in a contract or compact which can never be appealed to since it too 'isn't there', and never 'really happens'. If, following Hartman, we mean by a prosody such a structure of fiction mounted upon fiction, there is after all some excuse for many, if not all, of the muddles we have got ourselves into since free verse emerged to confound the old certainties of accentual-syllabic prosody. Indeed the puzzling thing is how those certainties ever emerged, how it came about that such a tissue of air-spun make-believe ever worked. For work it did, and it works still, with the accentual-syllabic metres: we know when a writer of blank verse has broken his contract with us, even though that contract was never drawn up and even though some of the terms of that non-existent contract are open to dispute.

What cannot fail to appal us is the extraordinary frailty, on this persuasive showing, of the basis on which we can talk at all about verse as a structured sequence of sounds. And indeed it is not only the crusted curmudgeons among us who may wonder whether the whole fine-spun structure has not dissolved into the air that it was structured from; whether in fact we have lost not just the ability to talk meaningfully about the sound-patterns of verse, but the capacity even to experience them. The sourest curmudgeons may suspect that the writing of free verse is itself a sign of this, not so much the cause of the collapse as the incontrovertible proof that the collapse has occurred. There is after all plenty of evidence that we are too confident in saying that we know when the blank-verse writer has broken his compact with us; that knowledge may in fact be shared only by a minority of readers, fewer with each generation. If so, the majority of readers have no longer a notion of any contractual obligations whatever: the poet can do whatever he pleases, and the reader has retained for himself only one right, which he exercises freely – the right to throw the poet's book aside.

Charles Hartman was far from entertaining such dire forebodings.

Though he knew that English prosody was in a mess, he believed that it could be cleared up; meanwhile for him poetry in English was certainly a going concern, and before the end of his book he was buoyantly welcoming a 'new wave', postmodernism in the American person of John Ashbery. And yet in a couple of places he too was dismayed by the precarious chanciness of the arrangements he was uncovering. William Carlos Williams for instance 'meant his three-line stanzas to be read so that each line occupies the same amount of time as the others. Lineation marks the isochronous units.' This was a prosody, Hartman, said, and it worked – for two reasons:

> First, it builds on the convention of line division, essential to and recognized in all verse. Second, *Williams became sufficiently well-known that through letters and essays he could establish single-handedly the convention that all lines take the same time – though only for his own poems.*

The italics here are not Charles Hartman's, but he can hardly object to them. For he remarks uneasily about this stratagem by Williams: 'His very success points up some of the interlocked problems of publicity and convention . . . It also hints that prosodic practice sometimes depends on published theory as much as theory on practice . . .' Well, yes indeed! But the case is even more complicated. For as Hartman had to concede, Williams's accounts of his prosodic practices were too muddled and slipshod to illuminate any reader; and accordingly, the poet's practices became clear only to those fortunate enough to read an unpublished dissertation by Emma Mellard Kafalenos at the University of Washington. Thus it seems that Williams's isochronous prosody 'works' (as a contract) only for those readers who have read Ms Kafalenos or else, later, Charles Hartman. And meanwhile, what of those thousands who had read Williams's poems without these aids? They had read poems which for them had no discernible prosody at all; but this lack had not prevented those poems from being applauded. And how can this be explained, except on the supposition that, for most readers, poets have ceased to be under any contractual obligations whatever?

William Carlos Williams may be thought a special case, inasmuch as what Americans applaud in him is much of the time inaudible to a British ear. But analogous situations are revealed with Charles Olson ('Like Williams, Olson had the public visibility to manage it'), and most intriguingly of all with that engaging crazy-man, Louis Zukofsky, who evolved a system that 'governs the distribution of "n" and "r" sounds according to the formula for a conic section.' This was, Hartman said, 'undeniably a metre' and yet 'not a prosody as far as the reader is concerned, because he does not share the secret.' But of course we the readers *did* now share the secret, since we had read Hartman's book, if not the essay by Hugh Kenner that first revealed Zukofsky's secret to a startled world. If Williams's prosody had now become public through the obscure conduit of Ms Kafalenos, Zukofsky's was no less public property thanks to Mr Kenner. And for all we know, dozens of aspiring poets at this very moment, British as well as American, may be studying conic sections, in the assurance, which Hartman could not deny them, that a prosody derived from such sources is as legitimate and effective as the iambic pentameter.

To be sure, these matters seem to belong on the wilder shores, or the lunatic fringes, of the American avant-garde. But British readers should surely beware of too smirkingly congratulating themselves on their native good sense. Zukofsky, it is true, never found many readers in his native USA, let alone in the United Kingdom. But the case is not significantly different with a poet so widely and appreciatively read as Eliot. Hartman was not the first to perceive that Eliot's prosody, at least up to *Four Quartets*, was consistently *vers libéré* rather than *vers libre*. But apart from the fact that few readers understood that distinction, and fewer were persuaded that they needed to find out, it was only a few years before Hartman that the point had been made. For years before that Eliot, just like Williams, had been read and applauded by thousands who discerned in him no prosody at all and were quite ready to do without it. This can only mean, as a matter of observable fact, either that the existence of a prosody is something that most readers take on trust, or else that they think verse is none the worse for not having a prosody behind it or within it. Either way, the British as much as the Americans seemed to have in practice abandoned the idea of a contract between poet and reader; it seems, they were happy to make a choice between blind faith and blithe insouciance. By 1980 for instance there was a sizeable amount of admiring commentary available on Ted Hughes; but one does not remember a page that asks whether this poet has a prosody, and if so what it is.

The complacent response to all this is to say that 'it is all in the ear anyway.' But as we have seen, prosody on the contrary depends very largely on purely notional structures of expectations, structures which determine what the ear shall register and what it shall suppress from awareness. Indeed in the bizarre limiting case of Zukofsky the prosody makes no appeal to the ear whatever. But surely a weightier objection is this: our grandfathers found it helpful and necessary to have a system, at bottom numerical, by which what their ears registered when reading verse could be checked against what other ears heard; we apparently have such faith in the nicety of our auditory awareness that we can dispense with such numerical, such 'mechanical', aids. Yet is this likely? Our ears are bombarded with mechanically generated and amplified noise, as the ears of our grandfathers never were – is it on the face of it probable that our auditory awareness is finer than theirs? Surely the opposite is far more likely. And if so, that side of modernism which vowed itself to unmetred verse must be seen to have failed. It relied, in Eliot as well as Pound, on there being in the reader's mind a rhythmical (also, incidentally, a syntactical) expectation, which the poet set himself to disappoint, offering in its place something more subtly satisfying. But if there is in the reader's mind, and in his ear, no expectation at all, the whole enterprise of free or 'freed' verse must fall to the ground. There is every reason to think that our ears are coarser than our grandfathers' were; and yet we regale ourselves with verse written on the assumption that our ears are finer.

Thus British poets and readers, who like to think that in metrical matters they are more conservative than Americans, cannot afford to be thus complacent. How many of those British thousands who have read Philip Larkin's 'Church Going' know that what they have read is iambic pentameters? And those who were possessed of this already arcane knowledge would have been startled to see from Hartman's scansion of some lines of the poem – a scansion more *outré* than it needed to be, but instructive all the same – how impudently and oddly (once we would have said, how loosely) Larkin handled his metre. Hartman's point was well taken, that a prosody so apparently conservative as Larkin's all the same showed, in that 'looseness', how the poet had grown up with *The Waste Land*; if it were not so, Larkin, we may suppose, would be a lesser poet than he is. That lesser poet, who at this juncture may as well be called Betjeman, would react to the challenge of unmetred verse in just the opposite way, by making his metres that much tighter, more drummingly insistent, less flexible. Thus we are forced to see that there is no warrant at all, when we speak of metres, for thinking 'strict' better than 'loose', 'regular' better than 'irregular'. And we are made to see also how we as readers agree to accept a convention, metrical or not, only so that we may see what the poet does with or within the convention; by the notional contract that he signs with us he undertakes to meet certain minimal expectations, but of course we hope that he will do more than that, and if his performance is limited to that we shall be dissatisfied. Betjeman's autobiography, *Summoned by Bells* (1960) is in blank verse; and so is his 'Sunday Afternoon Service in St Enodoc Church, Cornwall' (from *New Bats in Old Belfries*, 1945). But in the first case the poet satisfies only the minimal requirements he has contracted for, so that the metronomic recurrence of the pentameter shape only distracts us from the narrative, which would have been more interesting in prose; whereas in the 'St Enodoc' poem, the pentameter is varied and elaborated with a wealth of invention that may be called, intending the highest praise, Tennysonian. Unless the reader can recognize the convention, the terms of the notional contract, he may recognize the disparity but he cannot explain it, falling back instead on an unverifiable impression. And in fact it may be doubted whether, if we continue to be happily all at sea about metres and metrical conventions, we even *experience* the distinctions of value, let alone explain them.

However that may be, the persistence of accentual-syllabic prosodies in Larkin and many another British poet deserves more attention than Hartman and other transatlantic commentators have given to it. For if the varieties of free verse derive from new forms of contract between poet and reader (and this is what Hartman contended), we might have expected that the old forms of contract would have been discredited and would have fallen out of use. Plainly, this has not happened. But before taking heart from this, we might entertain the possibility that many readers today neither know nor care whether what they read or hear is in metre or not. Indeed in the 1970s the apparently equal popularity of Larkin and Ted Hughes – in many cases, it seemed, with the same readers – could hardly suggest anything else. Many people, it seemed, would have esteemed Larkin just as highly if, like Ted Hughes, he had employed no discernible prosody at all. There emerges once again the possibility that many readers in the 1970s had ceased to believe that there was between poet and reader any form of contract whatever.

It is easy to see why they might have been ready to do this. For some of them were plainly seeking a relation between poet and reader altogether warmer and more confiding than that of contracting partners to a transaction. This surely is the true significance of the poetry-reading by the poet, an institution obviously in keeping with the participatory democracy of the 1960s, which vigorously persisted into the 1970s – to the extent indeed that for the typical recipient of poetry in the 1970s, 'reader' was probably already a misnomer. Many observers noticed this, though most of them mistakenly welcomed it: people would rather hear a poet read than read his poems for themselves, and performing poets obliged with a rhetoric of buttonholing intimacy. Charles Hartman acknowledged this development, writing of 'directly rhetorical uses of form to establish a special community between the maker of the poem and the reader who "uses" it.' But his quotation-mark around 'uses' did nothing to dispel the squalid probability that at many public readings the audience was being used (exploited) by the performer, even as the audience emotionally exploited him. The poet on the reading circuit was plainly part of showbiz, purveying his art as a service. And Charles Hartman was trying to acknowledge, still within a framework of contract and transaction, a range of poetic procedures which in fact burst out of that frame and invalidated it. Accordingly, a book that began by being strikingly independent ended up as run-of-the-mill. For if Hartman had maintained the rigour of his earlier chapters he could only have reached the curmudgeonly conclusion that the 'special community' nowadays looked for between a poet and his readers, having put paid to the idea of the poem as public transaction, had put paid to, or at least had drastically imperilled, the practice of poetry in any sense that preserved continuity with previous centuries. For that continuity to be re-established, prosody had to be re-established as an indispensable and central concern both for the poet (including the free-verse poet) in his writing, and for the reader in his reading. Charles Hartman attempted such a re-assertion, but in the end he failed.

Bunting, Tomlinson and Hughes

In 1976 or 1977, Bunting told an interviewer: 'I like describing things I see . . .' It is a pity to have to refine upon an assertion so refreshingly direct. But the directness and the refreshingness are achieved by begging rather many questions. For instance, does Bunting really mean 'describe' (rather than 'convey', 'transmit', 'register', 'embody', above all – or before all – 'name')? And does he really mean 'see' (rather than 'smell', 'hear', 'touch', or – more comprehensively – 'feel', 'experience', 'perceive', 'apprehend')?

One reason for rummaging among these alternatives is to see where Bunting is at one with, and where he differs from, younger poets. That Hughes and Tomlinson are good enough poets to stand the comparison, should go without saying; indeed it might well be thought (though wrongly) that the senior poet had vowed himself to a simple-minded programme which his two successors were in different ways obliged to refine upon and sophisticate.

Consider Bunting on a flower, the blossom of the hawthorn:

> Dance tiptoe, bull,
> black against may.
> Ridiculous and lovely
> chase hurdling shadows
> morning into noon.
> May on the bull's hide
> and through the dale
> furrows fill with may . . .

And contrast, in *Remains of Elmet* (1979), Ted Hughes's 'Rhododendrons':

> Dripped a chill virulence
> Into my nape –
> Rubberised prison-wear of suppression!
>
> Guarding and guarded by
> The Council's black
> Forbidding forbidden stones.

The policeman's protected leaf!

Detestable evergreen sterility!
Over dead acid gardens
Where blue widows, shrined in Sunday, shrank

To arthritic clockwork,
Yapped like terriers and shook sticks from doorways
Vast and black and proper as museums.

Cenotaphs and the moor-silence!
Rhododendrons and rain!
It is all one. It is over.

Evergloom of official tittivation –
Uniform at the reservoir, and the chapel,
And the graveyard park,

Ugly as a brass-band in India.

Bunting's description mereiy three times over names the flower
('may'), whereas Hughes's poem has the air of showing how much
can be found in, or can be made of, or 'worked up out of', the one
word 'rhododendrons' (though also, to be fair, out of the visual
image of rhododendrons that Fay Godwin's camera had presented
him with). So much does the image, verbal or visual, spark off,
stimulate, provoke in Hughes's mind by way of association that by
the end, if the poem can be said to *describe* rhododendrons at all, that
description is certainly at the furthest remove from simply naming
them. What is sparked off in Bunting – what moves him, though by
one stage only, from naming to 'description' – is not associations but
a springing, tense and exciting *rhythm*: and more than that, a melody
– hence a metre, and submerged chimings of assonance and near-
rhyme. This suggests that a prosody is near to the centre of Bunting's
concerns, as (we are forced to think) it cannot be for Hughes. Rather
plainly there is room for a theoretical distinction between kinds of
imagination: one, fertile in associations and analogies, that may be
called 'literary'; and another, that goes immediately into prosody, to
be called 'poetic'.

A little later in *Briggflatts*, Bunting describes not what he sees, but
mostly what he once heard. The procedure is the same:

> Under sacks on the stone
> two children lie,

> hear the horses stale,
> the mason whistle,
> harness mutter to shaft,
> felloe to axle squeak,
> rut thud the rim . . .

Here, every verb simply names: 'lie' is what at this juncture the children do, 'stale' is what the horses do (the exact and therefore unusual word), 'whistle' what the mason does, 'mutter' what harness does to shaft, 'squeak' what felloe does to axle, 'thud' what rut does to rim. Contrast Charles Tomlinson (in 'Mackinnon's Boat', from *Written on Water*, 1972), telling us what lobsters do after they have been caught and are in the boat:

> Claw against claw, not knowing
>   What it is they fight, they swivel
> And bite on air until they feel
>   The palpable hard fingers of their real
> Adversary close on them; and held
>   In a knee-grip, must yield to him.

The lobsters first fight, then swivel, then bite, then feel, then yield. And how much more strenuous this is, in the demands it makes on perception and imagination – first in the poet, then in us – than a single-word naming of what lobsters in that situation do! (They, perhaps, 'claw'.) Yet strenuousness is not in itself, nor self-evidently, a virtue. For it exacts a price: not only does it slow the pace and muddy the narrative, it also, because such attentiveness is not normal, removes the poem, and the language of the poem, from the world of common discourse. Moreover, as with Hughes on rhododendrons, so with Tomlinson on doomed lobsters, we cannot suppress – we are perhaps not meant to suppress – the wondering and admiring sentiment: 'To have made so much of something so commonplace!' Both Hughes and Tomlinson in seeking conscientiously to go beyond the simple naming that Bunting understood by describing, risk the response from readers, 'What a show-off!' or else, more humbly but in the end more resentfully, 'Why couldn't *we* have noticed that much?' By provoking such responses, poetry may fulfil a useful educational function; and certainly, whether for this reason or some other, Ted Hughes's poems have been much in demand by educators. His large and loyal public has been recruited largely in the classroom. Bunting however seems never to have bothered whether poetry – his or any other – might be educational; and so for him rapidity and limpidity, melody and 'the common touch' are altogether more important considerations.

And yet the common touch is precisely what commentators have denied to Bunting, and deny him still. For a particularly rabid and therefore unrepresentative account, we may go to W. E. Parkinson in 1972, the year when Bunting became president of the Poetry Society:

> Bunting's work, . . must be mentioned because of its harmful influence on the work of the younger poets. His work and theirs reveals a lack of modern sensibility. *Loquitur*, a collection of poems written between 1924-35, and *Briggflatts*, a clumsy poem in the heroic mood, contained a hodge-podge of poetic styles (generally more effectively used by their originators), overworked and over conscious literary effects, collages of literary allusions reminiscent of Pound, and a meretricious display of erudition. Present also are the clues that point to an elitist view of life and art; the Art for Art's sake doctrine, 'Poetry is seeking to make not meaning but music' (a curiously anachronistic view of language); the facile rejection of modern society; contempt for modern man, present in *Briggflatts*, 'Chomei at Toyama', and 'How Duke Valentine Contrived'; over-weening pessimism, proud cynicism and the dishonest use of history conjuring up a former Northumbrian Golden Age that cannot be recovered. Bunting wallows in his illusions of the past, and like T. S. Eliot, Ezra Pound, W. B. Yeats, Oswald Spengler and Ortega y Gasset, apparently considers himself an embattled intellectual engulfed and threatened by hostile events while struggling to be the bearer of real cultural values. T. S. Eliot succeeds through his linguistic skills; Bunting is windy and often turgid rhetoric.[1]

Though not many would be so uncivil as this, nor so artless in displaying their ideological bias (not Marxist, merely British socialist), other commentators, by no means exclusively socialist, could be seen to harbour under their careful urbanity the same animosity towards Bunting, on the same or very similar grounds. Their opinions were of no importance for criticism, but certainly very telling and instructive for history: British populism, whether of the Right or the Left, saw the common touch anywhere but in naming, calling things and actions by their right names.

Of course if we take it as axiomatic that in the gutter press nothing ever *is* given its right name, and if we further find that

---

[1] W. E. Parkinson, 'Poetry in the North East', in *British Poetry since 1960. A Critical Survey*, ed. M. Schmidt and G. Lindop (Manchester 1972), p. 111.

the populace by its choice of newspapers has turned the gutter press into the popular press, then cynical populism seems to be vindicated. What is interesting about the 1970s and 1980s is that the highest reaches up-market were at pains to vindicate down-market usages and reading habits. For the characteristic endeavour of abstrusely learned speculators about language was, in those years, to establish that the idea of right naming had no substance; that the word 'misnomer' was without meaning. Since in each and every language a sound was matched with a meaning by at some point arbitrary convention, and since every such convention could be seen to be time-bound and space-bound and (often) class-bound, all standards of correctness were illusory, if indeed they were not instruments used by a dominant class to enforce upon subordinate classes their subordination. If enough people thought 'uninterested' was interchangeable with 'disinterested', then that interchangeability, underwritten by usage, became a law, and the notion of a distinction between them was relegated to the archaeological dustbin of history. Such speculators would make heavy weather out of reading either Tomlinson or Hughes, or any other responsible and educated author. But Bunting, so vowed to right naming, left them no alternative: he could only be proscribed and, he too, pitched into the dustbin.

Translations and Competitions

In 1976 the Oxford scholar and teacher John Carey published – in *The New Statesman*, where one had stopped looking for such things – an essay which attracted at the time some excited attention, mostly approving. It was called 'The Critic as Vandal'[1] . It looks now like a harbinger, in its demure and belle-lettrist fashion, of what was to be a much publicized concern of the 1980s: a 'crisis in English studies', which had most of the characteristics of a self-fulfilling prophecy since, if enough teachers like Carey confessed to doubts about what they were doing, then the doing of it was, as they declared, 'in crisis'. The crisis was shown to exist by the mere fact of so many implicated people declaring it.

Carey argued, going for evidence to three distinguished members of his own profession – viz. William Empson, C. S. Lewis and Christopher Ricks, to whom were added as his argument developed, the no less distinguished name of F. R. Leavis and the less distinguished one of William Kerrigan, author of *The Prophetic Milton* – that 'literary critics spend much of their time destroying the meaning of literature'. This was so because these critics could be shown to have fallen into the heresy of paraphrase, into substituting for the poet's words their own, as they tried to explain what it was that the poet (they supposed) was saying.

But the crucial question is whether paraphrase *is* 'heresy'. As Carey himself acknowledged, it was not always so regarded – for instance not by John Dryden who, in Carey's own words, 'believed not only that form and content were divisible but that, even in the best authors, the form might well benefit from a drastic overhaul which would leave the content unimpaired.' (The case in point was Dryden's adaptation of Shakespeare's *Troilus and Cressida*.) Against this view John Carey cited Coleridge's – which was, he assured his readers, axiomatic for modern critics:

> it would scarcely be more difficult to push a stone out from the pyramids with the bare hand than to alter a word, or the position

---

[1] When published by Oxford University Press in an extended version, the essay had a more decorous and less catchy title: *Wording and Re-Wording: Paraphrases in Literary Criticism* (1977).

of a word, in Milton or Shakespeare (in their most important works at least), without making the author say something else, or something worse, than he does say.

Carey was surely right: this *had* become axiomatic with modern critics, and for historically good and laudable reasons. But Coleridge's proposition is by no means self-evident; it is hyperbolical, and one may venture to think that in the light of common day no one really believes it. At all events, Dryden's quite different understanding of the matter has surely not been exploded by Coleridge's, but persists as – to put the case at its mildest – a viable alternative.

For after all, Dryden is arguably the greatest verse-translator in the language, whose adaptations of Shakespeare and Chaucer are in principle as much translations as his versions from Boccaccio and Ovid, Lucretius and Juvenal and Virgil; whereas one of the consequences of Coleridge's formulation, if we give it the seriousness that John Carey demanded for it, is to declare verse-translation an impossibility, or else an activity so misconceived that nothing can come of it except the humblest 'crib' or 'trot'. Robert Graves and Robert Frost ('Poetry is what gets lost in translation') had already lent their authority to this conclusion, which is indeed inescapable in the framework of a Romantic poetics like Coleridge's. Whether or not he knew or intended it, John Carey's eloquent re-statement of Coleridge's position was therefore, in the mid-1970s, profoundly reactionary. For at least since 1963, when Ted Hughes and Daniel Weissbort had instituted *Modern Poetry in Translation*, the translating of verse had been, more than ever before in the twentieth century, a major preoccupation for serious writers; and (to name but three instances) Michael Hamburger's versions from the German (e.g. *Paul Celan: Selected Poems*, 1972), Elaine Feinstein's of Marina Tsvetayeva (1971), and Peter Dale's of François Villon[1] might be judged great achievements not just of learning and ingenuity but of imagination. In this surely welcome development, one stage had been marked by George Steiner's *Penguin Book of Modern Verse Translation* (1966), as a later stage was marked by the very learned and sophisticated treatment of translation in the same polyglot critic's *After Babel* (1975); and it culminated in Charles Tomlinson's astonishingly ample and erudite *Oxford Book of Verse in English Translation*. But the persistence of attitudes like Coleridge's (or Frost's, or Graves's) meant that no one knew what to do with these books, what criteria to judge them by, still less how to applaud them at the rate they deserved. This meant that the bad translators, the *mis*translators (whose name of

---

[1] See Louis Bonnerot, in *Agenda* 11.4 and 12.1 (1973-4).

course was legion), went unrebuked, even as the good translators went uncelebrated and unrewarded. It seemed there was no way for any one to get out from under the Romantic inheritance so as to see the verse-translator as other than a more or less deluded drudge, at best a humble journeyman. And so the translating of poems was still thought to be an activity quite distinct from, and inferior to, the writing of them. This view was untenable in the light of the career of the modernist master Ezra Pound; but although in the 1970s respect for Pound increased quite rapidly in Britain, this was restricted to certain academic circles and still had no influence on reviewing and reputation-making.

One of the best verse-translators active in the 1970s was Peter Dale, and he is to be seen at near his best in what he makes of Rimbaud's 'Oraison du Soir':

> Je vis assis, tel qu'un ange aux mains d'un barbier,
> Empoignant une chope à fortes cannelures,
> L'hypogastre et le col cambrés, une Gambier
> Aux dents, sous l'air gonflé d'impalpables voilures.
>
> Tels que les excréments chauds d'un vieux colombier,
> Mille Rêves en moi font de douces brûlures:
> Puis par instants mon coeur triste est comme un aubier
> Qu'ensanglante l' or jeune et sombre des coulures.
>
> Puis, quand j'ai ravalé mes Rêves avec soin,
> Je me tourne, ayant bu trente ou quarante chopes,
> Et me recueille, pour lâcher l'âcre besoin:
>
> Doux comme le Seigneur du cèdre et des hysopes,
> Je pisse vers les cieux bruns, très haut et très loin,
> Avec l'assentiment des grands héliotropes.

In Dale's English this becomes 'Evening Prayers':

> I take things sitting down – angelic type
> at the barber's – fluted tankard in my fist,
> belly and neck curved, my Gambier pipe
> filling the air with veils that lift and twist.
>
> I'm burnt by the mild heat of a thousand dreams
> like the warm droppings left within an old
> dovecote. From time to time my sad heart seems
> sapwood where pollen bleeds its fresh dark gold.

Now when I've bolted down my dreams, I turn
and pull myself together just to cope
with ten to fifteen jars – a need that burns.

High and far out on dark skies I piss,
sweetly as our Saviour of Cedar and Hyssop,
winning approval of great heliotropes.[1]

A translation like this seems to satisfy the noblest and most exacting purpose that a translator may set before himself: that of extending the target-language and the target-culture, the translator's own, so as to make them accommodate ways of feeling such as that language and that culture had not previously discovered out of their native resources. For it is Rimbaud's achievement in such a poem to celebrate the adolescent's preoccupations with booze and sex (we fall into John Carey's heresy of paraphrase, but let it not worry us) inside a framework of inherited formality, that of the sonnet, of which the requirements are not just minimally honoured but gloried in and pushed to their limit. Consider only the vaunting audacity of rhyming 'hysopes' with 'heliotropes' – not just the clamorous fullness of the rhyme, but the antique and sacred resonances of 'hyssop'. Outside these early poems by Rimbaud (like 'Le Cabaret Vert', of which Dale's version can endure comparison with Pound's), there is – for a British poet like Tony Harrison who aims at such an effect – no precedent for such a combination. On the contrary, it was still assumed in Britain of the 1970s, a full century after Rimbaud stopped writing, that these basic pleasures could be celebrated and given their due only in verse which stridently proclaimed its liberation from all the formal conventions of the past. Accordingly, Rimbaud's supposedly more ambitious ventures, 'Le Bateau Ivre' and 'Une Saison en Enfer', had attracted more translators, partly because their apparently looser formal dispositions faced the translator with fewer problems, but also because their formal looseness conformed more comfortingly with what we had agreed to recognize as the avant-garde. Published in the 1970s, Dale's versions of this and similarly formal poems by the young Rimbaud thus had, for those who cared to think about it, immediately topical relevance to the matter of the life-styles then thought proper for the alienated or dispossessed sections of British society; the translation of a nineteenth-century French poem might speak immediately, if any one had been disposed to listen, to the bored and discontented teen-agers of Toxteth or Bermondsey. Though Dale in some of his poems and in his translations from

---

[1] Peter Dale, *Mortal Fire* (London, 1976).

classical Tamil (*The Seasons of Cankam*, Agenda Editions, 1975) used unmetred verse, it was plain, looking at his career as a whole, that what excited him most often was the tight structures of traditional verse. And in some of his work an inordinate love of that tightness had been damaging. But where his translation from Rimbaud was concerned, it was plain that reproducing the rhyming and metrical and stanzaic tightness of the original was not an option, but a necessity. For a translation of Rimbaud's sonnet into unrhymed free verse could only have been a travesty. (This was the case for instance with the elaborately structured 'octets' of Osip Mandelstam, translated into unmetred and rigorously bitten-short English by the late lamented Peter Riley.) Only a formally conservative translator like Dale could have done justice to the elaborately, indeed vauntingly formal shape that the young Rimbaud found for what was very informal, radically and rebelliously unconventional experience. And other examples could be found of how the poet-translator must subdue his own proclivities, or those most favoured by his age, so as to submit himself to the service of the poet he has undertaken to translate.

In the 1980 anthology of the Arvon Foundation Poetry Competition,[1] part of a manifestly profitable enterprise dreamed up by Ted Hughes or his advisers, one of the three or four best performances was surely Keith Bosley's 'Corolla', a sequence of nine exactly rhymed and metred sonnets, culminating in a splendid version of a Ronsard sonnet that had defeated Yeats:

> When you are old and lost in memory
> you might, seized by a sentimental fit,
> take down this book and blow the dust off it
> recalling: 'Bosley was quite keen on me.'

(Yeats, it will be recalled, came up with a wonderfully natural and crooningly memorable first line, 'When you are old and grey and full of sleep', but before the end had departed from Ronsard altogether so as to consider 'how Love fled/And paced upon the mountains overhead/And hid his face amid a crowd of stars' – a possibility that the tough-minded Renaissance poet never conceived of, and if he had conceived of it would not have entertained.) Bosley won a prize: the smallest offered, £100. And one wondered: what were the judges looking for – Ted Hughes and Philip Larkin, Seamus Heaney and Charles Causley – that they should have rated Bosley's

---

[1] *Arvon Foundation Poetry Competition, 1980 Anthology* ed. Ted Hughes and Seamus Heaney (Todmorden: Kilnhurst 1982).

heart-warming dexterity (feelingful as well as formal) below, for instance, eighteen solid unpunctuated pages of pornographic day-dream: Kenneth Bernard's 'The Baboon in the Night Club'? May we not suspect that somewhere in their minds was the assumption, which Coleridge and John Carey would underwrite, that verse-translation was of its nature inferior to verse-composition; that a poem which depended for its effect on a great poem of the past was by that very token inferior to a poem that acknowledged no such dependence?

Privately funded and munificent literary prizes had long been a bane of cultural life in the USA, France, Italy, and elsewhere. In the 1970s, Britain lamentably fell into line. Seamus Heaney wrote that the judges in the Arvon competition undertook their labours 'in a spirit of service' to 'a cause worth supporting'. One looked in vain for the traditional and salutary irreverence of the Irishman. Even English men and women could have represented to Heaney that 'a worthy cause' was precisely the most insidious and dangerous temptation for an artist; and a living Englishman, Sisson, could have taught him that since poetry is, like all the arts, necessarily 'élitist', the most disastrous of worthy causes are generated by societies that are, or like to think that they are, egalitarian. What else but abject egalitarianism could explain the award of £100 to a poem called (the title exhausted its significance) 'If I weren't a boring little middle class tit'?

If poetry is not a social service but 'bloweth where it listeth', if its socio-political value (supposing it has any, which may well be doubted) lies in saying what no politician of any party wants to hear, it follows that worth in poetry cannot be determined by that favoured device of egalitarian politics, the committee; not even when the committee is made up of poets so earnest and gifted as Hughes and Heaney, Larkin and Causley. From their deliberations, some of them stagily televised, there emerged as from any com-mittee (Heaney as good as admitted as much) a Lowest Common Denominator: a list of prize winners that placated them as a group, though in private it pleased no one of them. Good poems, one or two exceptionally good, had been submitted; and among the eighty-five poems in the anthology one in two at least deserved respect – a better bargain than one had any right to expect. But we learned to our consternation that the field had been originally nothing like eighty-five but, incredibly, 35,000! Thirty-five *thousand* poems had been read inside five months by each of the judges; it was enough to silence each of their four voices for ever after. The statistic was appalling. Did it mean that in the year 1980 more than 30,000 persons in the English-speaking world thought they had sufficiently mastered the principles of an ancient and intricate art, for them to compete for the laurel? Of course it did not mean that. It meant, it must have meant, that for most of these competitors poetry was not, and in their experience never had been, an art; that the ancientness of it, and the intricacy, had in their own sense of it been conclusively superseded. The four judges presumably knew that poetry was an art (though Hughes for one mostly suppressed this knowledge, except in the act of writing), but their performance as selectors did nothing to impress the unpalatable truth on the thousands of hopefuls already setting their sights on the next year's competition. It began to seem that in an egalitarian century the exclusiveness of art – of *any* art – was an affront that could not be tolerated. By 1984, the Arts Council was listing no less than forty-six 'poetry workshops' in London alone, these dubiously distinguished from just as many 'Write-your-own-poetry' classes; the writing of poems was clearly no longer considered an art but rather a hobby, a tactic of individual or group therapy. It could not be expected that the delicacy of Peter Dale's negotiations with Rimbaud and Corbière, of Peter Whigham's with Catullus, of Edward Dorn's and Gordon Brotherston's with Vallejo[1] , of Bosley's with Ronsard, would be appreciated in such a charitable context.

[1] Dorn and Brotherston, *Cesar Vallejo: Selected Poems* (Penguin Books, 1976).

Poetic Theory

Bunting in the 1970s was no longer writing poems, but was giving readings and from time to time interviews. In 1977 he replied to an interviewer, who asked him about his 'use of personae as a way of presenting material':

> Persona in the sense used by Pound and by Browning is almost foreign to me. I use very little of it. But if you mean by persona simply that the poet isn't always speaking in his own person, not everything he says is a personal confession, and so on, of course that is true. I don't go in for personal confessions. I like describing things I see, but if it goes beyond that, you can be fairly sure that it's not necessarily me that's supposed to be making these remarks.[1]

Nothing in this reply, so seemingly casual, is unconsidered. 'Personal confessions', for instance. 'Confessional poetry' had been a novel category much invoked in the 1960s, by readers who wanted to extol in particular the American poetry of Sylvia Plath on the one hand, Robert Lowell on the other. And there had been those who, ignoring Bunting's warning that *Briggflatts*, though 'an autobiography', was not to be taken literally, had construed the narrative of that poem as sentimental, since it seemed to say that a passage of unconsummated calf-love had condemned the rest of the poet's life to unfulfilment. (Yet who has not known such an experience and recalled it, however trivial in itself, as a prototype of the unfulfilment that shadows every life, however successful?)

As for the seemingly artless 'I like describing things I see', we have discovered already what distinctions, and what tangles of possible misunderstanding, that form of words papers over. So it is with the rest of Bunting's response to his interviewer: it is skirting round, where it is not plunging into, the hoariest of all questions about poetry, the question: how truthful are the things that poems say? Since poetry, as every one knows, deals in fictions, is what poetry says on a level with what advertisers say, or what an actor says from

---

[1] 'Basil Bunting Interviewed by Dale Reagan', *Montemora* 3 (Spring 1977), p. 77.

the stage? This question was very subtly and ingeniously answered by Philip Sidney four hundred years ago; tediously, it is a question that will not go away, but has to be asked afresh every time that the historical and social context for poetry alters even a little.

Bunting, it may be thought, hardly comes clean on this issue, but wants to stand betwixt-and-between. 'I like describing things I see' certainly narrows the possibilities: Bunting, he would have us believe, is like his American colleague George Oppen in wanting to make affirmations certainly, but not about large matters like Death and Prayer, Remorse and Memory, Soul and Society, only about things offered to his senses, and the patterns which such things make in his awareness of them. But much wider vistas are opened up, as Bunting goes on talking to his interviewer:

> When I became acquainted first with the work and then with the persons of Pound and Eliot what astonished me and made me so enthusiastic was that here were men who were doing and who had been doing all the time, though I had been unaware of it, the things which I had painfully worked out for myself were the things necessary to do with poetry, but we'd arrived by quite different roads at this conclusion. Only a very small part of my road to these ideas coincides with Pound's road or Eliot's road. The chief part of that would be that we were all three very enthusiastic readers of Dante . . .

Dante! There is the formidable name that cannot be avoided. What Dante affirms is, as every one knows, the dogmas of Christianity – along with, to be sure, certain other propositions that are heterodox or speculative. How can a non-Christian reader, like Pound but of course *not* like Eliot (Bunting, who never forswore his allegiance to the Society of Friends, remained to that extent within Eliot's Christendom), take *The Divine Comedy* seriously while privately denying the cardinal propositions which Dante's poem affirms or assumes? Many of us remember the answers that can be found to that, most of them beginning with Coleridge's 'willing suspension of disbelief'. But however that may be, Dante is only the extreme case of what confronts us with the vast majority of the past poets in our own language. Through hour on hour if we are at all studious, we are reading poets who either affirmed, or were prepared to affirm, what they took to be the truths of the Christian Revelation – truths (if that is what they are) which most of us, and most of our students if we have students, are *not* prepared to affirm. There is in this situation, of a Christian literature being read by non-Christian or post-Christian readers, a very patent reason for the readiness, greater

among Americans than among the British, to think that *all* the prop-
ositions advanced by poets are to be understood as provisional, as
fictive make-believe.

Did any one ever seriously propose that the affirmations made in
The Divine Comedy – whether by the pilgrim himself or by Virgil as
the pilgrim's guide – were to be understood only as make-believe?
The non-believer Ezra Pound must surely have understood them
thus, in order to continue frequenting the great poem at all, as we
know he did. But did any one ever assert that Dante was not, could
not have been, in earnest? At least one poet had said so. And he
was, of all unlikely things, a Jesuit priest: Gerard Manley Hopkins,
writing to Robert Bridges:

> This leads me to say that a kind of touchstone of the highest or
> most living art is seriousness; not gravity but the being in earnest
> with our subject – reality. It seems to me that some of the greatest
> and most famous works are not taken in earnest enough, are farce
> (where you ask the spectator to grant you something not only
> conventional but monstrous). I have this feeling . . . even about
> the *Divine Comedy*, whereas *Paradise Lost* is most seriously taken.[1]

That a mid-Victorian Englishman converted to the Church of Rome
should admire Milton's arch-Protestant poem to the detriment of
Dante's vast and complexly ordered image of Roman Christendom
. . . the phenomenon surely deserves more attention than it has
received. One reflection it prompts is that Hopkins, despite the
accident by which his poems were not published until the present
century, was indeed a *Victorian* Englishman, not a modern one born
before his time. And much of what is Victorian and admirable
about him is precisely, in his own phrase, 'the being in earnest'.
At all events there is no doubt where Hopkins stands in relation
to the question at issue: he is every inch an affirmative poet, with
little or (it really seems) *no* patience with poetry that affirms only
provisionally or under the mask of make-believe. And in a very
remarkable Chatterton lecture to the British Academy in 1975,[2]
Seamus Heaney had shown how this principle was not theoreti-
cal for Hopkins but informed every aspect of his poetic practice,
down to the very sounds, and the patternings of sounds, which he
cultivated so intensely and so idiosyncratically. Hopkins *will* take his

---

[1] G. M. Hopkins, *The Letters . . . to Robert Bridges*, ed. C. C. Abbott (London, 1955),
p. 65.
[2] Seamus Heaney, 'The Fire i' the Flint: Reflections on the Poetry of Gerard Manley
Hopkins', reprinted in *Preoccupations: selected prose 1968-78* (London, 1980).

stand, he *will* lay it on the line, he *will* stand by what he says . . . he insists upon that as his right, as also (no doubt) on the right to pay the price if he is proved or judged to be wrong.

The points at issue would appear just as clearly from considering affirmations in poems about politics or about morals. But it is in the area of religious belief that the issues emerge most starkly; as they do for instance in Robert Lowell's 'Colloquy in Black Rock.' This has been called 'one of Lowell's greatest poems' and it has been defined (by Hugh B. Staples in 1962) as 'an anthem celebrating the miracle of the Eucharist, expressed in terms of a personal awareness of Divine Immanence symbolized by the Feast of Corpus Christi'. 'A personal awareness . . .' Indeed nothing less seemed to be affirmed in the poem, in expressions like, 'I hear him, *Stupor Mundi* . . .' When the poem first appeared (in *The Sewanee Review* for Autumn 1944, thereafter in *Lord Weary's Castle* 1946) one had been led to believe that the poet was a believing and communicating member of the Roman Catholic Church, which he had joined in 1940. But in 1976, when in both New York and London the lines appeared unchanged in Lowell's *Selected Poems*, one was led to believe, through the same unsatisfactory but unavoidable channels, that he was not, and had not been for many years, either communicant or believer. It was impossible to think that this information about the poet's lapse into infidelity made no difference to a reading of this poem. For what the poem affirms is not merely credal assent but, as Hugh Staples had said, 'a personal awareness'. And so, when Lowell lost his Christian faith, he did not merely withdraw his professed assent; he conceded that an experience he had once presented, and continued to present, as indubitable was in fact dubious and delusory. A less light-minded or sophisticated generation might have been up in arms about it.

In fact Lowell had after a fashion cleared himself; for certain comments on his own poem 'Skunk Hour', and certain sections of his late collection, *Notebook*, had given us to understand that between *Lord Weary's Castle* and *Selected Poems* he had committed himself firmly to the view that the poet in Philip Sidney's words 'nothing affirmeth'; taking that to mean that whatever affirmation the poet formally makes in a poem is as much a device or a necessity of the developing structure as is any other feature of the composition – for instance, its cadences; in other words, that the affirmations are as fictitious, as provisional, as much a means to an end, as anything else in the poem. This was all very well. Yet in 1976 one could not help recalling that when W. H. Auden ceased to believe certain things he had believed in his youth, he had either suppressed or reversed the lines in which he had said such things, thereby rather comically incurring the wrath of bibliographers. Auden's solution, though admirably consistent and straightforward, did not seem quite right either. And so the dilemma persists: an ethical dilemma for poets who change their minds. What is a poet, when he surveys his earlier writings, supposed to do about his having once believed fervently what he now believes no longer? There can be little doubt that Gerard Manley Hopkins would have decided Robert Lowell was not 'in earnest', we must think, certainly not when he reprinted 'Colloquy in Black Rock' in *Selected Poems*, and probably not even when he wrote and published the poem in the first place.

The question arises on page after page of Lowell precisely because the rhetoric that Lowell mastered and early made his own, though it later underwent some quite drastic changes, always, early and late, committed him to seem to be making very emphatic and vehement affirmations indeed. Obviously, with a poet whose rhetoric is more sinuous and silkily low-voiced and ruminative, the question is not raised at all so often or so starkly. Thus (to move to another of our American contemporaries) it would be a very naïve reader of John Ashbery, and a reader very soon frustrated, who would look in Ashbery's poetry for affirmations that the poet will stand by, will take his stand upon. Quite simply, it is usually impossible to say what an Ashbery poem *is about*. As he has confessed himself, 'What moves me is the irregular form . . . that affects us whenever we try to say something important to us – more than the meaning of what we are saying at a particular moment.' And Lawrence Kramer, in an essay of 1977 of some importance for students of British poetry,[1] remarked that accordingly 'Because they almost never identify their subjects, Ashbery's poems affiliate themselves with each other more readily than they do with reality.' Here then is a poet who with singular purity 'nothing affirmeth', since he contrives not to make even provisional or make-believe assertions. Another thing to be said of him is that, since the question does not arise whether he writes as a Christian or not, the Christian, the non-Christian, and the post-Christian reader all start equal in approaching him. This is very democratic, as Americans understand democracy; and in committing poetry to be irreligious, it also permits or seems to permit poetry to be a-political. Does Ashbery then evade Hopkins' beady-eyed question: 'But is he in earnest?' It would seem that he does. And yet doubts arose when his admirer, Lawrence Kramer, went on to compare him with three of his British contemporaries: Ted Hughes, Philip Larkin, and Geoffrey Hill. Of these three, different as they are, Kramer decided that their writing 'seems to depend on

[1] Lawrence Kramer, 'The Wodwo Watches the Water Clock . . .', *Contemporary Literature* 18.3 (Summer 1977), pp. 319–42.

the assumption that reality transcends language negatively.' It was hard to understand what 'negatively' could mean in that sentence. But otherwise the drift was clear enough. What this critic was saying was plainly true, though much less certainly true of Hill than of Hughes and Larkin: these British poets, like British poets generally, wrote on the assumption that there was a reality which their language must be made to measure up to. And plainly it is only on this assumption – that there are names, bits of language, which must be accountably attached to things, bits of non-language – that one can speak of right namings and of misnamings, hence of statements that are true and others that are false. Accordingly this has to be the working assumption of any poet who believes that poetry, or *some* poetry, is 'sweetly uttered knowledge'. But the sophisticated Lawrence Kramer declared of this assumption that it 'may or may not be true, but either way it is one that fictions, if they mean to be supreme fictions, simply cannot make.' And at this point we may surely hear Father Hopkins, confronted with this insouciance ('may or may not be true'), and the blitheness with which reality is sacrificed to fictions, exclaiming: 'But he is not in earnest!' Moreover, it is Ashbery's admirer who is categorical and exclusive; who is sure that the poet who lays it on the line, who issues affirmations that he will stand by and stand over, is necessarily inferior to the poet who takes no such risks. The European observer does well to recall that in some societies the affirmations that it may fall to the poet to make are of the order of 'The Emperor has no clothes on'; and that the citizenry in those societies look to their poets to make those affirmations, because no one else has the duty to do so, or can find the courage for it. Akhmatova, Pasternak and Mandelstam are just three poets of our time who found that courage, and lived up to their sometimes dangerous calling.

Earlier in the interview with Bunting, his interlocutor had remarked searchingly:

> . . . you've said on a number of occasions that the poet is a man skilled in the use of words and that it is this which makes his writing of interest, not what he has to say. You have also stressed, however, that very often poetry fails because what the poet says isn't of interest, he hasn't seen his subject sufficiently clearly. How are these two notions compatible?

To which Bunting had replied:

> Oh they are tied together . . . unless a man knows bloody well what he's doing he's not going to do it very well, so a man whose

thought is floppy is not likely to produce anything but a floppy poem, not because the poem expresses thought, but because unless he is pretty clear about himself, about what he has to say, it's most unlikely that he will be able to say it in the most economical, the best sounding, the best carrying way; that's all. That's one of the reasons why poets are wise to do as they usually do and stick to commonplaces. . . .

Again, it is easy to be misled by Bunting's casual colloquialisms. Here we have a wholly new level of sophistication, a sort of finesse. For here, saying what he means or meaning what he says is presented to the poet not as an ethical but as an aesthetic imperative. Bunting seems to say that the poet should affirm only what he is prepared to stand by and stand over, because only in that way will he attain qualities like economy and 'soundingness'. We may be reminded of an American of an older generation, one who had no patience with Bunting; Yvor Winters, who was an important voice for some new British poets of the 1970s, notably Neil Powell, Dick Davis and Clive Wilmer:

> A poem is what stands
> When imperceptive hands,
> Feeling, have gone astray.
> It is what one should say.
>
> Few minds will come to this.
> The poet's only bliss
> Is in cold certitude –
> Laurel, archaic, rude.

Winters is often thought of, and he may have thought of himself, as a moralist. And yet all the three words in that clipped yet resounding closure – 'Laurel, archaic, rude' – are words for aesthetic effects, not moral principles. If we too are enamoured of those effects, effects which can come about only from 'being in earnest', we shall not believe that the poet like Wallace Stevens who aims at a supreme fiction is in principle and necessarily a truer poet than the one whose 'bliss/Is in cold certitude'. 'Our word is our bond' – in a few years Geoffrey Hill was to turn that familiar boast so upside-down and inside-out that we would be bewildered by what we had always supposed to mean simply: 'We mean what we say'. But however philosophers of language may explain to us that no one *can* mean exactly or wholly or exclusively that which he says, poets who have the illusion of doing that, or the intention of doing it, produce poetry that pleases in a special way. Bunting, much as he pretended to be interested only in making poems (and be damned to whether we liked them or not), was plainly a poet who aimed to give us those special pleasures. In this he showed himself, despite his many American affiliations, very much a British poet.

R. S. Thomas

Thomas's collection of 1972 had the arch and unpromising title, *H'm*. It was followed by *Laboratories of the Spirit* (1975) and *Frequencies* (1978). *H'm* marked a turning-point in Thomas's writing, and the turn that he made alienated some who had admired him. Their discontent was voiced by John Wain in one of his lectures as Professor of Poetry at Oxford:

> R. S. Thomas . . . is a particularly depressing example of the damage caused to a poet's work by the flight from form; his subject-matter has always been rather lowering (depopulation of the countryside, depopulation of the human heart through the decay of beliefs, etc.). But there was a time when the depressing nature of what Mr Thomas conveyed was irradiated and made bearable by his beautiful sense of rhythm and sound. The poems in *H'm* offer no such consolation.[1]

And Wain quoted in support of this contention 'Via Negativa':

> Why no! I never thought other than
> That God is that great absence
> In our lives, the empty silence
> Within, the place where we go
> Seeking, not in hope to
> Arrive or find. He keeps the interstices
> In our knowledge, the darkness
> Between stars. His are the echoes
> We follow, the footprints he has just
> Left. We put our hands in
> His side hoping to find
> It warm. We look at people
> And places as though he had looked
> At them, too; but miss the reflection.

Here, Wain contended, 'the lowered, daunted quality of the subject-

[1] John Wain, *Professing Poetry* (London, 1977), pp. 107-08.

matter is matched by the same characteristics in the expression';
whereas 'in the days when Mr Thomas made graceful, lyrical poems
about being daunted, he was telling us that the negative experience
was being contained in a mind, and expressed by a sensibility, that
was reaching beyond, attaining something positive.'

The response is clearly and forthrightly expressed, it is understand-
able, and certainly it was widely shared. But it is open to certain
objections. In the first place, and most importantly, it must be
questioned whether the subject-matter of 'Via Negativa' is, as John
Wain confidently takes for granted, 'lowered, daunted'. Thomas's
other poems suggested, and were to suggest, that a God who 'keeps
the interstices/In our knowledge, the darkness/Between stars' was a
concept not daunting but consolatory. The religious mind finds its
consolations in regions where the secular mind discerns only forbid-
ding bleakness, and just that paradox or seeming paradox is what R.
S. Thomas's later poems resolutely explore. If one's worst fear is that
technological man may extend his knowledge to the point where no
mysteries are left in the universe, then a God who can be relied on
always to reveal gaps in that knowledge is a God to be thankful for.
The way of negation, the 'Via Negativa' of the title, is thus one of
the ways to transcendence; this is what traditional Christian thinking
affirms, and the poem endorses that traditional understanding.

Secondly, one may question Wain's implicit assumption that
the poetry he calls 'lyrical' characteristically works by expressing
'lowering' apprehensions in a sweetly formal way that makes them
paradoxically exalting. That some poetry works on us in that way,
need not be denied. But to set up that way of working as a norm runs
the risk of overvaluing a suave melancholy, the poignantly managed
dying fall. It is a risk to which admirers of Larkin, that poet of very
'lowering' apprehensions, are particularly prone. The least one can
say is that the poet of *H'm*, though for that matter of earlier col-
lections also, had no interest in being lyrical on that understanding
of 'lyric'.

All the same, John Wain undoubtedly had a point: the R. S.
Thomas of the 1970s certainly went to great lengths to offend and
disappoint the reader's ear. As soon as we consider how to read
'Via Negativa' aloud, we can see where that offensiveness is: in the
enjambements, the run-overs. As the reading voice turns from the
third line into the fourth, and again from the fourth into the fifth, it
encounters after two syllables the jarring stop that had been denied it
(where it would not have jarred) at the end of the verse-line. There
are not much less jarring enjambements where the fifth line turns into
the sixth, and the seventh into the eighth; a particularly abrupt one,
on to a single syllable, where the ninth line turns into the tenth; and

another, only one syllable more lenient, where the eleventh line turns into the twelfth. Of course such abrupt or violent enjambements are an invaluable resource available to the poet; but when they are resorted to so frequently in a short poem (which is a sonnet only on the understanding that the sole requirement of a sonnet is that it be fourteen lines long), the trick seems to be a mere mannerism, one that denies even minimal integrity to the verse-line. Where the verse-line is concerned – and 'verse' comes from *versus*, the *turn* (from one line into the next) – John Wain's allegation, 'flight from form', seems not excessive. Wain called 'Via Negativa' 'a fine poem', but then, on second thoughts, 'a fine piece of writing'; it would be more accurate to say (teasingly, yet in all seriousness) that it may or may not be a fine poem, but it certainly is not a fine piece of verse.

This is not always the case. In 'The Calling', from *Laboratories of the Spirit*, the enjambements – not just between lines but between quatrains – are abrupt, even violent; yet in every case there is rhetorical justification. That is to say, they are expressive, and therefore an aid rather than an impediment to the voice that would read the poem aloud:

> And the word came – was it a god
> spoke or a devil? – Go
> to that lean parish; let them tread
> on your dreams; and learn silence
>
> is wisdom. Be alone with yourself
> as they are alone in the cold room
> of the wind. Listen to the earth
> mumbling the monotonous song
>
> of the soil: I am hungry, I
> am hungry, in spite of the red dung
> of this people. See them go
> one by one through that dark door
>
> with the crumpled ticket of your prayers
> in their hands. Share their distraught
> joy at the dropping of their inane
> children. Test your belief
>
> in spirit on their faces staring
> at you, on beauty's surrender
> to truth, on the soul's selling
> of itself for a corner

> by the body's fire. Learn the thinness
> of the window that is
> between you and life, and how
> the mind cuts itself if it goes through.

Here the line-endings over-ridden so imperiously are in the service of a saturnine, even savage, wit – consider how in the fourth quatrain the line-endings link 'distraught' with 'inane'. It is not how we imagine a Christian priest contemplating the flock he is responsible for; but in that case we had better (so Thomas's poem implies) revise our notions, and not suppose that either Christian charity or pastoral care precludes the Yeatsian arrogance that is invoked in the third and fourth lines. (Thomas alludes to Yeats continually; something too little noticed by those who have typed him as a Wordsworthian poet, grey and good and sober – that is not at all his character.)

Even so, Thomas's ruthless enjambements became in the 1970s such a prominent feature of his style – sometimes to affective purpose, more often not – that it was hard not to see this as a tic, a mannerism. It was as if this sole device constituted for him a prosody; and one was forced to protest that a respectable prosody must comprehend a good deal more.

Jack Clemo

1977 was celebrated as the Jubilee anniversary of Queen Elizabeth's accession to the throne. In June of that year a preacher asked himself on behalf of his congregation:

> . . . what does a ceremony like the coronation or a royal wedding have to offer me? First of all they are ceremonies centred on human relationships. It would be very good if all cultures were able to celebrate with communal rejoicing the nuptials of two people. The whole thing really does summon up the fairy tales of infancy: the beautiful princess marries and is happy. A royal wedding or a jubilee translates that archetypal aim of happiness into a contemporary reality ousting the economic and political orders of reality from our front pages. A girl gets married; that is a central fact of state. As a public ceremony one has only to compare it with an obscene row of tanks and nuclear weapons trundling past some grey group of power-hungry men to see that it belongs to a better and a more decent world. It is poetry not naked power.

The phrasing is not memorable. One records it only so as to set beside it a poem ('It is poetry not naked power', saith the preacher) in which the same or very similar sentiments are expressed otherwise. For the preacher had been anticipated by several years in a poet's response to the royal wedding that we may take it both of them had in mind: that of the Princess Anne. A severely incapacitated poet in Cornwall, indisputably proletarian both by his origins and in the style of his life, had participated – thanks to radio or else television, and the ministrations of his own devoted wife – in the wedding of the Princess Anne, and had written 'Royal Wedding':

> Sun sparkles on London crowds, though here in the west
> November fog sneaks round the dying shrub-stems
> Outside of one of England's humblest cottages:
> A century old, blunt granite, and industrial rubble
> Fumbling close by, with some garages.
> We who live wedded here
> Sit cleansed by Abbey music, fanfare,

And solemn voices flowing at the crest
Of another dream-drive among regal gems.

This is no hollow pomp, this is root and haven,
The sane oasis where hearts pause and listen
To the intoning tongue of half-forgotten springs,
The deep historic soundings
From the rock-base, at the courtly arrival.

Feel now, how mean and small
Is the modern desert, drably efficient
Swept by sullen agitation
Where the grey waste meets the red sand!
We have feared the ignoble trampling
Set as tomorrow's march for our people;
The alien expanse with no gracious order,
No traditional command,
But only the raw gasp of gravelly bluster
And machine-geared instinct, blind through separation
From the silken splendour of a reverent vow.

Bones of great lovers lie in this oasis:
Browning and Tennyson, who showed what the English meant
By marriage: rose-flush in a hushed garden,
Sheath of oak-shade, massive and wholesome,
Folding the plain vein, a pledge
Of ancient power and knowledge,
Northern and Christian. We need this
Revived, need voices to restore the flow,
Spread the crowned wisdom, let the chanting
Waters redeem the dry furrow.

It is hard to know what to make of such verses. Is it the sentiments
expressed which embarrass us, or the gaucheries in the expression
(those 'solemn voices flowing at the crest', for instance)? On the
cherished principle that in poetry form and content are inseparable,
the question must be ruled out of order. But in that case what do
we do with the artless and wretched verses that are to be found
sometimes on modern gravestones, or in the obituary columns of
provincial newspapers? The never long stilled complaints against
'academicism' as a blight on our poetry[1] would have point if they

---

[1] For a recent instance, Martin Booth, *British Poetry 1964-84: Driving through the Bar-ricades* (London 1985), p. VII and *passim*.

were issued in the interest of writing like this, where the faults
– explicitness at the wrong moments, lapses into reach-me-down
journalese – are patent, where none the less we find phrases undoubt-
edly memorable and vigorous: 'From the rock-base, at the courtly
arrival . . .', 'the raw gasp of gravelly bluster . . .' 'Folding the plain
vein . . .' Moreover the poem is more than the sum of its parts: it
is solidly and surprisingly constructed, and it addresses itself to a
matter – wedlock, and the idealization of wedlock – which is of
central and vexed importance. One gropes guiltily for a phrase like
'honest clumsiness' which older critics used, which recent critics have
ruled out of court for the good reason that it can be used to excuse the
inexcusable.

However it may be for the critic, the historian cannot ignore such
writing if only because it is very common, perhaps at any period,
certainly in the 1970s and 1980s, when the writing of verse had
become for many people up and down the country, even in aca-
demia, something more than a hobby yet less than a calling or a
constant preoccupation. At any rate it was in no one's interest, in
1975 when this poem appeared, to have its existence acknowledged,
let alone acclaimed. It could not serve the Left to have this proletarian
– no forehead-knuckling peasant, anachronistically surviving, but a
mutilated member of the industrial workforce – recording that he
found solace for his own condition, and significance for it, in the
institution and the rituals of monarchy. And as for the party of the
Establishment, this poet turned out to be a heterodox Wesleyan
Calvinist, and as such one who in true-blue Tory eyes had no
right to any monarchical sentiments at all. Among his fellow-poets,
the obvious place for him was with those who aspired to be both
popular and populist; but then it was widely held that dropping the
names of poets of the past was a patented device for excluding 'the
people' from poetry; and here was a poet from (to use their own
vocabulary) 'the workers', who none the less dropped the names of
Tennyson and Browning. Finally, among perfervid Cornishmen and
Celtic nationalists generally, how could they take to this unsolicited
tribute to a member of an allegedly alien nation, and a Hanoverian
dynasty? In such a self-answering question we have the record of this
poet's dealings with his British public: he broke across, and muddled,
all the comfortable categories of sociologists, psephologists, journal-
istic commentators, and party-managers. He just should not have
happened. But he did, and his name was Jack Clemo.

In 1975 Clemo was fifty-nine, and had been married for five years.
His finding so late the bride whom he had sought through thirty or
forty years, in the face of disappointments and physical afflictions
that had dogged him since early childhood, obviously had a lot to

do with his response to the royal nuptials. In other writings he had made it clear that he regarded his own belated marriage as proof of how God keeps His promises with those whom He has signalized as His Elect by burdening them with improbable miseries, precisely so that their witness to Him shall be that more startling. This was a private story, though the earlier unfulfilled stages of it had been recounted with great tact and taste in one of Clemo's several books of autobiography.

The man who wrote of 'the raw gasp of gravelly bluster' had been, he tells us plainly, much drawn in 1936 or so to British Fascism. And there are those who will think that to move over forty years from Fascism to monarchism involves no very extended pilgrimage. Others, who agree with T. S. Eliot that Fascism 'from a truly Tory point of view, is merely the extreme degradation of democracy', will think on the contrary that Clemo's journey was a long one. In any case the stages that Clemo passed through are of absorbing interest. They are also disturbing, because 1936 was not the only time in Clemo's life when politically, as he admitted, he 'might have got into a deal of mischief'. Clemo had meditated further on his Fascist sympathies and on how, during the Second World War, they had cooled:

> The religious aspect of an enthusiasm was the only one that could grip me for long. Thus I should have become a political misfit even among the Fascists had I been able to join them. Though I liked much of Nietzsche it was rather in Luther's sense that I accepted the dogma of violence. I believed that the true place for it was inside Christianity and that whenever it was applied outside Christianity it became perverted. The Nietzschean doctrine of the Superman was really a perversion of the Christian dogma of Election. The heroic age of the future was the Christian Millennium in which 'the saints shall rule the world.' I considered, therefore, that we could get nearest to an heroic age under the dictatorship of a Christian, a Cromwell or Calvin who would see to it that rebellion against God was no longer a paying game. The foundations of democracy were, in my view, undermined by its complete ignoring of theological truth. Its avowed purpose was to make life as agreeable for those who crucified Christ as for those who shared spiritually in His crucifixion, and this I knew must lead to moral apathy, religious impotence and chaos in all human relationships. I wanted, in short, a world run much as Calvin had run Geneva, a government that would not allow the proud and greedy and frivolous to persist in their illusion that they were on the winning side. If the Fascist and Nazi leaders

were attempting something on these lines I entirely approved of their policy.

Those who did not know Clemo's *Confession of a Rebel* – and it was little known, though it had been reprinted once since its first appearance in 1949 – must have thought they could not believe their eyes. For in 1970s England nobody was supposed to think any longer along these lines. It appeared however that some people did. Here was one of them; and who could say how many more there might not be?

Clemo should surely have made more salient the crucial perception that destroyed his callow equations of Calvin or Cromwell or Luther with Hitler or Mussolini. This perception came when he confessed: 'The subsequent history of the European dictators convinced me that totalitarian government in the twentieth century must be a very different thing from that which Cromwell and Calvin sought to establish. The Christian motive in such men is bound to be corrupted by the modern educational and political systems through which alone they could rise to power.' Just there surely, under the bland phrase, 'modern educational and political systems', lay everything that Eliot had pointed to when he spoke of Fascism as 'merely the extreme degradation of democracy'. And it was hardly good enough for Clemo to pass smoothly on (though with a little welcome comedy at his own expense) to say: 'This realization cooled my zeal for all political revolutionaries, and when the General Election came in 1945 the penniless proletarian and potential fascist of Goonamarris went gravely back to Trethosa school and voted for the Conservative candidate.' This recruit to the Conservative interest had been attracted, as he explains, by the flamboyance of Winston Churchill, believing that 'men who wrote and spoke like tenth-rate journalists were obviously not built on the grand scale nor endowed with faculties that could fire the enthusiasm of the nation . . .' Though Conservative leaders of the 1970s were doubtless glad to have the votes of Clemo and his likes, they would have been embarrassed to have them spell out such reasons for voting as they did. And yet the logic which led Clemo to this position out of his Nonconformist Protestantism seemed to be at least as strong as the logic that had led many Methodists and Nonconformists into the Labour Party.

In any case, when Clemo in 1945 had brought himself to vote for Winston Churchill's candidate, what was at stake was nothing less than his own sense of his national identity. Naturally enough, he felt as a Cornishman that 'my nature was very un-English'. More surprisingly, he decided that on the contrary it was in many respects 'Teutonic'; and he recorded with painful and valuable frankness how by 1945 anti-German war propaganda had exasperated him to the point where he could envisage that 'my patriotic loyalty would have to be sacrificed'. He was particularly exacerbated when propaganda explicitly or by implication presented Martin Luther as typically German; since Luther was a Christian hero with whom Clemo felt intense temperamental sympathy, even though 'Calvin had more exactly defined the creed which God had forced upon me'. It was the more moving when, within a few pages, he tersely recognized that in other countries such writers as he 'would be liquidated', and 'almost for the first time in my life I felt proud of being an Englishman'. Shall we be told to dismiss as 'racism' our satisfaction when a pro-German Cornishman was thus proud to declare himself 'English'? In that case we must dismiss in the same way a poem that seems to register the same turning-point, 'Service to England' from the collection *Cactus on Carmel* (1967):

> What have I done for this nation?
> I have wandered past its crossroads
> When the signposts were stripped for fear of invasion,
> And I mourned chiefly that the blunt text
> Had been unhinged from the pulpit stumps,
> That millions at their crossroads had no guiding finger.
> My brain turned black with a rage of loyalty,
> And my pen blazed at usurping codes.
>
> I have stumbled amid the victory flare
> After my land had been delivered
> Through assaults that were not mine;
> And my heart was barred off, a furnace of prayer
> For the tender conquest, the naked sign.
> I strove with the crippled ego
> Which had feared the cold glance more than the bomb.
>
> I am named in the ancient House
> Because I loved the plain sanctuary
> And sought to build my own English home:
> Loved and sought so fiercely behind the barricades
> That my vision grew cosmic, survived the raids
> And lived in language unique as my wordless vows.

In this poem, where the first stanza – it may be necessary to explain – turns on country signposts being dismantled in wartime so as not to help invading parachutists, the writing is still well below what Clemo can do at his best, though the three lines beginning 'I am named in the ancient House' surely express conclusively and movingly the patriotism of the English religious dissenters.

In *Confession of a Rebel*, Clemo had declared: 'It was impossible for me ever to take the cultured, civilized view of human rights – or of anything else. I demanded Christian gusto and scorned the weary dignity of the classic ideal. Ever since my childhood I had detested the Greek spirit and loved the Gothic . . .' This explains the terms in which, in 'Royal Wedding' he invokes the two Victorians, Browning and Tennyson. (In his work as a whole it is understandably the originally Nonconformist Browning, or rather that married couple, 'the Brownings', who count for more.)

And another phrase from the poem that takes on new and rather unwelcome meaning, in the light of this vehement espousal of 'the Gothic' as against 'the Greek', is in the lines: 'Of ancient power and knowledge,/Northern and Christian.' Though Clemo is pleasingly free of anti-Papist prejudice, it is plain that 'Northern' here means 'Teutonic' as against 'Mediterranean'. Thus, warmly as one might applaud when he said, 'The belief that the advance of medical science and the amenities of a Welfare State are part of Christian redemption is a fallacy', one could only be dismayed that nowhere did he make, nor see the necessity for making, a distinction between the *rationalism* that produces tyrannical Welfare States, and the much more noble and ample term, *rationality*. It was hard to understand how Clemo could admire the close reasoning of a Calvinist theologian like Karl Barth, while refusing to agree with John Wesley that Christianity is among other things a *rational* religion.

There remained however the vivid immediacy, the authority, of this record in verse and prose; and the admirable determination to thrust an initial perception into all of its implications, however inconvenient. Stone-deaf and white-blind, Clemo when he published *The Echoing Tip* (1971) and *Broad Autumn* (1975) was still living in the granite cottage in the china-clay area of Cornwall where he had been born in 1916. Lots of people were complaining in the 1970s that a voice of 'the common people' was never heard in British poetry; but when such a voice was heard, it turned out to be saying, like Clemo's, things that no one wanted to hear. And so it was ignored.

Anglo-Welsh Poets

Because Welsh nationalism is less of a political force than Scottish, not to speak of Irish, the outside observer tends to think that Welsh nationhood is something merely picturesque and sentimental, which the English can smilingly tolerate. In fact, just because the political assimilation of the Welsh has gone further than with the Irish and the Scots, and because accordingly the English are more ready to indulge what they see as endearing Welsh foibles, the Welsh writer's attitude to English culture is peculiarly exacerbated and in many cases peculiarly intransigent. It turns for him, far more than for his Irish and Scottish peers, specifically on the matter of language: for on the one hand Welsh is far nearer to being an alternative national tongue than Gaelic is for the Irish or the Scots; yet on the other hand, the English spoken and written by Welshmen diverges from metropolitan English, lexically and syntactically, much less than the English of Ireland or Scotland does. Thus the Welsh writer who writes in English feels especially guilty at doing so, at the same time as he cannot concoct a third option, such as Hugh MacDiarmid created for the Scots with Lallans. Anglo-Welsh, Anglo-Irish, Anglo-Scottish are three hyphenated compounds that ought to as it were lie parallel one with another; but this is not so – the three conditions, though similarly painful in a way that few English recognize, are in important ways unalike.

The predicament, and the pain of it, are touched on rather more often in R. S. Thomas's earlier poetry than later. But the dilemma had not been solved, and if Thomas set it aside in his poetry he had not set it aside in his politics nor in his sense of himself as an artist responsible to his nation. In 1978, in an address originally delivered in Welsh, he spoke of it heatedly, as some may think with anguish:[1]

> This devilish bilingualism! O, I know about all the arguments in favour of it: how it enriches one's personality, how it sharpens one's mind, how it enables one to enjoy the best of two worlds

[1] 'The Creative Writer's Suicide', in *R. S. Thomas, Selected Prose*, edited by Sandra Anstey with an introduction by Ned Thomas (Bridgend, 1983).

and so on. Very likely. But to anyone in Wales who desires to
write, it is a millstone around his neck . . .
A foreign language! Yes. Let nobody imagine that because there
is so much English everywhere in Wales it is not a foreign lan-
guage . . .
An Anglo-Welsh writer is neither one thing nor the other. He
keeps going in a no-man's land between two cultures . . .
Woe that I was born! Who has suffered, if I have not suffered? For
I bear in my body the marks of this conflict . . .

What emerges from this highly personal testimony is that Thomas
writes in English because his Welsh was too lately and laboriously
acquired for him to be critical enough of his own performances in
that language (he spells this out, and it does him honour), but that
accordingly he regards English as the medium to which an unkind
fate has condemned him. Nothing that Thomas says suggests that
he regards English other than grudgingly, even resentfully. This
is surely a very uncommon way for an artist to feel towards the
medium that he is shaping, and it is highlighted by the way in
which, when Thomas speaks of the poetic tradition in Welsh, he
dwells admiringly on its formal intricacies. For as we have seen
his way with such elegances inherited from the English tradition –
for instance, those of the English sonnet – is almost brutally rough-
and-ready.

There is a striking contrast, in certain Irish poets from the six coun-
ties of the north who attracted in the 1970s much admiring attention.
Not just Seamus Heaney explicitly, but Derek Mahon and Michael
Longley almost as plainly, were in love with English, with the
English language and with English poetry of the past as manifesting
that language raised to its highest power. Indeed in 1968-70, the years
of their first collections, these Irishmen made deft and accomplished
use of traditional English resources such as too many English poets
were then rejecting, often with contumely. The Irish, it seemed,
could embrace English without any suspicion that by doing so
they betrayed their Irishness, whereas the Anglo-Welsh poet could
have no such confidence. His namesake Ned Thomas sees Thomas
subscribing to the desperate view held by other Anglo-Welsh nation-
alist writers of the 1970s: 'one was writing poetry in English so as to
render that poetry unnecessary in the Wales of the future'.[1] Surely
no Irish nor Scottish poet was ever driven to this logical but lunatic
extreme of prolonging a tradition in the devout hope that it would
soon be extinguished.

[1] *op. cit.* p. 14.

These questions do not arise with the poet whom R. S. Thomas, from time to time, was prepared to consider as one of his Anglo-Welsh peers: David Jones, author of *The Anathemata*. One of the humiliating embarrassments for the hyphenated cultures in the United Kingdom is the over-abundance of borderline cases. The English reader is understandably though too easily bemused when John Buchan is presented to him as a Scottish writer, Louis MacNeice as Irish, Edward Thomas as Welsh. David Jones is not one of these; it is plain that his ancestral Welshness was crucial to his sense of his own identity, and also that that inherited allegiance was a principle of, and a motive behind, the one interminable poem which, as now appears, he spent most of his life putting together. As an Anglo-Welshman, he was in a very different situation from R. S. Thomas. London-born, having never achieved more than an inaccurate smattering of Welsh, and having spent very little time inside the borders of the Principality, Jones was moreover deeply attached to the British Army with which he had served on the Western Front in 1916, in a regiment where London Cockneys served side by side with Welsh-speaking Welshmen – an experience which he commemorated movingly in his long-meditated *In Parenthesis* (1937). From then on he seems to have devoted himself to re-creating, with a wealth of archaeological learning, that era in the history of the British Isles when Englishman and Welshman were not yet at odds, since both were citizens of Roman Britain. He avoided the Anglo-Welsh predicament by tracking back through recorded and legendary history to the point where the predicament had not yet arisen. For that reason, if for no other, one finds in Jones no resentment of the English donation to Wales, beyond a certain tetchiness with those periods of English culture when it seems to have attended more to other connections (e.g. French) than to the Celtic.

David Jones died in 1974. In that year Faber and Faber published *The Sleeping Lord & Other Fragments*, which they supplemented in 1978 with *The Dying Gaul & Other Writings*, edited by Harman Grisewood. In between, Agenda Editions published *The Kensington Mass* (1975). In *The Sleeping Lord* volume the most splendid piece was surely 'The Tutelar of the Place':

Tellus of the myriad names answers to but one name: From this tump she answers Jac o' the Tump only if he call Great-Jill-of-the-tump-that-bare-me, not if he cry by some new fangle moder of far gentes over the flud, fer-goddes name from anaphora of far folk wont woo her; she's a rare one for locality.

Not in theme nor in tone but in rhythm and the springing luxuriance of vocabulary this might remind us of Shakespeare's Iago:

> Our bodies are gardens, to the which our wills are gardeners; so that if we will plant nettles or sow lettuce, set hyssop and weed up thyme, supply it with one gender of herbs or distract it with many, either to have it sterile with idleness or manured with industry; why, the power and corrigible authority of this lies in our wills.

In the 1970s, as in most other decades, there was no lack of Falstaffian men of letters who could simulate the fruity bouquet of Shakespearean vocabulary, but at any time only a few writers like Jones can create the crucial aftertaste, the perception that the inventiveness, luxuriant though it is, is always apposite, answerable to the semantic requirement of reinforcing one solidly central meaning. The variety of semantic origins – 'tump' from the Anglo-Saxon, 'gentes' from the Latin, 'anaphora' from learned speech, 'she's a rare one' from colloquial – reinforces the main point: that, whereas 'Earth' or 'land' or 'place' is a concept and a noun common to all languages we may know about, yet for it to become an active imaginative and ethical principle in the life of any individual it has to be found a name that shall root it in some quite small patch of earth. Hence *Tellus*, 'earth' conceived of as feminine, is

> She that loves place, time, demarcation, hearth, kin, enclosure, site, differentiated cult, though she is but one mother of us all: one earth brings us all forth, one womb receives us all, yet to each she is other, named of some name other . . .

Plainly this constitutes a plea for minority and embattled languages like Welsh, a plea that has nothing to do with defending or rescuing present-day Welsh people from the incursions and adulterations of invading English. And not just linguistic usages but all local and parochial usages are proclaimed by this same logic to be indispensable:

> As when on known-site ritual frolics keep bucolic interval at eves and divisions when they mark the inflexions of the year and conjugate with trope and turn the season's syntax, with beating feat, with wands and pentagons to spell out the Trisagion.

> Who laud and magnify with made, mutable and beggarly elements the unmade immutable begettings and precessions of fair-height, with halting sequences and unresolved rhythms, searchingly, with

what's to hand, under the inconstant lights that hover world–flats,
that bright by fit and start the tangle of world–wood, rifting the
dark drifts for the wanderers that wind the world–meander, who
seek hidden grammar to give back anathema its first benignity.

'Anathema' – Jones's book *The Anathemata* had appeared as long ago
as 1952, and had been thought to be a complete and considered
work. But when his friends René Hague and Harman Grisewood
had sorted through the mass of drafts and manuscripts left by David
Jones at his death, there was to be no doubt that *The Anathemata*,
though so extended, was no less a fragment than 'The Tutelar of
the Place' and 'The Tribune's Visitation' and other self-declared
'fragments' published in 1974. All were equally parts of one poem
in the strictest sense interminable. Although David Jones's inability
to organize himself was to be amply documented in René Hague's
'self-portrait of David Jones in his letters', *Dai Greatcoat* (1980), the
inability to complete the poem was no fault of the poet's but was
inherent in the extraordinary or monstrous scope of his conception.
This seemed to range Jones along with Ezra Pound, author of that
similarly interminable poem, *The Cantos*; and so Jones got to be
called a 'modernist'. But all the evidence is that Jones had no
interest in, and little information about, programmatic modernism
in general and Pound's poem in particular. It was his theme, that
in turn dictated by his consciousness of himself as a special sort of
Anglo-Welshman, that ensured his great work should never be fin-
ished. 'With halting sequences and unresolved rhythms' – that was
to be, and had to be, the nature of what he was embarked on. And
if similar features characterized Poundian modernism, that was mere
coincidence. It meant, however, that Jones's poetry, no less than
Pound's, could never attract more than a coterie following; though
that following was so zealous, and in a case like René Hague's so
self-sacrificing, that the pejorative implications of 'coterie' seemed
quite out of place. On the other hand, Jones's having no more than
a coterie following meant that he had no safeguards against unwitting
self-parody, which he fell into quite often.

Some who would have excused Philip Larkin's exclusion of Jones
from *The Oxford Book of Twentieth-Century English Verse* pleaded
that, whereas at times Jones had indeed written beautifully, none
of that writing was in any strict sense poetry. It would have made
more sense, and better apology, if they had contended that whereas
Jones's writing was undoubtedly poetry, very little of it – and that
not the best part – was in verse. For the verse-line, and the niceties of
turning from one verse-line into the next, Jones very seldom showed
any susceptibility at all; and in his letters, whenever he is required

to comment on rhythm and metre and the relation between them, his remarks are puerile. In this, if in little else, he is at one with his fellow Anglo-Welshman R. S. Thomas: it is English verse that they do violence to, not English poetry.

Jones's stance however is Olympian. It is R. S. Thomas who has articulated and suffered through the predicament of the modern Welshman. The analogy with the Irish, partial though it is and potentially misleading, is illuminating. If we compare Seamus Heaney with his formidably accomplished and cosmopolitan fellow Northern-Irishman, Derek Mahon, the comparison cannot resolve itself into simple terms of better and worse. Rather, Heaney has chosen to enter himself in a league that Mahon, perhaps honourably judging himself unqualified, has chosen not to compete in: that is to say, the competition as to what poet is the voice of his people. Heaney and Thomas have chosen to act out, in their lives as recorded in their writings, the role and the predicament imposed in our times on the Welshman in the one case, the Irishman in the other. This is presumptuous, and in both cases the presumption has been fastened on, and derided, by the poet's compatriots: Heaney in Ireland, and R. S. Thomas in Wales, have been prophets without much honour in their own countries. But the presumption is allowable, and indeed necessary, in the case of those who aspire to be *national* poets. The national poet holds up a glass in which his nation shall see itself as it is, not as it figures in the beguiling image available alike for internal and external consumption; and so one has heard Welsh people complain that whereas R. S. Thomas's portrait of the Welsh was faithful, he should have registered it only in Welsh, not in a language that outsiders could read. In a similar way, Seamus Heaney is extolled much less wholeheartedly in Ireland than in the United Kingdom and the USA. Affronted by the presumption of a Heaney or R. S. Thomas, who impudently offer in their words and stanzas to enact the dilemmas not of themselves only but of entire nations, the reader may understandably prefer the beguiling modesty of Derek Mahon or (though the case is admittedly very different) of David Jones. But it is the presumptuousness of Thomas and Heaney that seems to keep the faith with great national poets of the past – or for that matter of the present, as in the case of many subjugated nations in Eastern Europe.

Poets' Prose: Hughes and Hill

In 1978, introducing Anne Pennington's versions from the Serbo-Croat of Vasko Popa (Popa, *Collected Poems 1943-1976*, Manchester), Ted Hughes wrote:

> I think it was Milosz, the Polish poet, who when he lay in a doorway and watched the bullets lifting the cobbles out of the street beside him realized that most poetry is not equipped for life in a world where people actually do die. But some is. And the poets of whom Popa is one seem to have put their poetry to a similar test.

The passage from Milosz that Hughes remembers will be found in *The Captive Mind*, 1953 (p.41):

> A man is lying under machine-gun fire on a street in an embattled city. He looks at the pavement and sees a very amusing sight: the cobblestones are standing upright like the quills of a porcupine. The bullets hitting against their edges displace and tilt them. Such moments in the consciousness of a man *judge* all poets and philosophers.

These four sentences from Milosz surely bear out John Bayley's suspicion that 'both Milosz and Popa would be deeply embarrassed by the curious claim Hughes is making on their behalf'.[1] Milosz says that the sight which so stirred Hughes's sympathetic imagination was 'very amusing'; and whereas Milosz is obviously being ironical in saying this, it is far from plain that he is directing his irony where Hughes might suppose. The bizarre comparison of the up-ended cobblestones with the quills of a porcupine is possible only to a detached aesthete, whose sensibility is at the furthest extreme from what Ted Hughes seeks to promote, and by implication claims to possess. And if, as Milosz says, such a moment of consciousness

---

[1] John Bayley, *Selected Essays* (Cambridge, 1984), p. 216. Bayley links with Milosz and Popa in their supposed embarrassment the Hungarian Jewish poet Miklos Radnoti, 'who died on a forced march to a German camp'. See Radnoti, *Forced March*, translated by Clive Wilmer and George Gömöri (Manchester, 1979).

'judges' all poets and philosophers (for instance, as Bayley justly specifies them, the Tennyson of *In Memoriam*, the Keats of 'The Eve of St Agnes', or the John Donne of 'A Nocturnall upon St Lucy's Day'), it is by no means clear, as Hughes assumes, that such poets of the past are judged only, in Milosz's estimation, *to be found wanting.*

This is a recurrent and indeed as it seems permanent difficulty that responsible readers have always found with Ted Hughes; his intelligence is all in his verses, whereas whenever he offers to explain or vindicate his verses he becomes puerile. Thus it was not surprising that the same reader who justly and temperately demolished Hughes's pronouncement about Vaska Popa, should also have intemperately denounced his 1977 book of poetry, *Gaudete*: 'This is poetry suited to a tepid, coddled, welfare society, dreaming of violence in front of the television screen, which is projecting its immaculate coloured details, blood or sunburn, wildlife or under-water, superbly shot by telephoto lens.'[1] So difficult is it, and a thankless labour in any case, to keep apart the sometimes splen-didly intelligent Hughes who writes poems, from the less intelligent Hughes who pontificates about them or about the poems of others!
  The same sentences from Czeslaw Milosz had a few years before attracted the attention of one of Hughes's distinguished contemporaries. This was Geoffrey Hill, who in *Agenda* (1971/72) had remarked of the Milosz passage:

> Granted that this is a parable and not a manifesto; even so this passage . . . excludes from acceptability all those unbaptised by an arbitrary fire. The passage purports to establish new terms of the utmost purity: things and moments. What it does, in fact, is to elevate the man-of-the-moment. However humbled one may be by this, it is still necessary not to be bullied by its absolutist elitist tone.

This is as characteristic of Hill as the sentences from the Vasko Popa introduction are typical of Hughes. For we may understand Hill to be refusing the moral and emotional blackmail just as John Bayley does, and for the same or very similar reasons. Yet where Bayley is clear and straightforward, Hill treats us to the distracting sonorities of 'excludes from acceptability' and 'unbaptised by an arbitrary fire'. Surely some more forthright, less pompous expressions were avail-able. And who is this pasteboard 'man-of-the-moment' set up for us to jeer at? Geoffrey Hill's prose had never been clear, but in the

---

[1] John Bayley, 'Smash and Bash', *The Listener*, 2 June 1977, p. 726.

1970s it inspissated itself more and more – and this not accidentally nor without forethought, but according to a perverse logic. The perversity was not to declare itself until, in 1984, Hill collected his essays and lectures as *The Lords of Limit*. That would reveal a writer so desperately aware of the duplicity of language – perhaps of all language, certainly of British English – that he would elevate opacity as the highest virtue and prime duty of all responsible writing, in verse and prose alike. *Mercian Hymns* (1971) did not answer to this description, but *Tenebrae* (1978) undoubtedly did. The most obvious instance of this opacity, in *Tenebrae* but also in earlier collections and later ones, was Hill's continual, perhaps compulsive, hovering around institutional Christianity (particularly in its recusant and Anglo-Catholic varieties) without his ever saying Yea or Nay to that faith, neither giving his assent nor plainly withholding it. Such ambivalence, and ambivalence in general, was often applauded, on the good Keatsian grounds that it is not the business of poetry to argue us into or out of any position, to have any such designs upon us. Yet an unsympathetic reader might think that poems which treat of the Church and its martyrs, while carefully preserving the speaker's ambivalence about them, earn the unflattering epithet, 'religiose'. However that might be, it was clear that whereas Hughes, all too forthright, had ironed the ironies and ambivalences out of Milosz's sentences, Hill had compounded them. And in their opposite ways both the English poets had mislaid the Pole's saturnine wit. Where Hughes embarrassed his judicious admirers by being so much more blunt and foolish in his prose than in his verse, Hill's English was even more all-of-a-fidget out of verse than in it.

The Edward Thomas Centenary

The poet Edward Thomas was born in 1878, and sixty-one years after his death in battle in 1917 the centenary of Thomas's birth was very properly and variously commemorated. The best tribute was undoubtedly R. George Thomas's magisterial edition, from the manuscripts, of Thomas's *Collected Poems* (Oxford University Press). But there were also biographies: William Cooke's *Edward Thomas: A Portrait*, and Jan Marsh's *Edward Thomas. A Poet for his Country*. The testimony of his widow was rounded out with *Time and Again: the memoirs and letters of Helen Thomas*. One of Thomas's prose works, *Richard Jefferies; his Life and Work*, was re-issued. And the admirably tenacious magazine *Poetry Wales* devoted to him an exceptionally enterprising and well assembled 'centenary issue'(Volume 13, no. 4).

These publications and others were so well received as to suggest that no British poet of this century, perhaps not even Thomas Hardy, enjoyed so secure a reputation as Edward Thomas, or was so generally loved. E. M. Forster had confessed to a correspondent: 'I am prejudiced beyond all explanation against the poetry, prose, personality, and papa of Edward Thomas . . .' And Robert Graves had written off-handedly to James Reeves in 1959: 'Edward Thomas? Can't read him myself.' But these adverse judgements – Forster's far from frivolous antipathy to the poet's father is highly relevant, and deserves study – were understandably drowned out by acclamation in a centenary celebration.

Though not many were ready to admit as much, it certainly helped Edward Thomas's reputation that the famously severe critic F. R. Leavis (who died this same year), forty years before, in his influential *New Bearings in English Poetry*, had conspicuously exempted Thomas from the strictures that Leavis directed at the poets he called, as they called themselves, 'Georgian'. But the trouble was and is, as Leavis recognized, that on a first or even a second reading Edward Thomas sounds much like any other 'Georgian', for instance John Drinkwater. Among the charges that have been brought against 'the Georgians', the one that is most damaging has to do with their pastoralism, their assumption that the English countryside as they experienced and loved it (nearly always south of the river Trent in fact) could and would remain essentially constant, despite the vast socio-economic changes that they were living through and were a part of. After much special pleading by Leavis and others, that charge lies as heavily against Thomas as against any of them. His 'Lob' may be the finest, the richest and most seductive and inventive, of all Georgian poems. Still, 'Georgian' in this sense is what it is:

> Robin Hood, Ragged Robin, lazy Bob,
> One of the lords of No Man's Land, good Lob, –
> Although he was seen dying at Waterloo,
> Hastings, Agincourt, and Sedgmoor, too, –
> Lives yet . . .

How much we wanted to believe that in 1978! How easily we could persuade ourselves to believe it as we read the poem! And yet how conclusively it was belied, the minute we lifted our eyes from the page, and thought of that country between the North and the South Downs which Thomas experienced as immemorially secret and settled and lonely, where in 1978 we barged along bumper to bumper between commuters' homes, to and from Gatwick airport. That the attitudes celebrated in the figure of Lob, whether or not they had survived virtually unchanged from Agincourt to 1915, should have survived the changes between 1915 and 1978 – the possibility has only to be stated for us to dismiss it. We just cannot believe what Thomas tells us, any more than we can believe Hardy when he assures us, of his 'maid and her wight', and his 'old horse that stumbles and nods', that these 'will go onward the same/Though dynasties pass'. It is not true, we have seen that it is not true; and so the pleasure that we take in these poems cannot help but be, to a large extent, the soothing pleasure of make-believe. That is perhaps a legitimate pleasure; but it is certainly not the pleasure that we get from great poetry.

No one can take that sort of pleasure, and perhaps few of us can take any pleasure at all, in Thomas's patriotic war verses, 'This is no case of petty right or wrong':

> But with the best and meanest Englishmen
> I am one in crying, God save England, lest
> We lose what never slaves and cattle blessed.
> The ages made her that made us from the dust:
> She is all we know and live by, and we trust
> She is good and must endure, loving her so:
> And as we love ourselves we hate her foe.

It is not good enough to call this embarrassing. We ought to probe our embarrassment far enough to admit that these lines move us painfully, in a way the poet did not intend and could not foresee. For insofar as the England here invoked is the rustic and manorial England that Thomas had celebrated in other poems like 'Lob', we surely have to say that his 'trust' that that England would 'endure' was misplaced. It has *not* endured; and we might even feel glad that he did not survive to see that England vanish. But in that case we murmur, 'How little he knew!' And that, once again, is not the response that we give to great poetry.

If we turn the page, however, we receive one of the innumerable shafts of illumination that R. George Thomas's meticulous edition spills down. For the next poem, dated just eleven days later, is 'Rain':

> Blessed are the dead that the rain rains upon:
> But here I pray that none whom once I loved
> Is dying tonight or lying still awake
> Solitary, listening to the rain,
> Either in pain or thus in sympathy
> Helpless among the living and the dead,
> Like a cold water among broken reeds,
> Myriads of broken reeds all still and stiff,
> Like me who have no love which this wild rain
> Has not dissolved except the love of death,
> If love it be towards what is perfect and
> Cannot, the tempest tells me, disappoint.

This gives a very different reason for going out to France and risking death in battle. And this reason, the death-wish, is there by implication at the end of 'Roads', dated fifteen days later again:

> Now all roads lead to France
> And heavy is the tread
> Of the living; but the dead
> Returning lightly dance:
>
> Whatever the road bring
> To me or take from me,
> They keep me company
> With their pattering,
>
> Crowding the solitude
> Of the loops over the downs,
> Hushing the roar of towns
> And their brief multitude.

Shall we say, of this opposition between 'the loops over the downs' and 'the roar of towns', that in a part of his mind Thomas knew that his manorial England was doomed, and that he wished for death so as not to survive her? Perhaps. At any rate, 'Rain' is quite unequivo- cal. And we, who have seen so much poetry wherein the strongest feeling is more or less suicidal (in Sylvia Plath, in John Berryman), are undoubtedly too ready to assume that this dark reason for risking death is truer, more searching and persuasive, than any patriotic reason for doing so. Yet in this case we are surely right; for the last two lines of 'Rain' move on a cadence at once more exquisite and more magisterial than anything in the patriotic verses. And the dark pleasure which this gives us – not exactly a painful pleasure, though a pleasure that comprehends and assimilates pain – is indeed a pleasure that we associate with great poetry; with the sort of great poetry that is profoundly nay-saying, a *fleur du mal*.

There are several other poets, overtly reassuring and affirmative, whom by 1978 we had come to esteem the more once we had per- ceived that under the sunny surface of their poems lay depths that were life-denying – the more compellingly so, for being hidden, compassionately or cynically, under a comforting surface. This had happened in our comprehension and estimation of Robert Frost. And Frost's association with Thomas was well known, though among Thomas's Welsh and English admirers one perceived a rather unpleasing disposition to play it down and to minimize the help that Frost gave. This doubtless owed something to the revelations, in Lawrance Thompson's extraordinary biography of Frost, of how self-serving and ungenerous that great poet could be. Yet Frost's own account of the relationship – in a letter of 1921, a human as well as historical document which *Poetry Wales* in 1978 admirably made available – there is no hint of playing to an audience or to posterity: 'Anything we may be thought to have in common we had before we met . . . There was never a moment's thought about who may have been influencing whom. The least rivalry of that kind would have taken something from our friendship. We were greater friends than almost any two ever were practising the same art . . .' With the troublesome false issue of 'influence' thus taken care of, one could profit by another item in this issue of *Poetry Wales*; R. George Thomas's judicious reconstruction of the sort of things Frost may have been saying to Thomas when the two poets walked together in Herefordshire at various times between April and October, 1914. Frost at that time was talking to other people about 'the sound of sense', meaning by that what comes over of a conversation that is heard 'from behind a door that cuts off the words'. Or again he says: 'We value the seeing eye already. Time we said something about the hearing ear – the ear that calls up the vivid sentence forms'. And, conclusively: 'I give you a new definition of a sentence. A sentence is a sound in itself on which other sounds called words may be strung.' Frost here perceives a sentence as being in itself either shapely or unshapely, as possessing in its syntactical structure a rhythm either satisfying or unsatisfying. As word-sounds are fitted to this overall sentence-sound, and as the sentence is strung across verse-lines, the inherent shape and rhythm of the sentence can either be enriched and heightened or (of course) impaired more or less grievously. And if, having secured this perception, we look back at the lines from 'Rain', we recognize that what we applauded as the exquisite cadence at the close has more to do with the culmination of an unwinding sentence than with anything that scansion might reveal about the structure of the pentameters: 'If love it be towards what is perfect and/Cannot, the tempest tells me, disappoint.' The last conditional clause, on which the poem and the sentence seemed about to die away, is surprisingly and strongly stiffened, at the last possible moment, by the firm parenthesis, 'the tempest tells me'.

When the sentence is strung not just across verse-lines but also across stanzas, there is even more opportunity to bring out and point up the shapeliness of sentences. This happens with the three (or four) sentences, and the four rhyming stanzas, of 'The Wasp Trap':

> This moonlight makes
> The lovely lovelier
> Than ever before lakes
> And meadows were.
>
> And yet they are not,
> Though this their hour is, more
> Lovely than things that were not
> Lovely before.
>
> Nothing on earth,
> And in the heavens no star,
> For pure brightness is worth
> More than that jar,
>
> For wasps meant, now
> A star – long may it swing
> From the dead apple-bough,
> So glistening.

It is idle to ask whether the shapeliness of this resides in the verse-line, in the stanza, or in the sentence. It is in all three of them, and in each only as modified by both the others. That assuredly is the sort of thing we say of great poetry. And a poem like this, so true to Frost's precept that 'a sentence is a sound in itself', makes it impossible to agree with those who would have it that Thomas moved outside or beyond Frost's ken as soon as he stopped shaping and condensing into verse perceptions that he had previously arrived at in prose.

'The Wasp Trap', it may be thought, stands in need of all three kinds of shaping – metrical, stanzaic and syntactical (and add a fourth, rhyme) – simply because the perception which it embodies is so fugitive, so elusive, even (so the unkind might say) so trivial. The prosody must be so elaborate because what the prosody must convey is so slight. This matter of the elusiveness of Thomas's perceptions was dealt with in *Poetry Wales*, in a strenuous and searching, though rather ill-written, essay by the editor, J. P. Ward. Ward, after a valuable examination of some of Thomas's character-istics, particularly what he calls 'his returning, recycling repetitions', decided that Thomas's concern was 'not to find *what* is elusive but rather to leave it so and therefore to capture the quality and feel of elusiveness itself.' One trouble with this is that it makes Thomas's objective sound rather like Mallarmé's, when the latter demanded always the nuance, the fragrance of non-existent nosegays; whereas in J. P. Ward's argument, Mallarmé had been ranged rather with those Anglo-American 'modernists' whom he lined up on the other side from Thomas. But a graver trouble is that, if this indeed was what Thomas was after, it will always seem to certain temperaments a marginal and unprofitable concern; and those who find it so will not necessarily be those whom Thomas shrugs aside in 'Aspens':

> Whatever wind blows, while they and I have leaves
> We cannot other than an aspen be
> That ceaselessly, unreasonably grieves,
> Or so men think who like a different tree.

For after all 'the elusive' is not a manifestly bounded nor self-evidently homogeneous category. Transcendent and Immanent, Noumenal and Phenomenal, Divine and Demonic – such pairs of words (there are others) represent attempts by the human mind to make distinctions amid 'the elusive', and to predicate something about some parts of it. Thomas seems to have been at all times wholly unfamiliar with, and unconcerned about, all such terms; and to have paid no attention at all to any of the disciplines which engender such terms and worry about them. Ontology, Epistemology, Theology,

Metaphysics, Psychology – all seem to have passed him by. For that matter, it is disconcerting to reflect that if Thomas had lived long enough to take account of Marx and Freud, Maritain or Spengler, we cannot be confident that he had the vocabulary to cope with any of them, for or against. Part of the blame for this must surely lie with Philip Thomas, the railway-clerk from Tredegar, author of *A Religion of This World: A Selection of Positivist Addresses* (1913). Edward Thomas's father, to whom the poet addressed a poem of implacable hostility (No. 99 in R. George Thomas's edition), who in 1915 dismissed his son's poems as 'pure piffle', pursued an intellectual odyssey that was cruelly summarized in two lethal sentences by Jan Marsh: 'Brought up a Methodist, Philip Thomas was intellectually a free-thinker, that is an atheist, but he could not abandon the habit of worship nor the respectability that went with churchgoing. Eventually he settled for the Unitarians, who had the least supernatural doctrine, until some time around 1910 when he took up with the Positivists.' Add to this devil's brew a hectoring personality like Philip Thomas's, and one surely has an infallible recipe for alienating (in more senses than one) a son who is to be a poet. Moreover, as Ms Marsh brought out very well, Philip Henry Thomas was not unrepresentative; those to whom Edward Thomas fled away from his father appear to have differed from that father only in having yeasty and excited feelings about English rural landscapes. And Thomas was not alone in his generation in learning from Edward Carpenter and his disciples to think that the oceanic feelings aroused by a prospect of the Kentish Weald or Salisbury Plain somehow bypassed the whole tradition of European thinking about the supernatural; from Plato and Aristotle through Aquinas and Berkeley to F. H. Bradley. One could say that this irresponsible muddling of categories not only damaged Thomas's poetry but as good as destroyed his marriage, for him if not for his wife. Jan Marsh assembles most of the pitiful evidence as to the latter, though of course the first-hand account is in Helen Thomas's two books of memoirs, *As It Was* (1926) and *World Without End* (1931). The damage done to the poetry can be recognized only by those few who understand in all seriousness that a writer's primary material, his palette, is his vocabulary. For reasons just glanced at, Thomas's vocabulary lacks nearly all the English words that stand for disciplined conceptual thinking about the things that preoccupied him most. The words that do duty for him as abstract nouns – notably 'Beauty', also 'Earth' and 'Nature' (these last apparently interchangeable) – have in fact as little assignable or definable meaning as his 'Heaven' and 'Hell', words which like many another irreligious writer he uses freely, though they can have had for him no *content* at all. These were words that bedevilled his prose, which he had to root out when he turned to the stricter discipline of verse. In the verse the lack of them had to be acknowledged as a constant pointing towards the unstated because, in the poet's vocabulary, unstatable; and in another way the lack of them had to be made good by such wincingly sensitive shapings of cadence as we can see in 'Rain' or 'The Wasp Trap'.

Because this was Thomas's dilemma, no writer influenced him much more balefully than Richard Jefferies. Walter Pater, to be sure, was a bad influence, as Jan Marsh and many another were ready to point out. Yet Thomas's *Richard Jefferies: His Life and Work* (1909), piously re-issued to mark the 130th anniversary of Jefferies' birth as well as the centenary of Thomas's, is as full of purple passages and self-consciously 'fine writing' as anything else that Thomas wrote. For instance, on the Wiltshire downs:

> They bring into the mind the thought that beauty – whether of a poet's lines, or of a melody, or of a cloud, or of shining water – is the natural and inseparable companion to passionate, bold, true-hearted acts and thoughts and emotions; and with that thought the question as to what great thought is expressed in these sculptured leagues of grassy chalk.

It is of course no question at all; Thomas knows as well as we do that whatever forces created the Wiltshire chalk uplands, they were not forces capable of 'thought'. Yet he drives on: 'Here, it sometimes appears, especially when the land has taken an alms of twilight, the creative forces must have reposed after mighty labours, and have had dreams which their deeds have not equalled elsewhere.' Thomas knows that the forces in question have as little capacity for 'dreams' as for 'thoughts', but nothing deters him from sounding the *vox humana* that he has had in mind from the first: 'And it is little wonder that we, who can create nothing except of snow or sand should be happy upon them, as if we hoped for a little while that their waves might lead us to whatever fancy has painted as desirable, lovely, and good.' *This* is what Thomas had to unlearn when he turned from prose to verse: not just bad habits, but vicious intentions; not just bad taste, but dishonesty. Small wonder that, even at his best, he learned the lesson only imperfectly. And yet Thomas's book on Jefferies had been applauded, by Q. D. Leavis, a critic not much given to accolades, as 'a classic in critical biography, to stand with Lockhart's *Scott* and Mrs Gaskell's *Brontë*'. How do we explain this, unless by supposing that Mrs Leavis, no less than Thomas himself, believed Jefferies when he said that if a person truly knows his own parochial world, and has 'come really into contact with its productions, and is familiar with them, and what they mean and represent, then he has a knowledge of all that exists on earth'? It is not true, it never was true, not for Henry David Thoreau any more than for Richard Jefferies. And those readers, American or British, who have taken for truths what in fact are irresponsible hyperboles, have to pay the price – as Edward Thomas did. His recognition of the price that had to be paid, and his eleventh-hour partial paying of it, constitute the pathos of his life as of his poetry. And Richard Jefferies was to blame, as much as Walter Pater.

Helen Thomas ended her life in the secure conviction that her dead husband 'is now among the immortals'. So he is no doubt, and no one did so much as his widow to put him there. But we can hardly think that Jan Marsh served Thomas well when she placed him on a strictly *insular* Olympus. She decided that 'Yeats, Pound and Eliot have been major influences, but they are on the wane; re-emerging is a characteristically English modesty, which appears almost as diffidence, avoiding the grand manner to concentrate on local achievements and the honest confession of human weakness'. Ms Marsh's comparisons with Hardy and R. S. Thomas and Larkin were just, and some of them were intriguing; but 'local achievements and the honest confession of human weakness' – this surely falls short of what is aimed at and sometimes achieved by all four of these poets, and certainly by Edward Thomas in a poem like 'Rain'. Thomas the poet disconcerted Harold Monro and Eddie Marsh, Gordon Bottomley and even W. H. Hudson, just as Thomas the reviewer had disconcerted them and their likes by applauding the early poems of Pound. Such a poem as 'Cock-Crow' is grievously misread and sold short if we project on to it pastoral nostalgia, just because it ends with an image from rural life:

> Out of the wood of thoughts that grows by night
> To be cut down by the sharp axe of light, –
> Out of the night, two cocks together crow,
> Cleaving the darkness with a silver blow:
> And bright before my eyes twin trumpeters stand,
> Heralds of splendour, one at either hand,
> Each facing each as in a coat of arms:
> The millers lace their boots up at the farms.

This has all the 'hardness' and 'dryness' that T. E. Hulme had asked for and called 'classicism', which Pound too was to ask for when he wrote 'The Hard and Soft in French Poetry', which he was to aim at when he took Gautier for his model in *Hugh Selwyn Mauberley*. It is as far as possible from self-expression. The poet's vivid feeling for his images, and for the constellation that he makes of them, is to be inferred only from the clarity, the compactness, and the rapidity with which they are juxtaposed, too flush one with another for any sliver or wisp of 'emotion' to emerge between them. The poem itself is like the heraldic scutcheon that it talks about, as impersonal as that, and as emblematic. None of the historical changes that we have seen since 1915 has any relevance to it. It is a great pity, and cause for wonder, that neither Pound nor any one else apparently should have recognized that, if Imagism means anything, it surely means a small impersonal masterpiece like this. And 'Cock-Crow' may seem to be in a wholly different mode from 'Rain', yet the two modes come together (along with much else) in the poem that begins, with magnificent metrical audacity in the handling of the pentameter: 'As the team's head-brass flashed out on the turn/The lovers disappeared into the wood.'

'Audacity' indeed is what characterizes Thomas time and again, and yet it was crucially missing from such assessments of him as the one that Jan Marsh offered. It seemed in 1978 that British readers were still hung up, as Marsh and Bottomley had been, on a sterile opposition between 'modernist' and 'traditionalist', now given a defensive chauvinistic flavour by being translated into 'Anglo-American' against 'English'. But surely the great poets of our century transcend this distinction, whatever side of the divide they started from. Pound recognized this about Hardy; and as Pound transcends the divide from the one side, so Thomas transcends it from the other. Though bad habits lingered on, so that on certain matters, notably bird-song, Thomas even to the end seems unclear whether what he says is literal truth or figurative hyperbole, nevertheless in him the British gave a great poet to the world, or at least to the English-speaking world. To say so is very different from treating him as an insular speciality, to be taken out and caressed only when no troublesome strangers are about. Too many of the tributes to Thomas that appeared in 1978, and have appeared since, seemed to answer to this description. And, astonishingly, a forlorn English pastoralism was still the stock in trade of many formally adroit poets who emerged in the 1970s.

Thom Gunn

Gunn's poems of the late 1970s were not collected until *The Passages of Joy* (1982), which appeared simultaneously with a volume of his selected essays and lectures, *The Occasions of Poetry*. We have seen how attentive readers had thought, on the basis of Gunn's earlier work, that his distinctive and great achievement was to have re-established creative connections with some aspects of Shakespeare, and of some of Shakespeare's great contemporaries, notably Marlowe and Donne. Gunn appears, not surprisingly, to have liked this notion, and Clive Wilmer endorsed it in his excellent and too brief Introduction to *The Occasions of Poetry*. But in *The Passages of Joy* this dimension of Gunn's imagination was no longer evident. In none of these thirty-seven poems was there any longer anything to show that their author had been attending to the songs from Shakespeare's plays, to Donne's *Songs and Sonnets*, or to Marlowe's translations and imitations of Ovid; they were 'contemporary' in an altogether less complicated and more obvious way. Although the title of the collection and an epigraph to one poem came (surprisingly) from Samuel Johnson's 'Vanity of Human Wishes', in all other respects these poems seemed to remember not much before Walt Whitman, and certainly nothing before Stendhal or Keats. Clearly, if Gunn had indeed been one modern poet with a sympathy for the English Renaissance, that was far from being as central to his enterprise as had been thought. Yet the achievement was still there, as was generally, though not universally, recognized: *The Passages of Joy* was as well written as ever, though it lacked the resonance that some readers had come to expect and to delight in.

And after all there had been plenty of signs, if only one had noticed them, that this was bound to happen. Re-reading in *The Occasions of Poetry* Gunn's important essay on Ben Jonson (originally 1976), some readers may have noticed, perhaps for the first time, how difficult Gunn found it to enter into Ben Jonson's world. One difficulty he did not surmount was his inability to share Jonson's Christian piety. But more revealing in relation to his own poetry was the difficulty he had with the famous forthrightness of Jonson's not necessarily Christian assertion: 'Not to know vice at all, and keepe true state,/Is vertue, and not Fate . . .' 'Jonson', Gunn commented, 'like so many of his contemporaries, looked up to the moral chastity of some one who *knew* what was right to do (and did it) rather than having to learn from experience.' The implication is, rather plainly, that whereas such 'looking up' was a possibility for Jonson and his contemporaries, it is no longer possible for us. And sure enough, when Gunn wrote about his own poetry or about twentieth-century poetry generally, it was plain that he recognized no philosophical or intuitive or revealed authority for morals, but only the authority of experience; that for him what John Keats called 'proving upon the pulses' was axiomatic, the only authority to be trusted. Yet it is surely true that in this the poet was at odds with most of his fellow citizens. For can it be doubted that knowing what is right, and then doing it, accounts for most of the decencies and braveries that we see from time to time enacted around us? Or that just such acting from conviction, rather than from experience, is still what most of our unsophisticated fellows recognize as virtue? It is only the intellectuals among us who believe, or affect to believe, that in any given situation right and wrong are always open to argument from experience. Gunn had always been a highly intellectual poet; but that is not the same as saying, what seems to be also true, that he is a poet of and for the intelligentsia.

The reason for this, for his having no choice in the matter, had been widely known for a long time, but in these two books Gunn took care that no one should be in any doubt about it. He was a practising homosexual, and in poem after poem in *The Passages of Joy* he proves on his pulses, from experience, that so far as he is concerned, homosexual practices (even, in some circumstances, of a notably promiscuous and mercenary kind) constitute 'what is right'. Among the essays, one on 'Homosexuality in Robert Duncan's Poetry' makes the same point. The appeal to experience, and alleged vindication by experience, are what Gay Liberation, when it is respectable, is all about; and Gunn's fearlessness about it, together with his ardent belief that the liberation is momentous and overdue and enlightened, was impressive, all the more because it was clear that he was naturally a reticent man who disliked self-exposure. Yet whereas inside the intelligentsia a majority may by 1980 have approved such Gay Liberationist sentiments, in the nation at large no such majority did so. Certainly in Ben Jonson's England such a secular experimental attitude to ethics was virtually unknown. And this seems to mean that, despite appearances, Thom Gunn's sympathies with any period before the Enlightenment can never have been more than skin-deep.

Clive Wilmer called Gunn 'this most chaste of modern poets'. He could not have had in mind Gunn's subject-matter, for at least one poem in *The Passages of Joy* was unequivocally lewd.

'Chaste', as Wilmer used the word, referred to Gunn's style, and in that sense it was exact. That had always been what was singular about Gunn's writing: the combination of unchaste subject-matter (one can be unchaste in other matters than sex) with a remarkably chaste, remarkably lean and unadorned, style. This fruitful tension was more marked in *The Passages of Joy* than ever before, chiefly because, unusually, many of the poems were in unmetred verse, where the tautness of formal control could show itself only in a diction that was, as always with this poet, terse and rapid and non-sensuous. Yet, enamoured though he was of liberation (and not just gay liberation – autobiographical pieces in *The Occasions of Poetry* showed him still starry-eyed about the acid-dropping Sixties), Gunn had never fallen for the simple-minded liberationist arguments for free verse as against metre; and in this collection the alternately rhyming pentameters in a poem called 'Crossroads' splendidly vindicated his belief that 'in metrical verse, it is the nature of the control being exercised that becomes part of the life being spoken about.' Similarly (that same fruitful tension in another key), though Gunn idealizes the 1960s, he does not like, and never did, a kind of writing that came in with that decade and has stayed around ever since:

> For several weeks I have been reading
> the poetry of my juniors.
> Mother doesn't understand,
> and they hate Daddy, the noted alcoholic.
> They write with black irony
> of breakdown, mental institution,
> and suicide attempt, of which the experience
> does not always seem first-hand.
> It is very poetic poetry.

This is a fair example of the firmness that Gunn's chaste diction can manage in free verse, but the acerbity (rather rare in Gunn but always welcome and well managed) gives it an adventitious lift. A purer example, because free of such special effects, is the last poem in the book, 'Night Taxi', which resists quotation precisely because its sixty-five lines of unmetred verse support one another totally, so that no excerpt from them carries any punch on its own. And just that effect surely is part of what is meant, stylistically, by 'chaste'.

The most learned essay in *The Occasions of Poetry* was also the longest and the best, on the Elizabethan poet Fulke Greville. Here not only was the learning impressive and well marshalled, but the critical intelligence was at full stretch as nowhere else. The criticism was methodical and trenchant in the manner of Gunn's old teacher, Yvor

Winters; but Gunn discriminated far more patiently than Winters ever did. The essay is masterly, with a mastery that has been over-looked because Greville is a poet who has never appealed to many, and probably never will. Gunn confronted that in Greville which he too found unappealing: 'The preceding outline ends as a description of attitudes that I find at best sterile and at worst obnoxious.' What was exemplary was Gunn's insistence, and his demonstration, that in poem after poem Greville validated poetically ideas that remain, in the abstract, obnoxious. This seems to represent an exertion of sympathy beyond what six years later Gunn was able to manage for Greville's contemporary Jonson; whether or not by 1980 Gunn could enter into pre-Enlightenment ethical attitudes, back in 1968 he certainly could.

He did so by way of Albert Camus, in whose image of *le malconfort* – 'the cell where one cannot stand, sit, or lie' – he found an exact analogy to Greville's 'that strait building, Little-ease of sin'. Gunn applauded Camus for saying, *Il fallait vivre dans le malconfort*, for 'the determination to live with that sickness, fully acknowledging it and accepting it as the basis for our actions.' Greville, Gunn says, 'could not make such an acceptance'. The rigour of this is extraordinary: Gunn calls us to live in Little-ease, while denying ourselves the Christian consolation that even the notoriously bleak Calvinist Greville could fall back upon. Obviously, for an unbeliever like Gunn neither sin nor depravity can have, strictly speaking, any meaning; but that distinction is quite consumed in his conviction that Greville's Little-ease, whether or not we call it 'sin', is the state in which we all live, and have to live. That is borne out by Gunn's poems. No one should be deceived by the title: *The Passages of Joy* isn't in the least a joyous book. The steely temper of it comes clear as soon as we return the phrase to its context in 'The Vanity of Human Wishes': 'Time hovers o'er, impatient to destroy,/And shuts up all the Passages of Joy.' The life in Gunn's poems is life in Little-ease; and he persuades us while we read that this is true whether we are 'straight' or (the pathetic incongruity of the word!) 'gay'.

The liberation or emancipation of homosexuals was only one of several 'progressive' causes which agitated poets and their readers in the 1970s. Two others were sexual equality and racial equality. And it is disconcerting to reflect that any poet who wanted in his or her verses to promote such causes would, it seems, have to make the same sacrifice that Gunn made in *The Passages of Joy*: the sacrifice, that is, of any profound resonances from periods earlier than the eighteenth century. This is so because all these 'causes' legitimize themselves on grounds unknown to, or unacknowledged by, earlier centuries: on the one hand, what I have called 'a secular experimental approach to ethics'; on the other hand, a doctrine of 'human rights', rights supposed to inhere in the individual by virtue of his being human and not, as Aristotle had taught, rights that accrue to him by virtue of his being a member of some one human community (for prime instance, the *polis*). As regards racial equality, we remember Shakespeare's Shylock in *The Merchant of Venice* and his Caliban in *The Tempest*, portrayals which seem to imply in the one case the equality of Jew with Gentile, in the other case equality of the colonized primitive with the white colonizer. But we think, too, that these are exceptions which prove the rule (and for just that reason are the more to be cherished); Shakespeare's century in general did *not* believe that all races were equal, even though all souls were perhaps equal in the sight of God. Equally, and notoriously, Shakespeare's century, and Milton's, did *not* believe that woman was equal to man. Sappho of Lesbos may serve as an archaic precedent alike for militant gays and militant feminists, and is a salutary reminder that certain equalities are better provided for in other cultures than Christendom, today no doubt as in the more or less remote past. But it certainly seems likely that militant gays, militant feminists, and militant anti-colonialists, if they belong in a society shaped by western Christendom, will find the earlier centuries of Christendom alien to them in important ways. And it seems true that just as arguments on these issues appeal typically to precedents no earlier than the eighteenth-century Enlightenment, so in poetry persuaded or agitated by such arguments the stylistic precedents will tend to reach no further back. In the 1970s one seemed to see this happening. Of course it could always be maintained that for the sake of achieving objectives so obviously just and overdue, the sacrifice of such resonances and continuities was a small price to pay.

PART THREE

The 1980s

Sisson's *Exactions* – Ivor Gurney Recovered – The Thomas Hardy
Industry – Geoffrey Hill – Jeremy Hooker and Tony Harrison
– Hughes as Laureate – Michael Hamburger – Sylvia Townsend
Warner, posthumous – Kenneth Cox's Criticism – Seamus Heaney's
Station Island.

Sisson's Exactions

C. H. Sisson had said: 'any form which finds its way into human speech, however articulated or disjointed, may find a place in poetry.' This sounded very permissive. And yet Sisson as a reviewer had not been permissive at all, but very angry about 'the already over-whelming number of transgressions in verse by people nature never intended for poets.' How could this be? The truth seemed to be in 1980 that Sisson could afford to be so permissive about syntax ('articulate *or* disjointed') because he was very exacting indeed about something else: about rhythm, and more precisely about *inventive-ness* in rhythm. Though Sisson sometimes writes verse that can be scanned, in his theory he is very much a free-verse poet. Most of his poems, like most of the nursery-rhymes he so much admires, resist scansion according to any of the standard accentual-syllabic metres. His praise of nursery-rhymes ('the original and most impor-tant element in poetic education', he said) was explicit in a review of Donald Wesling's *The Chances of Rhyme* (*TLS*, 12 September, 1980), where Sisson also declared, finely yet not altogether convincingly: 'To liberate the language, even ever so little, from the shadow of what has become familiar, and walk a few paces on firm ground, is still the business of the poet, as it always was.' If he had been implicated in the actual business of literary education, as Donald Wesling was, he might have thought that *familiarity* is the least of our worries, whether as educators or as poets. Most students of poetry, whether British or American, seemed to find the rhythms of past poetry so unfamiliar that they not only could not scan, they could not even *hear*, a rhythm so insistent as the Marlovian or Popian pentameter. Sisson, in fact, though he castigated with a proper vehemence our current barbarism, seemed to underestimate that barbarism, and the inroads it had already made. In this it may be he was a little mesmerized by Eliot and Pound, those modern masters to whom he was exceptionally loyal. It was all very well for Pound and Eliot in their day to attempt to give a new keenness to ears jaded by the too easily and too often satisfied expectation of the iambic pentameter; but such jadedness was not at all the condition of the ears that Sisson was writing for in 1980. And so it might seem that inventiveness in rhythm, simple rhythmical *novelty*, was in those circumstances much less of a prerequisite, or self-evident value, than he supposed.

The case was not different in respect of syntax. It was all very well for Pound and Eliot to compel their readers to recognize the legitimacy in poetry of syntactical structures that are incomplete or 'disjointed', for they aimed to disconcert in their readers a too inert expectation of complete sentences. But Sisson, whether he knew it or not, was addressing readers many of whom were as incapable of parsing a sentence as of scanning a line. Since the expectation was not there to be disconcerted, no one was disconcerted into any new keenness.

But Sisson, in a strikingly old-fashioned way, tries in the act of composing not to take any account of 'the reader'. To take account of him, of the public to which the poem would ultimately be offered, was (as he saw the matter) to act as rhetorician, not as poet. But in all such theories there is inevitably a peeping under the blindfold, or between the fingers held over the eyes; for the poet must be aware of *some* putative reader, if not when he writes the poem, at least when he publishes it. And so it is fair to ask, if not what sort of reader *Exactions* is addressed to, at least what sort of reader is well placed to enjoy it. And some of the lineaments of that reader have already emerged. He will be a reader who delights in nursery-rhymes, and particularly in the unpredictable off-balance rhythms that nursery-rhymes favour; who for the sake of those rhythms (not just for the pleasure he takes in them, but for the trust he has in them) will happily tolerate a lot of what looks like nonsense:

> As I was walking by the mirabel sea
> Down-a-down, the mirabel sea
> There came a monster walking to me
> Hey down
>
> I wept intransitively, there was no-one
> Who could be the object of my tears
> Down-a-down, but the mirabel sea
> Hey down
>
> There were tears tears tears but they were only the
>   salt sea
> Down-a-down, the salt sea
> Only a tear and no eye to weep it
> Ho down
>
> Exactly as I said, she said it was, he said
> But say as they all say it is still the same

> Hey down, by the mirabel sea
> Murder is laughing but that is not exactly
>
> Down, by the mirabel sea

Moreover, this ideal reader will be very suspicious indeed of the ordering of experience that the grammar of the sentence pretends to enact for us. Hence, here, the word 'intransitively', and the extreme sparsity of punctuation – only commas, not one full-stop at all, not even after the last word of the poem. In most of these poems, punctuation was sown more thickly, and most were in sentences that could be parsed. But we were left in no doubt that this was no more than a concession, that the syntactical ordering was not to be trusted, since it held good only for language, not for that brute experience which language only pretends or affects to be ordering as it orders itself:

> So I address the musing mind
> Which has no mind to speak
> Which can hear nothing, see nothing
> And has no heart to break.
>
> The key of the kitchen is frenzy
> And the cook stands by the door
> Pobble-de-hope fair stranger
> What is the ladle for?
>
> A fortune for your porridge
> The hope of a transitive verb
> Is only to find its object
> But the best word here is, Starve.

The nursery-rhyming mind, the auditory imagination, which comes up with 'Pobble-de-hope' out of 'hobbledehoy' and 'do as you please', which creates 'A fortune for' out of 'A fig for', has earned – by such sideways rhythmical dartings – the right to jeer at the doggedly linear logic which, finding a transitive verb, has to look ahead for its object. And indeed the mind can dart sideways, as well as thrust forward; but can the one capacity be exploited, only at the cost of repudiating the other? The reader who will respond most readily to *Exactions* is the one who will reply to this last question, resoundingly: Yes!

What has just been quoted is the third out of eight sections in a poem called 'Burrington Combe'. The concluding section is exceptionally beautiful and moving, worthy of Thomas Hardy:

When I walk out there will be nothing missing
That I can see;
The pond will be there with its fish,
The rosemary

Spreading itself over the garden
As if still aided by my hand;
The mulberry-tree I planted, and the cherry,
The old apple-trees and

The plums stretching up against the wall
Over which the church-tower still looks;
Starlings and swallows, the swans flying over,
And always the rooks.

And that distance into which I shall have vanished
Will still be there;
It was always dear to me, is now
In the thickening air.

No distance was ever like this one
The flat land with its willows, and the great sky
With the river reflecting its uncertainty
But no more I.

Yet in this poem (still unscannable, for all that it is in rhyming quatrains), we cannot fail to notice how firm the punctuation is, how definitely it marks out the grammar of the sentences. Without that, how could we take the force, as we should, of the triumphant audacity that ends the second quatrain on the rhyming word 'and'? Or, more momentously, consider how the poem ends with 'I', not 'me'. It is not that he will no longer be reflected by the river; but that he will no longer reflect the sky's uncertainty, as the river has and will, and as he has done in the past. What makes his last mordant and momentous point is grammar, nothing else. And so we may legitimately reflect that articulate forms of speech can compass certain effects that are outside the scope of the inarticulate, unpunctuated and disjointed forms.

And yet the hope of finding an object for each transitive verb is easily satisfied. 'Uncertainty', for instance, is a grammatically satisfactory though humanly desolate object for the verb 'reflects'. The trouble is not here, not in the verb nor in its object, but earlier, in the subject, the 'I'. So long as the subject of the sentence, the first person (for Sisson rarely uses the second or the third), is irresolute, tentative, merely provisional, none of the transitive verbs on which it launches itself can find any object that is not correspondingly irresolute, as 'uncertainty' is. And for many years Sisson, alike in his verse and his prose, had recognized and acknowledged frankly that this was where his troubles started – in the fluctuations of his 'I', his inability to find a stable and continuing identity for himself. There may have been philistines who suspected, rebelliously, reading Sisson's 1976 collection *Anchises*, that this problem of identity was a problem not experienced but notional: something brought over into poetry, and imposed upon the poetry, out of readings and thinkings in the more arid habitat of epistemology. In *Exactions* such philistines got their come-uppance:

> Nobody hears what we say
> – Nobody, nobody;
> The echo has gone away
> – Body.

Here the problem of an insecure identity was helpfully placed in a social, not epistemological, context. If we speak earnestly and yet every one who hears seems to misunderstand us, if what we say comes back to us in echoes that travesty what we intended, how can we fail to suspect that the voice which spoke, our own, is altogether less clear and ringing, less unmistakable, than we had supposed? And if our voice is thus shown to be split and uncertain, how can we not suspect that the same is true of that personal identity which the voice utters? Since the voice on this showing quite evidently lacks 'body', has demonstrably failed to embody the perceptions and conceptions that it sought to articulate, the personal identity which thus voiced itself is itself brought into question. Thus we might suppose C. H. Sisson to think, reflecting for instance on the bizarre misprisions revealed in letters to the *TLS* after he had published a review there. A more arrogant man would confidently blame the stupidity, or the bad faith, of his readers; but if Sisson the reviewer and essayist is sometimes arrogant, Sisson the poet is not. And indeed he schools himself to a humility that few of us can emulate. For he asks what happens to the objective world when the subjective world of the 'I', the perceiving agent, turns out to be so unstable as he has found it to be. Most of us, poets and non-poets alike, would conclude that stability in the 'out there', the objective, depends upon stability in the 'in here', the subjective, the perceiving agent; and would suppose that, once the perceiving sensibility is unstable, what it perceives is similarly unstable, phantasmagoria, a fluctuant projection on to a world that is only by hypocritical convention supposed to be objective and constant. But this is precisely what Sisson denies:

> There is not Nothing if not I
> For 'I' is only emptiness.
> And what comes flooding in? The Time,
> The Place: the Matter, nothing less.

The time, the place . . . Though Sisson is learned and sophisticated about epistemology, about the 'I' and the 'not-I', and has experienced (not just read about) an anguished scepticism as to how the 'I' can accurately perceive the 'not-I', still the dimension that he moves in most feelingfully is not this, but another: the dimension of the historian, and the patriot. Thus in this quatrain what is called 'the Matter' is surely, at least in part, what the Middle Ages called 'the matter of Britain'; just as the verses which begin 'Nobody hears what we say' go on to speculate about 'Earth', and to say:

> England rides on her back,
> Born and born and born
> Till the last extremity
> Of Christ's morning.

Ultimately Sisson will gladly put up with uncertainty about his own identity (in this world, let alone the next) in the confidence that his own identity, dubious or not, can and will be incorporated in the larger identity called 'England', whether known through recorded centuries or in the seasons wheeling over a particular patch of England that looks down on the battlefield of Sedgemoor and on King Arthur's timeless Avalon. Most of his English readers, it may be suspected, while more confident than he is of their personal identities, fall short of his confidence in their corporate identity as Englishmen. And those who, on the contrary, suppose themselves patriots as he is should probably ask themselves if what they call 'patriotism' is anything more than self-congratulating insularity. For patriotism like Sisson's is rare, and not to be attained (by intellectuals) except through studious labour.

In any case it would give quite the wrong impression if we seemed to say that Sisson's patriotism has afforded him a stay or anchor that saves him from the abysses of scepticism that threaten the rest of us. On the contrary, the drama of *Exactions* is precisely in the spectacle of Sisson hauling himself out of a scepticism which is, in the poems printed first, more abysmal and terrifying than most people have experienced or can contemplate without extreme discomfort. The turn-around (though it is nothing like so spectacular or conclusive as that suggests) seems to come in a poem called 'The Garden of the Hesperides':

> However, something has happened. The thin air
> Is certainly thinner and finer than before:
> I can see things. It is not that there is light
> Anywhere in particular, unless it is every night
> Has its moon, everyday its sun,
> Equal everywhere. Trees tower and streams run
> Everywhere lighted. Animals come out
> In bright daylight fearless, minnow and trout
> Agitate in a water clear as air.
> What is the meaning of this? The meaning is where
> The objects are, it does not bother me.
> All of us are disproven, but gently.

Nothing, we are meant to understand, has been solved. The identity of the perceiver is as insecure as ever it was (and his subscribing himself 'Englishman' does not help matters). The change is all in 'it does not bother me': if the stable identity of the perceiver is a delusion, then what he seems to perceive is no doubt delusory – but in that case the multiple delusion is probably a spectacle mounted for some purpose that we cannot conceive, by a Power that is equally inconceivable. And in that case contentment lies in accepting the terms of the contract – in accepting delusory appearance as if it were reality, since for us, conditioned as we are, that is what it is.

This resolution is offered to us as, at best, something discontinuous and momentary. Any more secure apprehension of it is presented in the wistful tense of 'could be' – as in 'Narcissus':

> If I could only find a little stream
> Which leapt out of the ground over black pebbles
> And wore a hat of light on every ripple,
> I should not care for the imaginary
> Problems of I and Me, or Who and Why.
> This corner of the world would be my mind;
> What it saw I would say, if it were cloud,
> Blue sky or even wind told by an eddy:
> But what I would not see is this body,
> Aged, severe and, written on it, REFUSE.

('Refuse' can be accented on the first syllable, as a noun, or on the second, as a verb; and this uncertainty, so far from being an enriching ambiguity, is surely a flaw in the poem.)

If that came back into my little stream
It might be I should wake shrieking from my dream.
To what? Ah, what is there for us to wake to?
When pain is past, that is our hope or pleasure.
But nail that nothing now, keep me in vain
Beside the water, not seeing any shadow,
Only translucence, only the pebbles and earth,
A weed swaying, a fish, but nothing human
Or bearing any resemblance to man or woman,
Nothing compels our nature to this shape
For a stone will resemble the friends we make.
The mind is not peculiarly under skin
But might lie loose upon a high mountain.
A corner of a cloud might do for mind,
The bright border perhaps, with the moon behind,
The wind, recognized by its wandering billow
Scattering to surf as the moon comes and goes.
I thought I was a man because I was taught so.

Literary historians might characterize this poem as an utterance of the high Modernist mode, improbably promulgated as late as 1980. (Consider how it repeatedly approximates, without ever fulfilling, the requirements of the heroic couplet; very much surely as Pound in *Hugh Selwyn Mauberley* repeatedly approximates, without fulfilling, the requirements of Théophile Gautier's quatrains.) Those whose interest in poetry is less academic can delight for themselves in how every ripple of rhythm here wears a 'hat of light', as does every ripple of the stream (imagined, never actual) into which one might look without seeing one's self there mirrored. What is imagined, and proposed as admirable, is a condition of perceptiveness free of egotism, such as the human perceiver cannot attain to, except momentarily, even in old age. What is proposed to us as admirable is something that (the poet admits) we cannot attain to except momentarily, and in special circumstances. In saying so, he is entirely within his rights; and the poem is surely lovely as well as masterly.

There is one other thing that the ideal reader of *Exactions* must have, beyond those defined already. He must have a passion for, and an instructed interest in, what is called 'the plain style'. Sisson's verse-style is predominantly, and had been since *In the Trojan Ditch*, 'plain'. This had given offence, it offends still and will offend in the future. 'It is', said John Dowland, 'a precious jewel to be plain.' That preciousness was not much esteemed in Dowland's generation, nor has been in any other up to our own – witness the anguished complaints about Sisson's intransigently plain version of *The Divine*

Comedy (1980). This afforded no purchase to those who wanted Gothic picturesqueness on the one hand, nor to those others who yearned for the sob in the throat. We may be ready to think that the distinction between the plain and the 'sugared' style became meaningful only in the English Renaissance; and that pre-Renaissance poets, Chaucer as well as Dante, could be plain and yet luminous in a way that current idioms cannot manage. Certainly plainness is no guarantee of honesty. Honest Iago spoke plain. It is a rhetoric like any other, as Sisson knew at least as long ago as 'the Usk'. It is, however, the rhetoric that he has chosen to cultivate, and by 1980 his command of it was assured. It is a rhetoric which depends upon assumptions of continuity between the English of poems, the English of prose, and the English of considered and heartfelt speech. A reader would be well placed to receive the astringent pleasures that *Exactions* offered him, if he had agreed to consider English in poetry as only a further tightening of English as practised by for instance Swift and Defoe in prose, and by any one of his fellow citizens speaking under the stress of extreme experience.

Ivor Gurney Recovered

Gurney had never been lost sight of. Historians of choral music seemed to agree that some of his settings and song-cycles were masterly. And Gurney had often been respectfully remembered in the company of Brooke and Grenfell and Sorley, Owen, Rosenberg and Sassoon, Graves and Blunden and David Jones, among poets of the Great War. On the other hand, neither Edmund Blunden's selection of Gurney's poems in 1954, nor Leonard Clark's selection of 1973 (for which Clark himself put up some of the money) had attracted the attention they deserved. It seemed that categorizing Gurney as a war-poet had blocked the recognition that he was a great deal more than that. The publication in 1982 of the *Collected Poems of Ivor Gurney*, though 'Collected' still did not mean 'Complete', should have been enough to show that neither 'war-poet' nor 'nature-poet' did justice to Gurney's *oeuvre* as we now had it, incomplete indeed but much more amply represented than before, and at last textually reliable, thanks to the devoted labours in the Gloucester Public Library of the poet-editor P. J. Kavanagh. And yet, though Kavanagh's edition was buttressed by a biography and a selection of the poet's letters,[1] there was little acknowledgment that Gurney's finest work made of him a post-war poet, the voice of a disgruntled or painfully disenchanted peacetime. It was still widely supposed for instance, against the evidence, that the mental affliction which confined him to a mental hospital for the last fifteen years of his life was the result of his experiences in the trenches. And it was dispiriting that when one poet of the 1980s, Geoffrey Hill in an F. W. Bateson Memorial Lecture, admirably rose to the challenge of the Kavanagh edition (*Essays in Criticism*, April 1984), the piece, closely attentive though it was and intricately argued, still considered Gurney for the most part in the wartime context of Brooke and Rosenberg, Hilaire Belloc and General Sir Ian Hamilton and Eddie Marsh.

It is hard to find excuses for the indifference that had greeted the earlier selections. Both Blunden and Clark had printed for instance

---

[1] Michael Hurd, *The Ordeal of Ivor Gurney* (Oxford, 1978); *War Letters by Ivor Gurney*, ed. R. K. R. Thornton (Manchester, 1982).

'Townshend' – a poem that honours a man who was patron to Ben Jonson:

> Knowing Jonson labouring like the great son he was
> Of Solway and of Westminster – O, maker, maker,
> Given of all the gods to anything but grace.
> And kind as all the apprentices knew and scholars;
> A talker with battle honours till dawn whitened the curtains,
> With many honourers, and many many enemies, and followers.

The third line here conveys what one school of critics calls 'a limiting judgement'; and this had been anticipated in a poem to Beethoven that similarly had appeared in both Blunden's selection and Clark's (and also in *Music and Letters* in 1927):

> You had our great Ben's mastery and a freer
> Carriage of method, spice of the open air . . .
> Which he, our greatest builder, had not so:
> Not as his own at least but acquirèd-to.

The judgement on Jonson limits him indeed, but only in the sense that it defines and characterizes his excellence: not in any way to devalue 'our great Ben', 'our greatest builder', 'labouring like the great son he was'. Nothing more clearly marks off Gurney in his generation. Many of that generation vowed themselves, as Gurney did, to emulating the great Elizabethans and Jacobeans, but no one else gave pride of place to the most *laborious* of those masters. Labour, hard study and relentless practice, making, *building* – the emphasis is constant, even if it points more to what Gurney wanted to do than to what he did. Certainly there was no time for that, no chance of it, in the trenches or on leave from the trenches. Gurney was explicit about that in one of his letters. And that is surely the chief reason why our focus ought to shift from *Severn and Somme* (1917) and *War's Embers* (1919). These were the only two collections published in Gurney's lifetime, but he revealed himself as a great poet only later, after the war was over. And before P. J. Kavanagh's edition it was impossible to recognize this.

What is true of Gurney holds also – it could be argued – of other Great War poets like Rosenberg and Owen. In both these cases, surely, we see poets trying to respond to unprecedentedly harrowing and horrific experience, before they had had time to achieve technical mastery, and writing in circumstances that prevented their acquiring it. Both Rosenberg and Owen are in important respects *incompetent* writers, and although W. B. Yeats gave other reasons for excluding them from the *Oxford Book of Modern Verse*, it is possible to think that he excluded them because he noticed their incompetence. No one will deny that time and again the urgency of what they had to say overcame their incompetence in the saying of it, so as to produce irreplaceable poems. Yeats, we may think, should have noticed that. But it is surely wrong to infer that urgency of concern can at all times bypass the need for that learned mastery of which Jonson stands, not just in Gurney's mind but in general acceptance, as the great exemplar. In this way the attention paid, by one generation after another, to the Great War poets from Brooke to Owen has had the unfortunate effect of reinforcing a preference, not just British but more generally post-Romantic, for the amateurish in verse-writing over the professionally accomplished. This is not to say that fascination with the Great War poets is morbid and should be discouraged. For the story must be told time and again how poets showed themselves unable and unwilling to supply their public with what that public expected and demanded. But Brooke and Owen (and Rosenberg and the wartime Gurney) belong in that history, of the poet's relations with his audience, not in the history of the art as such. There are those who will say that the art as such has no history apart from the history of the artists' dialogue with their publics. But Gurney's declared commitment to Jonson in the art of poetry, as to Byrd in music, suggests that this was a view he could not agree with. So far from being a nature-poet, Gurney is a poet of, and ultimately a martyr to, Art. He knows, and repeatedly asserts, that all the beauties of his beloved Gloucestershire are fugitive and therefore unconsoling unless someone like himself – and there *is* no one else, as he knows exultantly – can catch and seal them in the art of music or the art of poetry, or in the two arts married.

The strenuousness of this conception of art is not only asserted in the poems, it is enacted there, as in the wrenched compactness of 'Given of all the gods to anything but grace', or (the same point re-phrased) 'not as his own at least but acquirèd-to'. Both phrases are perfectly clear, yet each is as far from current speech as any of the archaic inversions of Robert Bridges or Elizabeth Daryush. The feel of them, however, is quite different; as with Hardy sometimes, Gurney's locutions are muscular contractions of the run of English speech, whereas Bridges's and Daryush's archaisms are for the most part slackenings. It seems that for Gurney, much of the life that there is in English speech has been injected into it by lonely, learned and masterfully artificial speakers like Ben Jonson. Our conviction that life in our speech is to be found on the contrary in what is casually spoken, and as casually overheard, in a corner of the saloon bar or at a neighbourhood barbecue – this may be the most likely, at all events the most respectable, reason why the poet Gurney has never yet got the recognition which, as he knew, he deserved. Again, 'a freer/Carriage of method'. This too has never been heard in any saloon bar: but how much more of the history of our tongue, how much more resonance, how much more *life* it has, than anything that might be heard there! Gurney doubtless never read G. M. Hopkins's declaration that the language of poetry should be always 'the current language . . . heightened'; but the margin that Hopkins left for 'heightening' is enough to vindicate Gurney's diction most of the time.

Gurney's third collection, *Rewards of Wonder* (1919-20) was rejected and never published. The publishers were right to reject it, and Gurney was right to be undeterred. As we read it in the Kavanagh edition, *Rewards of Wonder* seems to represent a violent mutilation by this erstwhile lyrical poet of his lyrical voice. There is one exercise after another in headlong, mostly couplet, rhyme, much of the time intolerably strained and grotesque, looping up extremely hetero-geneous matter into six-foot or even seven-foot accentual lines. One such poem is called 'What I will pay' (he means, for artistic mastery) and what Gurney will pay is unceasing work, and emulation of 'Beethoven, Bach, Jonson', all so that he may 'write fair on strict thought-pages'. The harvest of this violence, the reward for which this price was paid, would come later.

It came soon, in the more than a hundred poems that Kavanagh dates between May 1919 and September 1922, when Gurney was committed to a private asylum. Not many of these are consum-mated masterpieces. We shall be told that Gurney was too big a poet to bother about perfection. But all poets worth their salt, and Gurney among them certainly, aim at perfection. However, when poems are coming at the rate of one or more a week over a period of two years, there is just no time for perfecting them. Accordingly, this work is rich in magnificent torsos, passages of breathtaking mastery following starts that are merely and hastily roughed in. What strikes first is Gurney's unfailing touch with what Barbara Herrnstein Smith had by 1982 taught us to call 'closures'. Even in *Rewards of Wonder* this had been evident, when brutally rhymed pieces would abandon rhyme so as to end on a heart-breaking cadence. Similarly, in these slightly later pieces many a rough-and-ready performance is all but redeemed at the last moment by a closing line that is much more than a summing up or a sweet coming-round. Gurney now has at his command any number of distinct styles, and he chooses one or another according as the occasion requires: the ceremonious stateliness of 'Sonnet to J. S. Bach's Memory' can be let down to turn a graceful compliment on the bicentenary of a local newspaper. In the same way the lyric voice, so savagely extirpated from *Rewards of Wonder*, can now be re-admitted because the poet has a sure sense of when it is appropriate, when not. The influences – Hopkins in 'George Chapman – The Iliad', Edward Thomas in 'On Foscombe Hill' and 'Up There' and possibly 'Imitation', Jonson in 'We Who Praise Poets', Whitman and possibly D. H. Lawrence in 'Felling a Tree' – are discernible but never for certain, because so thoroughly assimilated and turned to purposes that the originals would not have contemplated. 'Felling a Tree' draws on the Romanticism of Whitman and/or Lawrence to enforce a thoroughly classical, because Roman-imperialist, sentiment. (Gurney is keenly aware of the Roman archaeological presence under the turf of his Gloucestershire.) And similarly 'We Who Praise Poets' is not Jonsonian pastiche, because its Jonsonian diction is carried on a more than Jonsonian restiveness and barely controlled turbulence in the metre. Of the ten or so poems of this period that *are* perfected, Blunden or Clark or both had picked up several. They had missed 'We Who Praise Poets', and also 'The Valley Farm':

> Ages ago the waters covered here
> And took delight of dayspring as a mirror;
> Hundreds of tiny spikes and threads of light.
> But now the spikes are hawthorn, and the hedges
> Are foamed like ocean's crests, and peace waits here
> Deeper than middle South Sea, or the Fortunate
> Or Fabled Islands. And blue wood-smoke rising
> Foretells smooth weather and the airs of peace.
>
> Even the woodchopper swinging bright
> His lithe and noble weapon in the sun
> Moves with such grace peace works an act through him;
> Those echoes thud and leave a deeper peace.
> If war should come here only then might one
> Regret water receding, and earth left
> To bear man's grain and use his mind of order,
> Working to frame such squares and lights as these.

The runover, 'Fortunate/Or Fabled', is magisterial, and so is the audacious handling of the pentameter three lines from the end. Moreover, Gurney is in earnest: so far is the Severn valley from being a cherished constant standard by which history's vacillations are judged; it is itself, and rightly, a symptom and register of man's history – let it be inundated afresh, and removed from man's dominion, if that dominion eventuates in what Gurney had seen in wartime France.

P. J. Kavanagh is very good on the Great War as Gurney experienced it. Gurney's is the war of the common infantryman, as against the subalterns' war of Owen or Grenfell or Sorley, Sassoon or Blunden or Graves. Because he is not of the officer class, he feels no responsibility for the horror, hence no guilt about it, and so his revulsion from it is manageable. He is nearer to David Jones; one 'soldiers on'. His revulsion and protest came later, when post-war England made light of its soldiers' sacrifices: 'How England should take as common their vast endurance/ And let them be but boys having served time overseas.' As Jeremy Hooker had already noted in 1980, the crucial word is 'honour': England refuses to honour the draft that Gurney, as soldier, musician and poet, has drawn upon her.[1] And so the poems of this phase sound increasingly a note that may be called confessional or querulous or both. But 'querulous' will not do for the crescendo of accusation in 'The Not-Returning', 'Looking There' and 'Sonnet – September 1922', all three of them consummated statements. As we have seen, the draft upon England was still not honoured as late as 1973, and it was not certain that it would be honoured ten years later.

The next poems, written in asylums, reveal immediately a development least to be expected by anyone who has followed Gurney's career to this point: his style becomes plain.

> Why have you made life so intolerable
> And set me between four walls, where I am able
> Not to escape meals without prayer, for that is possible
> Only by annoying an attendant. And tonight a sensual
> Hell has been put on me, so that all has deserted me
> And I am merely crying and trembling in heart
> For death, and cannot get it. And gone out is part
> Of sanity. And there is dreadful hell within me.

That is addressed 'To God'; and although it is the cry of a soul in torment, it is also poetry. Nor does the plain diction come only with anguished themes: we find it in 'Cut Flowers', or in 'The Mangel-Bury', which starts out with the astonishing plainness of 'It was after war; Edward Thomas had fallen at Arras . . .'

By this stage we are no longer reading for pleasure, in any ordinary sense. If there is gratification (as there is), it is of the unearthly and

[1] Jeremy Hooker, 'Honouring Ivor Gurney', reprinted in *Poetry of Place* (Manchester, 1982).

inhuman sort that has to do with the indomitable spirit of Man, or suchlike unmanageable notions. And in any case Gurney is by now deranged. After the appalling plainness of a poem called 'An Appeal for Death', there come thirty poems which are, with only one or two exceptions and marginal cases, unhinged, incoherent. Blunden and Clark were to blame for printing many of these, and even Kavanagh, who wrote finely, 'It is a period from which an editor would like to rescue him,' seemed to think some of these pieces could be salvaged. We have all heard about 'the lunatic, the lover and the poet': but not Shakespeare nor anyone else can excuse us for being light-minded and unfeeling about the madness of mad poets. There are those who positively welcome such disorder, as if it authenticated a poet's vocation. But great poetry is greatly sane, greatly lucid; and insanity is as much a calamity for poets and for poetry as for other human beings and other sorts of human business.

Astonishingly, the piteous story had still not run its course. There was, it seems, around September 1926, one more spurt of poetic energy; and it produced, along with more of that painful incoherence to which we are too ready to accord 'rough power', work of a quite unprecedented kind which Kavanagh called 'timeless classical utterance'. 'Classical' can be given a quite precise meaning. For in one of several poems where Gurney tries, with some success, to reconcile himself to what he sees as England's ingratitude, he adjures swallows to abandon England in favour of 'the shelves/Of Apennine . . . or famed Venetian border'; and in a series of short but exquisite pieces that might even be called 'imagist', Gurney evokes with plangent severity Graeco-Roman or Mediterranean emblems like Pan or 'a cup of red clay Sparkling with bright water'. The failure of this manoeuvre is also recorded – in a piece called (the title tells its own tale) 'Here, If Forlorn'. Kavanagh wrote of those poems that 'though sometimes good, they seem bloodless compared to the previous work' – and the sentiment is understandable, though it will not be shared by readers who set less store by 'blood' than by pure diction.

A confident yet respectful reader can find many trails worth following through the various and ample terrain of Gurney's poetry. One such may be isolated. It would start from a group of poems on American themes, all of which Blunden and Clark significantly and regrettably passed over. These pieces are entirely sane, because judicious: on Whitman, on Thoreau, on Washington Irving, on George Washington's America ('Portraits' – perhaps the finest meditation by an Englishman on American history), Gurney passes firmly a commonsensical but in no way deflating judgement, just such as he had pronounced on Ben Jonson. 'The New Poet' and 'To

Long Island First' should have derailed in advance the attempt
that was predictably made to enrol Gurney in the service of a
supposedly indigenous alternative to 'modernism'. The last poem
in P. J. Kavanagh's edition, written from the lunatic asylum, is
one example out of many of how this English poet and musician,
much too poor ever to visit the United States or to dream of doing
so, nevertheless recognized American poetry as an alien body that
his British tradition must somehow accommodate. Gurney's title is
drawn from Whitman: 'As They Draw to a Close':

As they draw to a close,
These songs of the earth and art, war's romanzas and stern . . .
The seaboard air encompasses me and draws my mind to sing nobly
    of ships . . .
Or the look of the April day draws anthems as of masters from me –
(O, it is not that I have been careless cf the fashioned formal songs!)
For rough nature, for gracious remincer, I have sought all my days:
For men and women of the two-fold asking, for democracy and
    courtesy wherever it showed –
For the honour of flags well-borne at the head of regiments digne . . .
Of what underlies my songs, the precedent songs, as they draw to a
    close I think,
Of failures rough crude half formless (yet I understood rarely why)
Of the blurred pictures of rare colour here and there shown on my
    pages . . .
Yet I have deserved well of men, and the book *Leaves of Grass* will
    show it –
Their homes and haunts nobler that I lived. (Hear the laugh ringing
    from the tavern . . .)
The meeting in market-place or hall, the workers together will
    remember me.
(In their talk are words like earth or panelled rooms, Baltimore,
    forced-march, page and maker-look –
The winds of the north still stir their eager questing minds.)

The seed I have sought to plant in them, trefoil, goldenrod &
    orchard-bloom,
These O precedent songs you also have helped plant everywhere in
    the world –
When you were launched there was small roughness in the touch of
    words,
A woman's weapon, a boy's chatter, a thing for barter and loss;
But I have roughed the soul American or Yankee at least to truth and
    instinct

And compacted the loose-drifting faiths and questions of men in a
 few words.

This poem, written some time between 1926 and Gurney's death in
1937, is deliberately Whitmanesque throughout – not just in the long
and looping rhythms, but also for instance in the cavalier appropria-
tion of non-English words (*romanzas, digne*). And Gurney, it appears,
through his years of incarceration dreamed of a work that should be
called *Leaves of Grass*, in deliberate emulation of Whitman's Ameri-
can masterpiece with that title. Yet we can hardly think that we
have here a case of a British poet successfully assimilating American
poetry at its most intransigently unBritish, into a British tradition.
For we have to attend to the parenthesis in the fifth line: 'O, it is
not that I have been careless of the fashioned formal songs!' And
indeed Gurney had not been thus careless; on the contrary *Severn
and Somme* and *War's Embers* include lyrics, handled with the grace
and accomplishment of musician as well as poet, which are clearly
'fashioned' and 'formal' in the manner of a Renaissance lyrist like Ben
Jonson. On the other hand, however we may and must admire 'As
They Draw to a Close', 'fashioned' and 'formal' are not words we
can apply to it. Surely Gurney's continuing commitment to that
fashioned formality is made in a parenthesis precisely because in
the Whitmanesque mode he has adopted for this poem the acknowl-
edgment cannot be made except parenthetically – no marriage can
be effected between that Renaissance mode and the post-Romantic
mode of Whitman. Accordingly in all Gurney's tributes to Whitman,
which are frequent and fervent, there is always such a parenthesis,
a saving clause or a limiting judgement. When Gurney says, 'For
rough nature, for gracious reminder, I have sought all my days', he
surely means us to acknowledge the persistent seeking but with no
implication that the search was successful. For the gracefulness or
'graciousness' is precisely what Gurney has had to forego in order
to make room for Whitman's 'rough nature'. Similarly in the next
line, when he addresses 'men and women of the two-fold asking, for
democracy and courtesy', if we give to 'courtesy' its full Italianate
sense, it means 'formality'. And how to join that formality with the
democracy that he is equally devoted to, is a problem that Gurney
has wrestled with but does not pretend to have solved. The asking
is 'two-fold'; and the two demands cannot be reconciled.
   All the same, Gurney had surely earned the proud boast that he
makes, addressing his own poems:

When you were launched there was small roughness in the touch of
 words,

A woman's weapon, a boy's chatter, a thing for barter and loss:
But I have roughed the soul American or Yankee at least to truth and
  instinct,
And compacted the loose-drifting faiths and questions of men in a
  few words.

In a largely self-educated poet who appears never to have read T. S.
Eliot (*The Waste Land* appeared in the year when Gurney went out
of his mind), these lines are astonishingly perceptive about what had
happened to the diction of English poetry in his lifetime, and about
how he (Gurney) had helped to change it. In the world of British
poetry when Gurney began writing ('When you were launched',
as he says to his poems) the Jonsonian grace and formality were
sought after indeed, and sometimes achieved, but only at the cost
of effeminacy or callowness such as Jonson would have scorned.
Gurney's claim to have 'roughed' (or roughened) the diction and the
rhythms of that English poetry is a claim that must be allowed.

The Thomas Hardy Industry

R. S. Thomas, in a not very considered nor memorable quatrain, had declared himself about the poetry of Hardy:

> Then Hardy, for many a major
> Poet, is for me just an old stager,
> Shuffling about a bogus heath,
> Cob-webbed with his Victorian breath.

The lines had been more provocative in 1970, when Thomas published them, than they were ten or fifteen years later. For in 1970, largely because Philip Larkin championed him, Hardy was quite generally thought to be the great poet that independent witnesses like Yvor Winters and John Crowe Ransom had always considered him. In 1978, however appeared *The Older Hardy*, the second volume of an exhaustive and admirable biography by Robert Gittings; and this, though it nowhere directly assailed Hardy the poet, undoubtedly tarnished the image of Hardy, the man. Although there is no rule that says a great poet must be a lovable individual, the public likes to love what it is asked to admire, and the lovableness of Hardy had been much insisted on. He had been presented as stubbornly and naïvely sincere, resolutely independent and veracious. There had already been signs that this image was too good to be true. It had been established for instance, at least for those who read bibliographies, that the two volumes of supposed biography published in Hardy's lifetime over the name of the second Mrs Hardy were in fact dictated autobiography. Moreover, this was an autobiography more remarkable for what it left out than for what it divulged. Terry Coleman and Lois Deacon in *Providence and Mr Hardy* (1966) had uncovered Hardy's youthful love-affair with his cousin Tryphena Sparks – a matter that would not support the speculations that Coleman and Deacon spun out of it, but which certainly showed that the heretofore received account of his life could not be trusted. Gittings, correcting and supplementing these hints out of his own researches, drew the portrait of a man who, so far from wearing his heart on his sleeve, was exceptionally devious and secretive. Hardy, we were made to see, had been at very great pains not just to conceal much of his past but deliberately to mislead about it, and now fifty years after his death the specious fabric was unravelling. Among the most damaging revelations were what Gittings had found out about Hardy's behaviour to his first wife Emma in the last weeks of her life. It had been known, ever since the publication in 1963 of Emma's artless *Some Recollections* (ed. Evelyn Hardy & Robert Gittings, 1961) that the couple had been on bad terms for years before Emma's death, but now it appeared that Hardy's conduct towards her, maddening though she was, had been towards the end mean and heartless, and her place had been filled with unbecoming promptness by Florence Emily Hardy, whom in her turn Hardy neglected and exploited.

None of this behaviour was either criminal or vicious, and perhaps most artists' lives would show similar blemishes. The difference was that Hardy had for so long successfully covered up, and also that his admirers had too often presented him as a blessed, blessedly rustic and blessedly English, exception to the rule that great artists are perhaps necessarily egotistical and often devious as well. Now, with a certain vengefulness, we were reminded that Hardy's friend Edward Clodd had decided: 'he was a great author: he was not a great man; there was no largeness of soul.' And it is true that Clodd's charge 'no largeness of soul' reaches damagingly beyond allegations of egotism and furtiveness. Peter J. Casagrande in an interesting though laborious essay, building on Clodd's verdict, argued that Hardy knew he lacked magnanimity, and worried about it, in *The Return of the Native* and elsewhere.

Casagrande's essay appeared in the first issue of *The Thomas Hardy Annual* (1983). There was already a 'Hardy Newsletter', also a Thomas Hardy Society, which published its own *Review*. Moreover, however they might lack magnanimity, Hardy's novels and poems had for years been securely installed among books that schoolchildren and college students would be required to study. One contributor to the *Annual* spoke without irony of 'workers in the Hardy industry'. Another, P. N. Furbank, seemed to have strayed out of some more urbane and sceptical gathering when, ruminating on the batch of books he had for review, he murmured to himself: 'What about the theme of *rain* in Hardy's verse: an essay there too . . . ? 'Maybe', he told himself, 'some one has written it.' If so, there would in the future be a quick way to find out; for Richard H. Taylor elsewhere in the *Annual* announced that each year he would provide a survey of recent Hardy studies, remarking happily, 'Guidance into the rich pastures of Hardy scholarship becomes increasingly essential.' Clearly the Hardy industry, now that so many people had invested in it, would sustain itself by its own momentum; and though it might for a while be disconcerted by Robert Gittings' unamiable portrait, there was no need for any Hardy scholar to be demoralized.

'Hardy scholar' goes along with 'Hardy studies'. Hardy studies is what Hardy scholars do. And since there are so many of them whose publications must be 'kept up with', it is plain that the Hardy scholar need not, cannot afford to, move out of the cosy circle of *Hardy Newsletter* and *Hardy Review* and *Hardy Annual*, backed up by local and regional and national and international Hardy conferences or meetings of the Hardy Society. Certainly he would not have time to read many books by or about another author. The phenomenon was not new in the 1980s, but the absurdity of it, the philistinism implicit in it, and the bland complacency with which the academic profession countenanced and institutionalized the absurdity, sparked an overdue and properly indignant protest from within Academia. Books and symposia by younger teachers of literature began to tumble from the presses, declaring their profession to be 'in crisis'. The remedies they proposed were either implausible or else worse than the disease, not least when one detected behind them, predictably, the political agitator fishing in troubled waters. But those older members of the profession were surely wrong, who protested that there was no crisis until the dissidents declared it. A profession which envisaged with equanimity essays like 'The theme of rain in Hardy's verse', and an array of reviews, newsletters and annuals in which such pieces should find print, was surely in crisis, if it was not in terminal decline. When a mean-minded government began to cut off funds to university departments that generated such trivia, the squeals that were heard about threats to academic freedom and disinterested enquiry could hardly sound anything but hollow.

Of course if there was a Hardy industry, there was also a Pound industry, a Joyce industry, an Eliot industry, a William Blake industry and how many more. Undoubtedly these were symptoms of the same malaise. If the Hardy industry seemed a particularly flagrant case, it was because all these other poets were in a rather obvious sense *difficult* authors, as Hardy clearly is not. Pound and Blake patently call out for exegesis, and perhaps will demand it for ever more – which is a pity, and surely says something about these authors that is not to their credit. It is one of Hardy's great virtues that he gives the exegete hardly anything to do. His poems are formally intricate, not always in ways that declare themselves on the surface; and he often engages, far more than has yet been realized, in dialogues with his predecessors, not just Browning and Shelley and Swinburne, but past masters like Virgil and Dante. These are matters for the critic; and there will always be room, perhaps indeed a crying need, for good criticism of Hardy's poems. But there is no need for commentary, beyond what the biographers have provided. Accordingly if there was a Hardy industry, it was in several senses, all unflattering, very much a *cottage* industry. And most of what passed in the 1980s for Hardy criticism was the sedate riding of hobby-horses.

Geoffrey Hill

Geoffrey Hill's *The Mystery of the Charity of Charles Péguy* (London, 1984) was a work of monumental pathos, celebrating a vanished world (Péguy's), and intimating that we were the poorer for its vanishing. The monumentality was typical: Hill seems always to have wanted to create a monumental art – in this following one of his American masters, Allen Tate, and disregarding another, John Crowe Ransom who, writing out of the same cultural milieu as Tate, eschewed the monumental as consistently as Tate strained after it. It was notable that in *The Lords of Limit* (also 1984), Hill included an essay on Ransom which seemed to argue that in the end Ransom betrayed himself and his vocation. It might be said that whereas Allen Tate was a badly flawed major poet, Ransom was an exquisite minor one; and Hill, it had always been plain, was a very ambitious poet, not interested in achieving acclaim only as a minor master.

All the same, monumentality is not the same as ambitiousness. Metrically, for instance, Hill had always been very *un*ambitious. Though he patently aspired to be measured by the standard of the presumptuous modernists, he had never followed such as Pound and Eliot in breaking down the inherited accentual-syllabic metres so as to accommodate the broken or disjointed cadences of British or American speech. And the poem about Péguy was no exception; one of its least noticed accomplishments was that it consisted of four hundred lines of iambic pentameter, handled very inventively so as to avoid monotony. That standard metre had been turned to very various purposes through the centuries, but Hill, one recognized, clung to it so as to aim at just one of those purposes, the most monumental. For in *The Mystery of the Charity of Charles Péguy* Hill's pentameters were reaching after, and sometimes attaining, Christopher Marlowe's 'mighty line', his 'drumming decasyllable':

> How the mood swells to greet the gathering storm!
> The chestnut trees begin to thresh and cast
> huge canisters of blossom at each gust.
> Coup de tonnerre! Bismarck is in the room!

On the other hand, this same quatrain suggests how, if in metre

Hill is conservative and seemingly unambitious, in diction he is nothing of the kind. 'Coup de tonnerre' is an undemanding instance of the French interlarded in Hill's poem so generously that some people were inclined to wonder in what sense the poem could be said to be written in English at all. Presumably there were some readers who, lacking French, felt excluded, and resented their exclusion as a piece of élitist arrogance. Certainly there were others who took the interlarded French as so much acceptable local colour in a poem that was, after all, about an historically recorded Frenchman trying to act responsibly and decently in an historically specific French context. But Hill, if he was consistent, would have had to disown and exclude the second set of readers as much as the first. For every time we encounter a phrase like 'coup de tonnerre' in a context that we have been led to suppose is English, the effect is to halt the run of an English sentence in the interest of a poised parenthesis. The French expressions, in fact, might as well have been set off inside inverted commas. And Hill, in another essay in *The Lords of Limit*, had shown himself characteristically acute and uncompromising about how in poetry such inverted commas, actual or implied, perform. In this essay, called 'Our Word is Our Bond', Hill considered the effect of the quotation-marks in Pound's *Homage to Sextus Propertius* and *Hugh Selwyn Mauberley*: ' "inverted commas" are a way of bringing pressure to bear and are also a form of "ironic and bitter" intonation acknowledging that pressure is being brought.' Even as Hill defines the effect of inverted commas in verse, he uses them in his own prose, and in a way not significantly different. And this is characteristic of Hill the essayist; his prose is always, though in a special way, 'poetic', and even those who tolerated the inverted commas in his verse might legitimately protest at how almost compulsively he had recourse to them in prose. At all events we are forced to see how little patience Hill has with the naïve reader, and how few (virtually no) concessions he is prepared to make to him. His haughty disregard of such naïveté appears even more clearly in another thing he says about Pound's use of quotation-marks: 'the effect is not that of avoiding the rap but rather of recording the rapping noise made by those things which the world throws at us in the form of prejudice and opinion . . .' Such a passage, which typically makes a fine and necessary point in a very involved way, gives sufficient notice that, whenever Geoffrey Hill uses or alludes to a common idiom like 'taking the rap', he will turn it upside-down or inside-out, or at very least will extend it with a deliberate literal-mindedness to a point where we can no longer hold on to the straightforward meaning that we thought it had for us. Such probing scrutiny of reach-me-down expressions is indeed, we may think, one of the things we expect of the responsible poet; but if there is never a phrase used by the poet without being subjected to such scrutiny, if we are so continuously wrong-footed and made to seem foolishly guileless, the effect is of congestion and of every word being a-fidget. This sometimes happens in Hill's poetry, more often and less tolerably in his prose; none of his words, we come to think, can be taken at their face-value. And yet some of his most devoted admirers seemed to applaud the opalescent sonorities that from time to time he contrived for them, while neglecting to pay the price that he scrupulously demanded – of recognizing that such gratifying resonances were part and parcel of a way with language that he would expose, at other points, as heartlessly casuistical or sportive.

It follows that the innocently simple-minded reader who ventures into the charged area of Hill's language finds the path is through a minefield. Two of the important matters considered in *The Mystery of the Charity of Charles Péguy* are undoubtedly patriotism, and martial valour. This made the poem topical, for the Falklands War in 1982 had for a short time made it possible to speak of such matters once again. But those who thought the poem simply endorsed these as indubitable values were as wide of the mark as those (there were some) who read it as decisively denying them, who interpreted the poem for instance as a polemic against militarism. Patriotism and martial valour were treated monumentally; but the upshot of the poem was a monumental uncertainty, or ambivalence, about both of them.

Jeremy Hooker and Tony Harrison

One of the best collections of the 1970s had been Jeremy Hooker's *Solent Shore* (Manchester, 1978). Hooker, born in 1941, can hardly be thought representative of his generation of poets. He had for instance resided through several years in Wales, and (less important but still significant) he had been educated at Southampton University, not Oxbridge. Moreover he was untypically in earnest. Indeed to those who knew him only through his prose (*Poetry of Place*, Manchester, 1982) his earnestness could seem oppressive. Part of the distinction of *Solent Shore* was precisely that the exigencies of verse-form prompted Hooker to a sprightly variety of tone beyond what came naturally to him:

> Yachts on the leaden estuaries
> are wingless, larval.
> Leeward of the island
> rusty bums of tankers
> squat in the swell.
> This full-bodied water
> bears its trademark in oil.

One looks a long way in Hooker's prose before finding such a rapid and nimble change of tone as that from 'larval' to 'bums'. Yet Hooker's prose is very valuable and interesting because so much of it is a commentary on his own poetic progress, and so it is revealing about the motives that impel him, some of them surely shared by his contemporaries.

Nothing for instance is much more telling than, in the 'Afterword' to his *A View from the Source: Selected Poems* (Manchester, 1982), his confession: 'An irony of which I am painfully aware is that distance from my place has sharpened my sense of it, and made my poems of Southampton, for example, not what I wish they were, a citizen's, but an exile's.' Why should it have surprised and pained Jeremy Hooker that he could shape his memories of growing up by Southampton Water, only when he recalled them in his exile in mid-Wales? Did he not know that James Joyce could re-create his native Dublin only from the distances of Zurich and Trieste? That

Eliot and Pound could re-create their native North America only out of long-term expatriation in Europe? That even his cherished master David Jones could create or re-create his ancestral Wales only from the comfortable distances of Harrow and Kensington? It seems it was not just technical matters that the Modernists had failed to transmit to Jeremy Hooker's generation, but more far-reaching considerations about the conditions of artistic life in the twentieth century, and the cost of it. The necessary alienation of the artist from the community that he seeks to speak for – this a lesson promulgated not at first hand by the modernists but learned from as far back as Flaubert – is a lesson to which Hooker only reluctantly attends. For him in the last resort 'belonging', being a 'citizen', seems to matter more than uttering the truths that he has in his keeping. Accordingly, when he moved on from *Solent Shore*, his poems ceased to register scenes drily, with hard edges, from a distance, and tended to become pleas or cries for help out of his alienated condition.

Hooker's *Poetry of Place*, a collection of his essays and reviews from 1970 to 1981, is an attractively generous celebration of those influences and models that he is aware of as having helped him. But it is remarkable that none of them can easily be credited with the distinction that he achieved in *Solent Shore*:

> Where the shoreline ends
> At the horizon, the far sky's
> Pronged with orange flames
> From the refinery.
>
> Today the clouds bear east,
> Forming a broad, shadowy space
> Of dark green mudlands,
> Staked out with old stumps,
> With rows of masts along
> Estuaries and creeks.
>
> It might be almost any time,
> As one slow hulk of cloud
> Lags to the west, mirrored
> Like an oil slick off the Needles.

If we admire this as 'a vignette', we shall be thought to imply that the author had no special concern for the scene that he depicts. But this will be supposed only by those who cannot believe that a writer has such a concern unless he beats his breast and avows it. The odd thing is that Hooker himself may be one of them. For his writing both before *Solent*

Shore (*Soliloquies of a Chalk Giant*, 1974) as well as after it (*Englishman's Road*, 1980), is full of just those protestations in the first person which are very profitably excluded from *Solent Road*. And such protestations are by no means absent from those predecessors whom Hooker most honours, notably Edward Thomas and Ivor Gurney. What seems most likely is that Hooker found the style for *Solent Shore* not anywhere in literature but by meditating the procedures of landscape painters like his own father or Paul Nash. (Not that his procedure is therefore to be called 'pictorial' – the force and felicity of 'lags' is entirely verbal, not available to any painter's brush.) Either that, or else the severity of the style comes of the resolve to avoid nostalgia – a temptation that Hooker was certainly determined to resist. Not that however but protestation, what Auden called 'the loose, immoderate tone', seemed to be what he was prone to.

Telling how it was to come of age in the 1960s, Hooker narrates that as an undergraduate he called himself a Communist ('this was political romanticism'), and that he responded to the CND movement 'with religious fervour'. Weaning himself from putting these matters directly into his verse ('My ambition', he tells us, was at that time 'to write the English *Howl* of my generation'), he did not therefore change his political sentiments. Rather he came to the view 'that it is impossible to write about anything without revealing one's social and political convictions . . . ; if they are not made explicit by the work, they will be implicit in the nature of its materials and the manner in which they have been handled.' In this he is surely right. But it follows that we may infer his politics from passages and features of his writing that are not overtly political. Such is the yearning to 'belong'; for the reluctance to accept social alienation as the artist's lot is rather plainly related to the exaltation of 'solidarity' – with kindred, with trade, with class, with local community, sometimes though rarely with nation – as the highest good, to which all other goods must if necessary be sacrificed. This is a characteristic posture of British socialism, as articulated for instance by Raymond Williams, to whose novels Hooker has devoted a mostly admiring essay. Faced with a choice between that and the alienated *hauteur* prescribed for the artist by modernist aesthetics, most British poets have like Hooker opted for the first alternative. But only a sort of haughtiness towards the public – which is to say, necessarily, towards 'the community' – could have produced the best poems of *Solent Shore*, so austerely determined not to expound, not to explain.

Four years older than Hooker, Tony Harrison too is the graduate of a provincial university (Leeds). And for him too a central preoccupation is alienation from his origins, the distress of no longer 'belonging'. Harrison indeed is raucously explicit:

> I thought it made me look more 'working class'
> (as if a bit of chequered cloth could bridge that gap!)
> I did a turn in it before the glass.
> My mother said: *It suits you, your dad's cap.*

This appears to be a peculiarly British, or even peculiarly English, theme. And we cannot help but envisage the non-British reader who should protest in bewilderment that, in view of the range and sorts of human misery world-wide, the woe of having been educated beyond one's kindred and one's station must surely be accounted among the least grievous. Grievous, however, is how Tony Harrison experiences it. And he was certainly aggrieved in *The School of Eloquence* (1978) and *Continuous* (1981). The conflict of feelings is understandable, and faithfully teased out: on the one hand he pities his parents for their inarticulacy; on the other hand, since pity is not what one wants to feel for parents, he rages at his own articulacy (in many languages, for he is a notable polyglot) and, so far from feeling grateful for the liberation which that and his education have brought him, he resents it as what has made a breach between himself and those he loves. Such satisfaction as his skills give him is chiefly vengeful: 'So right, yer buggers, then! We'll occupy/your lousy leasehold Poetry.' 'Yer buggers' shows that Harrison wants his vengeful alienation to determine not just the content of these poems but also their diction. Too much has been made of this, however, by Harrison himself and by London reviewers: the West Riding urban vernacular that he gestures at is not in any real sense a dialect, for it differs from standard English chiefly in pronunciation, not much in vocabulary or syntax. National criteria of correctness in pronunciation can certainly, among the English, be exploited to wounding effect, though this happened less often in 1980 than thirty years before. But Harrison's harping on the slights and mortifications he suffered on this count had the effect, surely gratifying to his tormentors, of showing that every one of their shafts struck home, that the wounds still smarted and bled. This is just one of the anomalous or at any rate uncontrollable consequences of a sort of writing that in the 1960s, its heyday, was called 'confessional'; and *The School of Eloquence* is a late come instance of such writing as practised years before by Robert Lowell and Sylvia Plath and John Berryman. Harrison admitted as much by a poem in his *Selected Poems* (1984). This is called 'Confessional Poetry', and seems to record an occasion on which a fellow-poet, Jeffrey Wainwright, tried without success to alert Harrison to some of the anomalies in his enterprise. The trouble with all such enterprises – whether by Plath, by Lowell, or by Harrison[1] is that the poetry asks to be taken in the first place as 'a human document'. The story that we read from *The School of Eloquence*, particularly as amplified in the *Selected Poems*, is indeed interesting and touching. But its interest is documentary, not intrinsic to its nature as poetry; and so we are bowled over on a first reading, but less so the next time, and the next. This, it may be, was part of what Jeffrey Wainwright tried to point out. Of course, since human appeal is so much more straightforward than poetic appeal, such poems and sequences of poems will be widely admired. And this has happened with Harrison, whose poems to and about his parents enjoy more repute than other unconfessional pieces, both earlier in his career and later, which in fact deserve more respect.

Among such unjustly disregarded pieces must certainly be counted some from his first collection, *The Loiners* (1970), in which Harrison drew – not 'confessionally' – on four years he spent in Nigeria. These poems were boisterously lewd, but in being so they only spelled out the plain implications of many well-loved poems by Kipling about the behaviour of expatriate Britons in colonial or (by Harrison's time) ex-colonial territories. And like Kipling, Harrison could wring a genuine pathos out of the lewdness:

> Sunday Scotsman Northwards, autumn trees all rusting up;
> My fifth *Light Ale* is swashing in its BR plastic cup.
> Coming back to England; there's no worse way than this
> Railroad North from London up to *Worstedopolis*.
> Britannia, Old Mother Riley, bending down to pray,
> The railway line's the X-Ray of her twisted vertebrae.
> I'm watching England rolling by; here a startled grouse
> Shoots out from a siding, and there Sabbath-idle ploughs.
> Clogged in soggy furrows are seizing up with rain.
> Life's either still or scurrying away from the train.

> *Anxious, anxious, anxious, anxious, perhaps the train'll crash.*
> *Anxious, anxious, anxious, Doctor Adgie, there's a rash*
> *The shape of bloody Britain and it's starting to spread.*
> *My belly's like a blow-up globe all splotched with Empire red.*
> *Chancres, chancres, Shetlands, spots, boils, Hebrides,*
> *Atlasitis, Atlasitis, British Isles Disease!*

---

[1] Or by D. J. Enright, in *The Terrible Shears: Scenes from a twenties childhood* (London, 1970). See Enright's *Collected Poems* (Oxford, 1981).

The rot sets in at Retford and the stations beyond;
Coffles of coupled, rusty coaltrucks chalkmarked COND.
But at each abandoned station shunned like a suicide
There's that loveliest of flourishers, the purple *London Pride*.
Though why the 'proud' metropolis should monopolize weeds
Beats me, when we've got millions more all over mucky Leeds,
Springing up wherever life is teetering on the brink
Like pensioned-off yours truly's pickled in his drink.
With a bit of help off Bitter, I can do it on my own.
They can stuff their pink *Somalgins* and their *Phenobarbitone*,
O those lovely bubs that almost touched black chin and shiny knees
Leaping up and down to drumming like hoop-jumping Pekinese!
Ay, it's a pity all that's over. From now on every night
It's *Whatsoever Thy Hand Findeth To Do, Do It With Thy Might.*

Anxious, anxious, anxious, anxious, perhaps the train'll crash.
Anxious, anxious, anxious, Doctor Adgie, there's a rash
The shape of bloody Britain and it's starting to spread.
My belly's like a blow-up globe all blotched with Empire red.
Chancres, chancres, Shetlands, spots, boils, Hebrides,
Atlasitis, Atlasitis, British Isles Disease.

Veni, vidi, vici, Death's cackling in my ear.
And there he is a Caesar with an earth-caked Roman spear.
Queer sorts of dozes these are, where I'm nodding off to dream
Of being chased by Caesars and I wake up with a scream.
Must be that pork-pie I've eaten or the British Railways Ale.
Night behind the window. My coaster's tan gone deathly pale.
It's *me*! It's *me* the fauna's fleeing. Nothing'll keep still.
My adrenalin moves Nature now and not God's heavenly will.
Lean closer as the darkness grows. My vision's fogged by breath
Clouding up the window as life's clouded up by death.

Anxious, anxious, anxious, anxious, perhaps the train'll crash . . .

The remorselessly unsubtle yet compulsive rhythm recalls Betjeman,
as the combination of formality with coarse sentiment recalls
Kingsley Amis. But this comes about, surely, because all three
poets are indebted to Kipling, whose greatness and fecundity as a
poet at last, in the 1970s, began to be recognized. And if Harrison, like
Betjeman and Amis, seems sometimes to *bully* his metrical schemes
and his rhyme-schemes into compliance, as Kipling at his frequent
best did not, yet his reliance on such schemes, or his preference for
them, says something about him as about Amis who utters, for what

little it matters, political sentiments directly opposed to Harrison's. Harrison's fidelity to scannable verse, and most of the time to rhyme, is sometimes explained by his academic conditioning in the classics, Greek and Roman. But this seems implausible, for Kipling knew precious little Latin and no Greek. Rather it seems to derive from a craftsman's ethic built into Harrison's West Riding inheritance, a value put on overt expertise and tidiness; as when he addresses three of his north-country forefathers:

> Fell farmer, railwayman and publican,
> I strive to keep my lines direct and straight,
> and try to make connections where I can . . .

And to be sure, if there should ever come a time when such as Tony Harrison's father can read his verses with understanding, would it not help them that those verses rhymed and could be scanned?

Hughes as Laureate

Ted Hughes wasted no time in vindicating the choice that Grey Gowrie and other advisers to the Crown had made when in December 1984, he was declared Poet Laureate. His first performance in his laureate capacity was unlike any Laureate's poem ever, and triumphantly overcame all the constraints and preconceptions that had inhibited his predecessors. The poem, ninety lines long, celebrated the christening, on 21 December 1984, of Henry, second son of the Prince and Princess of Wales. Published two days later in *The Observer* (23 December 1984), it was entitled 'Rain-Charm for the Duchy', and sub-titled, 'A Blessed, Devout Drench for the Christening of Prince Harry'. Overtly what it told of was the poet's experiences as a massive rain-storm broke weeks of drought in the West Country.'

> The car-top hammered. The Cathedral jumped in and out
> Of a heaven that had obviously caught fire
> And couldn't be contained.
> A girl in high heels, her handbag above her head,
>
>   Risked it across the square's lit metals.
> We saw surf cuffed over her and the car jounced.
> Grates, gutters, clawed in the backwash.
> She kept going. Flak and shrapnel
>
> Of thundercracks
> Hit walls and roofs. Still a swimmer
> She bobbed off, into sea-smoke,
> Where headlights groped. Already
>
> Thunder was breaking up the moors.
>   It dragged tors over the city –
> Uprooted chunks of map. Smeltings of ore, pink and violet,
> Spattered and wriggled down . . .

The poem moves from these vivid and unaffected vignettes of sudden torrential rain over the city of Exeter into an entranced litany of West Country rivers, great and small, as the poet imagines each of them awakening to the intimation that the drought is over: Lyn and Mole, Taw and Torridge and Okement, Tamar and Tavy, Dart and Teign and Exe (each river distinctively characterized). And the poem ends with the poet imagining how the denizens of those rivers, though of the off-shore seas also – that is to say, the fish – respond to this momentous and thunderous event:

> And I thought of those other lightnings, the patient thirsting ones,
> Aligned under Crow Island, inside Bideford Bar,
> And beside the Hamoaze anchor chains,
> And beneath the thousand, shivering fibre-glass hulls
> Inside One Gun Point,
>
> And under the Ness, and inside Great Bull Hill:
> The salmon, deep in the thunder, lit
> And again lit, with glimpses of quenchings,
> Twisting their glints in the suspense,
> Biting at the stir, beginning to move.

It is hard to think of a better verse for a new-born baby, royal or not, than 'Biting at the stir, beginning to move'. Those people were wide of the mark who surmised knowingly that this was a poem Ted Hughes had already written or worked at, which he adapted to the public occasion. Even if this were true, the deftness and fittingness of the adaptation would itself be imaginative and compel admiration, particularly in the appropriateness of the tone, at once awe-struck and elated. Everything, even to the title and sub-title, was wonderfully in keeping: the Duchy for instance of Cornwall, owning large tracts of land throughout the West Country, is one of the fiefs reserved for the Prince of Wales, heir to the throne; and 'drench', though it can mean a downpour of rain, means also a draught of medicine forcibly administered to an animal – an affecting analogue for what any unsuspecting baby must experience, taking the shock of water on its head from the baptismal font. Other associations – from the fish-like life of the foetus in the amniotic fluid, through to the breaking of the waters in child-birth – are obvious. Much of the distinction of Hughes's poem (as of other poems by him) is in the way such radically physiological considerations are brought insistently into the poem while being, by a nice decorum, never explicitly stated or named. And how proper it is, how in the right sense democratic, that for this public poem of the 1980s the poet should figure not as a land-owner nor as husbandman (both of which he is), but as a motorist caught by a rainstorm in a city street! (For the monarchy, if it is to persist, has to commend itself to an urbanized nation; and its long-standing association with broad acres and horse-breeding does not help.)

It was impossible to think that Philip Larkin could have risen so adroitly to such an occasion, any more than John Betjeman ever did. In the 1960s Larkin had been described as 'the unofficial laureate', and no one had demurred. Twenty years later, during a long delay before Betjeman's successor was announced, Larkin's name was still the most favoured, to the extent indeed that his appointment was in some quarters thought a foregone conclusion. Though he let it be known that he rightly feared the possibility, yet in the event it must have hurt that he was so pointedly passed over. One hopes he did not read the astute journalist who explained that 'Philip Larkin was the favourite to be Laureate because he promised, in his own special downbeat way, to continue the Betjeman tradition'; whereas, so this writer declared with obvious satisfaction, 'the old dispensation, the cosy sociable world of John Betjeman and his teddy bear, has been left behind.' Of course this is not criticism, only a chart of turns in the tides of fashion. But this anonymous writer was shrewd, not least when he remarked of Hughes that 'in the country at large there will be less surprise about his appointment than in London's literary circles.' This was surely true. And yet the uninformed reader would be wrong if he inferred, reasonably enough, that Larkin was, or had been, a poet of the metropolis. On the contrary, Larkin had been, rather more insistently than Hughes, a voice from the provinces – in this as in much else different from Betjeman the proudly impenitent Londoner. Larkin's world, in fact, had been neither cosy nor sociable, and it was unthinkable that his childhood teddy bear should have figured in it. A resolutely provincial poet extolled in the metropolis, a raucously anti-academic poet cherished in the academies, a morosely private poet who became the darling of the publicizing media – Larkin's career was a tissue of anomalies. The career, as distinct from the poetry (some of which will surely endure) calls out for sensitive and searching study. Several hypotheses and relevant considerations present themselves: first, Larkin, though he never served in World War Two, was of the generation which did so serve, and so his registration of post-war Britain has an authority denied to Hughes who in some poems seems to regret having been excluded, by being born too late, from the carnival of violence which World War legitimized; second, 'post-war' means for the British 'post-imperial', and, though it cannot be proved, it could be argued that the melancholy which pervades Larkin's poetry is a sadness at the loss of imperial vision – something which did not, and could not, enter into Hughes's poetry; third, Larkin with the help of such as John Wain and Robert Conquest *made* his public, whereas Hughes just *found* a public that had always been there and waiting; fourth, whereas Larkin made it offensively obvious that he had no interest in nor concern with American readers, Hughes on the contrary was launched on his career by an award from the New York Poetry Centre for his *The Hawk in the Rain* (1957); lastly, and perhaps most tellingly, Larkin is a poet of *culture* (though of a culture wilfully and disingenuously narrowed), whereas Hughes is a poet of *nature* (though of a nature insistently seen as amoral).

When in 1984 Charles Tomlinson published *New York Scenes*, an unusually educated blurb remarked that his world was 'a surprisingly unalienated one for the late twentieth century'. This made sense; the equanimity with which Tomlinson gilded scenes from rural England (of which there were several in this collection, despite its title) had come to seem at times inordinate. And Tomlinson was on paper a candidate for the Laureateship, though no one supposed him a serious contender. The proof of the pudding was, it may be thought, in the eating: the zest and élan with which Hughes wrote 'Rain-charm for the Duchy', something that Tomlinson no more than Larkin could have equalled, surely showed which of these poets was the least 'alienated'; which of them was most at home with and in tune with his audience; which of them in short was capable of being a *national* poet, as the Laureate is required to be. It was seldom that either Tomlinson or Larkin expressed in poetry sentiments to offend the British public, but their unexceptionable sentiments were often uttered with an inflection – wry or Olympian or just abnormally intent – which distanced them from their readers. Hughes was different, his tone was straightforward. As a journalist remarked approvingly, 'The new Laureate is a stern, uncompromising poet who speaks of "the Muse", "inspiration", and of negotiation with . . . dark forces . . .' 'Uncompromising' means 'undoubting'; Hughes was as little alienated from his poetic calling as from his public, as little in doubt about the one as about the other. And of course there can be a shallow modishness about the assumption that the late twentieth century is peculiarly 'alienated'. All the same, Hughes's unwavering tone was certainly in his period a rarity, so much so as to prompt the question, seldom or never asked, in what sense he can be called a *modern* poet at all. This question was often asked about Larkin, and it was sometimes answered by saying that he was not, and did not want to be, 'modern'. Thus *The Times* obituary (December 3, 1985) declared flatly, 'In reality he was the last neo-Georgian.' (Larkin the anthologist had invited this label, and perhaps it would have pleased him – which does not mean that it is right.) Hughes is so much a Lawrentian poet that, if we remember how D. H. Lawrence collaborated with the *Georgian Poetry* anthologies, we may think 'neo-Georgian' fits Hughes's case at least as well as it fits Larkin's.

Michael Hamburger

In 1984 George Oppen, one of the original 'objectivists',[1] died of Alzheimer's disease in San Francisco; and at the end of 1985 Michael Hamburger published in memory of Oppen an admirably suave and monumental poem which he called 'To Bridge a Lull':

> Alone in your genus, ectopistes,
> Your flocks were thunder clouds
> That discharged themselves on forests,
> Clattering down, breaking thick branches
> With the weight of your roosts or nests
> When you broke your journeys, rested.
> In thousands then you were slaughtered,
> Smoked out with sulphur, clubbed
> Or shot on acres white
> With your acid dung. So many
> That herds of pigs were turned loose
> To fatten on carcasses left
> When their keepers, Indian, colonist,
> Had bagged all they could eat.
> At a mile a minute, billionfold,
> Long-tailed and purple-necked,
> Powerful flyers, you travelled
> Between Mexico and Quebec,
> Able to rear, it was thought,
> At any season, wherever
> Abundance of fruit or seed
> Matched your multiple hunger,
> One male, one female, and those
> Mature within half a year.
> And then you were gone;
> And then in tens, not thousands
> Were seen again and counted;
> And then were not seen again.

[1] See An 'Objectivists' Anthology, ed. Louis Zukofsky (1932).

Ectopistes. Vagrants. A dead name I write
To bridge a lull. Absurdly let
Lips, tongue that will be dumb
Address what is not, never could make out
The spoken or the written vocable, dead.
And hear the clatter still,
Come down to ravage forests razed
By your self-ravaging destroyers
Whose obsolescent words I write.
And see the sky blacked out
Not where your millions passed,
Light breaking as you hurtled to escape
Eagle or hawk, armed with their talons only,
But by a larger, lingering darkness that's unbroken.
A stillness, cold, your kind could share with mine
Fills with your flocks, absurdly
Brings back what dead men called you, passenger.[1]

Although the poem touches deftly enough on the migrant quality of Oppen's life, it is apparent that the focus of interest is not on the individual called George Oppen, any more than the 'I' of the poem is to be understood as the German-Jewish-naturalized-English individual, Michael Hamburger. What we hear is 'The Death of the Poet', not a live man but a live *poet* mourning not a dead man but a dead *poet*, and doing so accordingly by way of the distinctively poetic activity, that is to say, the rifling of dictionaries. From the rare Greek word 'ectopistes' through to the half-suppressed solution to the riddle, 'passenger *pigeons*', Hamburger's poem is entirely within the domain of language, of verbalism. This does not constrict it; recalling, as surely we are meant to do, the pointless extermination of the passenger pigeon in the first two centuries of European settlement in North America – something described and deplored as far back as James Fenimore Cooper – we read this poem in memory of an American poet as, in important respects, an anti-American poem. This point is obscured, and the poem itself is obscure, only because this twentieth-century poet, with a humility hardly known in earlier centuries, claims for himself and for his calling no more than that he is a practised merchant and manipulator of words – words like 'ectopistes', words like 'passenger'.

This vision, of the person who writes poems as an eccentric, at all events a highly specialized being, has been with Michael Hamburger

[1] *Agenda* 23, 3-4, pp. 71-2. Reprinted in Michael Hamburger's *Selected Poems* (Manchester, 1988).

from the first. In his earliest collections (for instance *Flowering Cactus*, 1950), it often took the form of declaring himself Poet with a capital P, swathing himself in the mantle of special bardic privileges after the fashion of Holderlin or Wordsworth; and this set him at odds with the poets who clustered around Philip Larkin in the anthology *New Lines* (1956), who invoked 'the poet' indeed but always in lower-case, and who by their idioms were at pains to establish that the poet was not significantly different from the man next door. At that time, and for long after, the British poetry-reader was grateful for that assurance; and during the long period when Larkin was popular, Hamburger's more presumptuous conception of his calling could only with difficulty get a hearing. Indeed even in the 1980s when, as we have seen, Hamburger's elevated conception of the poet's vocation was expressed much less explicitly, the enormity of it was still discerned and still resented. Thus, a review of his *Collected Poems* (1985) protested that '. . . there are difficulties because the poet denies us direct access to himself by hiding continually behind the mask of the "poet" '; that 'instead of letting us journey with him as fellow companions who want to explore, challenge the route, and initiate our own courses, he takes us along with him grudgingly, often reducing us to mere bystanders'; in short that 'He is not one of us. Nor does he try to be'.[1] Though Hamburger's professed politics outside of poems was anxiously, even over-anxiously, 'democratic', his presence in his poems was, for a reader like this, not sufficiently confiding and fraternal. The bearing and presence of Hamburger, the figure that he made in his poems, was not haughty at all but on the contrary very 'low-key'; the haughtiness or even arrogance that this reviewer nevertheless discerned derived from the poetic enterprise itself, as Hamburger conceived of it.

There is a paradox here which few English-speakers were aware of, though poets and readers in other languages had been much exercised about it. It consists in this: there is a kind of modern poet who practises a humility hardly known in earlier centuries, whose humility however looks like, and in part is, arrogance. George Oppen was such a poet in English; another, in French, was Francis Ponge, who can provide an explanation for the paradox: 'I don't mean only that we reject the literary *donnée*, the *literature anterior to us*, no, our nihilism bears on the possibility of being a writer, on the justification of such an activity. That's to say, in fact we want to be this (a writer), but not with an easy mind'.[2] The humility is in the

---

[1] Patricia McCarthy, reviewing Hamburger's *Collected Poems* (1985) in *Agenda* 23, pp. 3–4.

[2] Francis Ponge, *Pour Un Malherbe* (Paris, 1965), pp. 80–81.

writer's uneasiness about his own activity; the arrogance is in the assumption or the perception that this uneasiness was unknown to nearly all writers before modern times. To nearly all, but not to all. For Ponge was writing 'Pour un Malherbe', and in that past master of French poetry, François de Malherbe (1555-1628), he discovered an ancestor who, so he thought, shared this unease of the moderns and therefore had much to teach them: 'To the degree that Malherbe disdained Literature, even as he assigned to it rules that could not be more strict, he is very near to us . . .' Thus Ponge's rejection of literature anterior to himself and his contemporaries does not mean what we might suppose; in the presence of Malherbe (and of certain other masters from the French past – Montesquieu, Lautréamont), Ponge is very humble indeed.

Hamburger, who was exceptionally well versed in foreign poetries, had written about Ponge (though not, interestingly enough, about Oppen) in his wide-ranging survey of 1969, *The Truth of Poetry*, subtitled 'Tensions in Modern Poetry from Baudelaire to the 1960s'. There, speaking of Ponge as a writer of 'poetry that has no other content than things', whose free-verse poems essay to capture, one by one, things so diverse and commonplace as bread, shells, pebbles, cigarettes, Hamburger came by the crucial perception that 'The ego that captures them is fictitious, a mere carrier of language.' And it is thus we must speak, surely, of the ego in 'To Bridge a Lull'; humble in its readiness to sink its individuality, yet arrogant in its implied claim to release and articulate the wisdom of mankind as stored up or frozen in dictionaries. Just this is the poetic enterprise as Ponge conceives of it and attempts to practise it; and, if we believe him, it was the enterprise also of Malherbe. What no one denies in any case is that Malherbe was, for good or ill, the legislator of or for French *classicisme*; and indeed Ponge was vehement about this – a modern classicism, to which Ponge vowed himself, would take Malherbe as its model. To the extent that French *classicisme* corresponds to English 'classicism' (the fit is not perfect, but not without substance either), it seems that we might or must call 'To Bridge a Lull' a classical poem, written by a poet who on this showing must be called a classicist. It is remarkable that the poet who arrived at this destination should have begun his career refusing to abandon the rhetorical liberties of the English and German romantics.

Elsewhere in *The Truth of Poetry* Hamburger had remarked that 'much English poetry seems trivial to French readers'. Of course the question is moot whether French readers have the right to this sentiment. Hamburger considered this, and concluded that the right was dubious. But one reason for the French reader's loftiness has emerged from the testimony of Francis Ponge:

English-speakers have not yet acknowledged (that is to say, articulately) the problematic nature of the poetic activity in our day. In particular they have never or very seldom questioned the notion that the characteristic procedure of the lyrical poet is to station himself in a physical or mental landscape, and then have emotions about it. This is Philip Larkin's procedure in a much admired poem like 'Church-going' where, as many commentators have observed and as Larkin himself gave notice, nothing is to be gained from distinguishing between the author and the *persona* who speaks the poem, since in fact there is no such *persona* – Philip Larkin, the man, utters the poem *in propria persona*. The directness of this engagement with his subject has understandably appealed to many readers, and few of them have paused to consider that by such a procedure the matters observed in the poem are made subordinate to the quirky sensibility of the observer. By what right, if any, the lyrical sensibility can thus subjugate to itself the physical or historical realities which it chooses to play upon – that question, which has much exercised French or for instance Polish poets sine 1945, is never or very seldom considered by English-speakers. A poem like 'To Bridge a Lull' shows that Michael Hamburger has considered it, and has acknowledged the force of non-English objections and reservations.

In this he was not quite without precedent. At least one English poet before him had taken note, if not of Ponge, certainly of Malherbe. This was Bunting, who wrote in a private letter in 1953: 'I've been thinking . . . about how and where I got whatever I know and feel about poetry, and the more I think the bigger Malherbe's part in it seems . . . Horace gave the first inkling of how it was done (odes). Malherbe produced all I afterwards found in Ez's writing except what I'd already got from Horace.'[1] If we believe Bunting when he says that Malherbe's influence on him preceded that of 'Ez'(Ezra Pound) – and to be sure, as early as 1932 in *The New English Weekly* Bunting was already citing Racan's *Vie de M. de Malherbe* – we must be astonished by the independence of his judgement. For in 1926 St John Lucas, introducing a revised and expanded version of his *Oxford Book of French Verse* (originally 1907), could still write of 'the cold cleverness of Malherbe', and could expatiate, writing of Ronsard's and the *Pléiade*'s invention of poetic genres, 'To Malherbe we owe the perpetualizing of these forms reduced to their lowest terms of mechanical accuracy by a frigid intelligence.' Inflamed, Lucas went further:

[1] Quoted by Peter Quartermain in *Conjunctions*, 8 (1985).

Ronsard and Malherbe will be remembered together as the supreme examples of the ancient truth that the letter kills and the spirit makes alive. The Pléiade is immortal; Malherbe will be recalled only as the uninspired prophet of a dawn that had already risen, as the thin voice of an epoch which stole the lyrical forms of its despised forerunners and found nothing lyrical to say.

So much for the man whom Ponge was to extol as 'the Johann-Sebastian Bach of French literature'. Fifty years later, after Ponge had made his impassioned plea, D. G. Charlton could still tell his British readers: 'However, even in practice, he was seldom more than a conscientious craftsman. His influence was to help to make of French lyric verse, for nearly two centuries, something elegant and harmonious, but lacking the imaginative inspiration of true poetry . . .'[1] Lucas, and less excusably Charlton, are echoing, several generations in arrears, the sentiments of the French nineteenth-century historians of literature, Brunetière and Faguet, whom Ponge does not forget to excoriate. The nearest English analogue is the one that Renée Winegarten points to, in her *French Lyric Poetry in the Age of Malherbe* (Manchester, 1954), the first book in English to attempt, though timidly, to revise the received account of Malherbe; the partially analogous figure in English poetry is Ben Jonson, whom it was once common form to deride for thinking that he could correct Marlowe (as Malherbe corrected Desportes), and for wishing that Shakespeare had left himself time to revise and polish his verses. It was in the face of a consensus thus unquestioningly based on a romantic idea of the lyrical afflatus that Bunting first found, and then declared, Malherbe as his master. As late as 1969 he was recommending to the students of Newcastle University Malherbe (along with Dante!) as a model for 'precision of language'[2] It looks as if this English poet may have anticipated French poets in rehabilitating this one of their classics; and it looks too as if Bunting's *Briggflatts* is most truly seen as, on the grand scale, a monument of that modern classicism of which Hamburger's 'To Bridge a Lull' is another and admirable example.

---

[1] D. G. Charlton, *France. A Companion to French Studies* (1972, 1979), p. 324.
[2] *Courier* 4 (5 February 1969), Newcastle-on-Tyne.

Sylvia Townsend Warner, Posthumous

Early in *The Truth of Poetry*, Michael Hamburger had called to the witness-stand John Dryden:

> To Dryden the words that make up a poem were 'the image and ornament' of the thought which it was the primary function of that poem to 'convey to our apprehension', though Dryden was writing about verse translation, and even his practice as a poet and translator of poetry does not always accord with so rigid a definition. The modern poets . . . differ from Dryden in having no use for ornament . . .

Hamburger was not the first to use Dryden in this way as a whipping-boy, or at least as an exemplar of all that modern poetry has set its face against. Yet his scrupulous qualification ('his practice . . . does not always accord . . .') gives us warrant for thinking that Dryden's ways of writing are not so irrelevant to the modern poet as might appear. And in fact, Hamburger's qualification must be extended: if we read Dryden not as the scholars do (very properly, for their purposes) but as if John Dryden were our contemporary, there is hardly a verse of his, or a passage of his verses, which answers to 'so rigid a definition'.

A case in point came up when an octogenarian poet in 1975 responded to her interviewers:

> I'm more at home with seventeenth-century poetry than with any other. I'm a very great admirer of Dryden, because Dryden can say anything. He makes the most ridiculous statements and he can always bring them off. The line in 'The Hind and the Panther' that I particularly like – it's the last line of a section: 'The Lady of the spotted-muff began.' Now that is a line which is purely nonsensical and yet Dryden is so stately in his control of the medium and so sublime that one hears it almost with awe. When that line comes, one is merely delighted: Here is a splendid line.[1]

[1] *P. N. Review* 23 (1981), pp. 36-7.

Reading along with the scholars and restoring the line to its context, one discovers that 'Lady of the spotted muff' is a periphrasis for 'Panther', and that 'Panther' in turn is to be construed as the Church of England, here in conversation with the 'Hind', the Church of Rome, in accord with the bestiary-fable that has already for instance identified the Baptist Church with 'the Boar'. But having unpacked the emblematic fable in this way, have we arrived at 'the thought' to which 'the Lady of the spotted muff' is merely 'ornament'? Surely not; for the reason behind Dryden's choice of this periphrasis rather than some other just as logically apt, is still to seek. The 'muff' for the panther's paws is a discovery still as bizarre, as almost surreal, as when we first encountered it. And the comical-sinister effect is, we find if we bother to look, the culmination of a score or more lines all devoted to building up this same impression of demure yet dangerous comedy, as with deftly slight yet telling changes of focus we move from couplet to couplet or line to line. Of course none of this is 'ornament': Dryden's poetic theory supplied him only with a vocabulary that could not measure up to his practice.

No word from the 82-year-old Sylvia Townsend Warner was unconsidered. For instance 'sublime' – 'Dryden is so stately in his control of the medium and so sublime . . .'. Surely the sublime rules out any such toying with comedy? Not so; there was one moment in European art, the moment that we call 'the baroque', when – in architecture and sculpture as in literature – artists characteristically sought and sometimes achieved the sublime precisely by skirting the ludicrous. (Dryden's contemporary Crashaw notoriously teetered on that brink, and sometimes tumbled over it.) And it is notable that when Dryden explicitly claimed the sublime for himself – the first English writer to do so – it was in respect of a couplet which reported of Milton's angels in *Paradise Lost* that they 'Unguarded leave the passes of the sky/And all dissolv'd in hallelujahs lie'. Not only does this stop barely short of the ludicrous, Dryden in his defiant vindication of the lines showed that he was well aware of this – 'I have heard', he makes an imagined interlocutor say, 'of anchovies dissolved in sauce . . .'[1] Fired by Warner's enthusiasm for Dryden, and unpacking the justness of her few seemingly casual sentences, we may well remember Francis Ponge in *Pour Un Malherbe* deciding that 'the only classicism we may tolerate is that which is no more than the string of the baroque strung to its tautest.'

This superbly intelligent reader is she of whom *The Times* decided:

---

[1] Dryden, Preface to *The State of Innocence*.

'Sylvia Townsend Warner had a limited sense of the possibilities of poetry – her structures and procedures are conventional to a fault . . .'[1] Certainly Warner does not essay the baroque (whatever a twentieth-century baroque might be), nor does her verse anywhere sound like Dryden's. But that may be just the point: her inwardness with a verse-register so remote as Dryden's suggests very forcibly that her choice of a quite different register for herself (it is near to Robert Graves's, though no reviewer said so) was indeed a *choice*, not something she haplessly drifted into because she knew no better, or because her domicile in Hardy's Wessex made her Hardyesque by contagion. In fact there is nothing that is Hardyesque, though much that is Gravesian, about the late poem (first printed 1978) December 31st. St Silvester':

> Silvester, an old harmless pope,
> Stands at the year's end and gazes outward;
> And time his triple crown has shredded
> And winters have frayed out his cope.

> He is white as the weathered blade-bone;
> Bleached in the rim of his name like winter honesty
> He rattles on the stem of history
> And is venerated at Pisa alone.

> But green in his hand is a twig of olive;
> For in his reigning days he devised a reign
> Of peace with the Emperor Constantine;
> And he watches the years to see it arrive.

There is nothing to be done for readers who cannot see or hear that the 'rim' of the sixth line comprehends 'rime', or that in the next line 'rattles' implies dried seed-pods. The same readers will think that the half-rhymes are there only because the poet could not devise full ones, and they will not see, reaching back from the poem, a melancholy and compassionate view of all the history of Western Christendom.

Where Thomas Hardy is a presence in Warner's poems, he figures there only with a crucial difference. Claire Harman made the essential distinction: 'There is . . . an air of learned mischief . . . which is far from Hardyesque.' Denis Donoghue made the point

[1] *The Times*, 29 July 1982. Robert Nye reviewing Sylvia Townsend Warner, *Collected Poems*, ed. Claire Harman (Manchester, 1982).

more obliquely when he reviewed the *Selected Poems* (1985): 'Sylvia Townsend Warner was a novelist by profession and a poet at times, so she thought her poems the best of her. They are very fine, especially those which come in forms and manners which Hardy did most to establish and Ransom to guarantee.'[1] How could a Tennessean poet of the 1920s have 'guaranteed' the forms and manners that had been established by Hardy? The insular mind jibs and is bewildered. But any admirer of John Crowe Ransom sees what is meant: the quaintness of diction which Hardy practised unwittingly is by the later poet incorporated by deliberate design, so as to create an ironical though feelingful distance between himself and his reader. So too with Warner:

Though you should sorrow as only the young can sorrow,
Though you make tears your wine and your bread despair,
Though you lie down as to death and abjure the morrow,
Yet, come that tomorrow, you will rise up fair.

Sleep will unarm you for all the sad brain's diligence,
Betraying you tenderly as a mother can,
Sleep will betray you to the body's insolence
And you will revive not your own but your body's man.

Your limbs shall be strong, your triumphing flesh shall be mantled
With youth like the mantled cream-bowl, your eyes shall be bright:
Though the eyelid's nacre declare where the tears have trampled
We beholding shall own the blazon of an amorous night.

The quaint archaism 'own the blazon' opens up a space between the poet and us in which we wonder: Is the man in the poem being exalted? envied? jeered at? pitied? (With a Lesbian poet like Warner, the questions are pressing, though not to be answered crisply.) Hardy's quaintnesses do not work like this, but Ransom's do. Which is not to say that Warner had read the American poet – she could have got to this point on her own while pondering Hardy, with or without the help of Graves. She and Ransom achieve the pathetic, as Dryden achieved the sublime, by risking the comical. It seems rather disgraceful that whereas English readers like Robert Nye damned her with faint and baffled praise, this most English of poets (for *that* was the register she chose) should have been glimpsed at something like her true worth only by the Irishman Donoghue:

---

[1] 'Ten Poets', *London Review of Books*, 7 November 1985.

Poetry consisted, for Sylvia Townsend Warner, in the turning of an experience, real or so fully imagined as to be real, toward the decisiveness of song. Many of her poems seem to ask to be set to music by Delius, Vaughan Williams, Finzi or Peter Warlock; especially those about peopled and unpeopled landscapes, the first cuckoo in Spring, faith gained or lost, and doves come flying. As if waiting for them to be set, she gives them a provisional music of her own, in keeping with the sentiment that we should gather rosebuds while we may.

In fact a few of her poems had been set, fifty years before, by John Ireland. Among the more than 70 uncollected or unpublished poems discovered by Claire Harman – an astonishing harvest which by 1986 no one had bothered to rake through or gather in – there is poem after poem which aches for musical setting. Typical is 'East London Cemetery' (originally, 1927):

> Death keeps – an indifferent host –
> this house of call,
> whose sign-board wears no boast
> Save Beds for All.
>
> Narrow the bed, and bare,
> and none too sweet.
> No need, says Death, to air
> the single sheet.
>
> Comfort; says he, with shrug,
> is but degree,
> and London clay a rug
> like luxury,
>
> to him who wrapped his bones
> in the threadbare hood
> blood wove from weft of stones
> under warp of foot.

These heartfelt formalities were too recondite for Women's Liberation. Though the feminist Virago Press reprinted some of her novels, in the anthologies of women's verse Sylvia Townsend Warner did not supplant Kathleen Raine nor the endearingly eccentric Stevie Smith.

Kenneth Cox's Criticism

Kenneth Cox was born in 1916. So it is to be supposed that he had another career behind him when in 1966 he emerged as a powerful critic of poetry, with 'The Aesthetic of Basil Bunting'. This appeared in William Cookson's *Agenda*; and re-reading it, one perceives that it could have appeared nowhere else. Perceiving that, one may perceive also, not reluctantly but with some surprise, that *Agenda* can be considered the most important literary magazine in Britain over the past thirty years. In the short term that claim must seem to be extravagant, particularly if 'most important' is taken to mean 'most influential'. And yet in a longer perspective it may well appear some day that *Agenda* has exerted more influence than magazines much better funded and better distributed.

It began in 1955 when William Cookson, then sixteen, sent some verses to Ezra Pound, who responded by sending a four-page publication called *Strike*, edited by William McNaughton. Two years later, when Cookson was editing a Westminster School literary magazine, *The Trifler*, he sent Pound a copy in which he had reviewed *Rock-drill*. Pound responded with animation. He was then still incarcerated in St Elizabeth's Hospital in Washington D.C. After his release in 1958 and his return to Italy, Pound arranged for William Cookson and his mother to visit him there. And, wrote Cookson, 'the idea of *Agenda* grew from this visit'. There could hardly be a more telling example of how the continuity of literary culture, the passing on of necessary wisdom from one literary generation to another, is effected in our days subterraneously, quite independent of the fellows of Oxbridge colleges, who in widely read publications make or break literary reputations, week by week or month by month. In 1979/80, in an *Agenda* designated 'Twenty-First Anniversary Ezra Pound Special Issue', Cookson printed the letters that Pound sent him at this period, in which we see the veteran poet bombarding the Oxford undergraduate Cookson with generous, copious and highly specific advice, none of it apposite to the British situation that Cookson was bemusedly trying to influence nor, so far as we can see, to Cookson's own taste and temperament. No matter! Cookson consistently thereafter conducted *Agenda* as a distinctively Poundian magazine, committed to espousing and explaining writers who either

had won Pound's approval, or might have been expected to win
it: for instance David Jones, Hugh MacDiarmid, Wyndham Lewis,
Bunting, Louis Zukofsky. And it did not disturb William Cookson,
nor apparently *Agenda*'s readers, that in nearly every issue writing
by or about these difficult masters has appeared cheek by jowl with
tremulous water-colours in verse by Oxonian poetasters, their work
duly applauded in the review-pages by others of their kind. This is a
pity; in particular it is a pity that Cookson has never assembled, per-
haps never tried to assemble, a team of responsible reviewers, nor has
allowed his reviewers enough space. But in the end this does not mat-
ter. The water-colourists evidently appeal to one part of Cookson's
sensibility, as the Poundians to another. What we have in any case
is a magazine conducted (and maintained through thirty years – how
funded is Cookson's secret) in serene indifference to 'the public', to
what is in or out of fashion. In matters like typography, proof-
reading and indexing *Agenda* has not become much less amateurish
than it was to start with; but if in these ways it can hardly qualify as
what is called 'a scholarly resource', the fact remains that it has con-
sistently published documents, both primary and secondary, such as
no student of twentieth-century poetry can afford to ignore. Among
such documents are undoubtedly some pieces by Kenneth Cox.

Cox and Cookson may be called mavericks, but with a difference.
At a time when the expected postures of the maverick – flashiness,
audacity, brutal belligerence – were being courted and welcomed
by main-line journals like *The London Review of Books*, Cox's and
Cookson's maverick independence expressed itself in an unwonted
courtliness, equanimity, even a touch of pedantry. Thus, when Cox
wanted to stress Bunting's debt to the Border ballads rather than to
Ezra Pound's precedent, he wrote of the ballads: 'The re-emergence
of this tradition may be of interest to those critics who stress Mr
Bunting's acknowledged obligations to Ezra Pound and who ask
to what extent and in what manner the example of the American
master can be assimilated to a native heritage'. Such walking on stilts
marvellously served T. S. Eliot's subversive purposes in his prose of
the 1920s, but forty years later the stratagem had been rumbled and
seemed quaint. A later Eliot is equally audible, at times: 'there is also
to be found in his verse a slower movement keeping time not with
the movements or gait of the body but with the longer stronger
movement of the sea.' Such flatulence infects not just Cox's phrasing
but even his understanding of certain poems, as we shall see. But
these uncertain mannerisms are insignificant when set beside Cox's
peroration:

Skills and accidents by which we make contact with poets distant and past, or by which we seem to establish a relation with the non-human world, convince us that in cultivating the art we are not just playing with words, toys of our own invention, but that we do indeed perform, in ways we cannot understand but know for sure, parts in a rite able to dignify and perpetuate our common life. It may also be allowed that in obeying its laws we do a little to appease the dead.

Where else in 1966 (or since, for that matter) do we find the essential dignity and necessity of poetry affirmed with such nicety and yet such gravity, such weight?

The poem by Bunting that Cox seems to misread is *The Spoils* (1951). Of this he wrote:

> The dominant theme of this poem is that of opposition between the calculating and the reckless. The calculator (moneylender, administrator, policeman) imposes arbitrary rule and measure; the reckless (singer, soldier, seaman) gives without counting. The difference between them is determined by the presence of death. The calculator works to an end beyond the scope of an individual lifespan, but it is the risk of death that gives zest to life: without death life is not worth living. This bourgeois-romantic dichotomy is counterpointed by a secondary opposition running in the contrary direction. In spite of the care and precision of their operations the art of the calculating is rhetorical and false: *Roman exaggeration and the leaden mind of Egypt*. But the art of the gay in the shadow of death is cool and fine: it is by taking risks that we preserve proportion.

Although oppositions of this kind are certainly at work in Bunting's poem, they are dispiritingly familiar, as the sad phrase 'bourgeois-romantic dichotomy' acknowledges. What is certain is that the verse which Cox quotes in italics belongs in a passage that the poet intended should carry a much more specific and unexpected meaning:

> For all that, the Seljuks avoided
> Roman exaggeration and the leaden mind of Egypt
> and withered precariously on the bough
> with patience and public spirit.
> O public spirit!
>
> Prayers to band cities and brigade men
> lest there be more wills than one:
> but God is the dividing sword.

The importance that Bunting gave to this passage was to appear in 1974, in reminiscences of Yeats which appeared in (where else?) *Agenda*. Here Bunting at one point writes of Yeats's, also Pound's and Eliot's, sympathy with Fascism:

> What these poets and many other writers really had in common was a love of order. With order in society it matters little whether you are rich or poor, you will not be harassed by perpetual changes of fortune . . .
> . . . Weighing this up, if it is worth weighing at all, you must of course allow for my conviction that 'God is the dividing sword', and that order is no more than a rather unfortunate accident that sometimes hampers civilization. But my purpose is only to remind some critics that Yeats's love of order is something he shared with Dante and Shakespeare and probably far more than half of the world's great poets, as well as with nearly all the philosophers and historians.

Three years later, when an interviewer pressed him on these sentences about Yeats, Bunting explained: ' "God is the dividing sword" is a quotation from my poem "The Spoils" . . . That order is an unfortunate accident you can verify at once by seeing what happened when the Roman Empire succeeded in establishing itself a "pax Romana" on Mediterranean lands. Everything went flat. Things had been going fine up till then.'[1] As always with Bunting, in prose or in conversation, the throw-away colloquialisms are misleading; Bunting's verdict on the *pax Romana*, the 'Augustan peace', is deeply considered. It sets him irreconcilably at odds with another poet who had been in some technical respects his master: not Yeats, and not Pound, but Eliot. For Eliot, editor of *The Criterion* and author of 'What is a Classic?' (1944), had declared himself fully persuaded by Virgil's vision of the *imperium* of Augustus as a world-rule divinely appointed, that appointment acknowledged through later centuries by the appellation, 'The Holy Roman Empire'. The great duty and travail of European civilization from Virgil's day to ours was, so Eliot thought, the wedding of that inspired institution, the *imperium*, with another, the *ecclesia* – a consummation that Eliot went so far as to think had been foreseen and foretold by Virgil in the famous Pollio eclogue. In all this Eliot was proudly aware of thinking along the same lines as Dante and many medieval jurists; it remained for Frances Yates and Frank

---

[1] Dale Reagan, in *Montemora* (1977), excerpted in C. F. Terrell (ed.), *Basil Bunting. Man and Poet* (1981), pp. 409-10.

Kermode[1] to show how the conception had been held to through
the post-Reformation centuries, in English not just by a poet like
Dryden who has been frequently tagged 'Augustan', but also by
an Elizabethan Calvinist such as Spenser. Bunting was surely not
exaggerating when he quietly acknowledged that his own repu-
diation of such visions of world-order (devoted though he was to
Dante) set him at odds with 'more than half of the world's great
poets, as well as with nearly all the philosophers and historians.'

On the other hand, Bunting does not reject such visions of order in
the interests of an anarchic or bohemian individualism. And the lines
about the Seljuks make this clear, for in them Bunting is praising
– temperately to be sure, and with reservations – one sort of civic
order, that of Persia in the eleventh and twelfth centuries under the
originally Turkish Seljuk dynasty. The Seljuk rulers are praised for
not seeking to impose a monolithic public order like that of the
Roman Empire or of ancient Egypt.

The purpose of this exposition is not to triumph over Kenneth
Cox for not having available to him, in 1966, documents that
would point to what Bunting had in mind. What is important is
to establish that Bunting did have, as every great poet must have, a
politics, and a philosophy of history. Cox cannot be blamed for not
noticing this, for no one else noticed it. It went unnoticed, we may
think, because no one understood the English tradition that Bunting
was always speaking for and speaking out of. The Quakerism that
this bibulous and sometimes profane poet professed has been treated
with, at best, a sort of baffled respect. Yet Bunting insisted on it, for
instance in his reminiscences of Yeats. It may help to recall that the
Society of Friends is one of the Nonconformist communions. For the
Seljuks' civic order, it seems fair to say, is akin to that advocated by
responsible spokesmen of those communions down the centuries: an
imposed conformity or uniformity is what they must and will resist,
even as they deny that such uniformity is a prerequisite of any effec-
tive order in the state. 'God is the dividing sword' because He divides
the 'gathered churches' of Dissent from the majority not so 'gath-
ered'; and also, perhaps less happily, because He divides one such
ingathering (for instance, Presbyterian) from another (for instance,
Baptist). The divisions that He makes compassionately acknowledge
the diversity of human gifts and callings; and the divisions are not
such as to prevent Baptists and Presbyterians and Anglicans from
making common cause in the maintenance of public order, so long
as that order is sufficiently elastic. The demoralized silence of the
Nonconformists on these issues, and their acquiescence in being

---

[1] See Frank Kermode, *The Classic* (London, 1975), *passim*.

dragooned into the silent majority of the political Left, seem to have lamentably distorted British thinking about politics since long before 1960. Bunting, for those who would listen, gave the Nonconformists once again a voice.

In 1974 Cox reviewed for *Agenda* C. H. Sisson's *In the Trojan Ditch*. He may have had some difficulty with the assignment, for *Agenda* had by implication firmly committed itself in favour of Sisson during long years when no other magazine of any note would publish his poems. Certainly, though the tone was respectful and welcoming ('A review can only indicate the vigour and variety of Sisson's writing'), Cox with remarkable suavity managed to combine this with searching questions and discomforts about some of Sisson's procedures. Thus, remarking with witty penetration that Sisson is 'a recalcitrant sectary like Milton, a Non-Juror or an Old Believer', Cox pointed out that such people run the risk of an unappealing querulousness – 'an injured nobility, the obsessiveness of the crank'. Sisson accordingly had problems with his diction, and came up with solutions that Cox did not much like. 'Sisson favours hyperbole, a figure which suits the crusty, magisterial style often affected by Latinists. He also uses various kinds of play or guise where the voice may sound self-conscious or equivocal. Either way leaves the centre hollow and diminishes credence.' This is very searching and demanding criticism, such as one reserves for authors of real importance, and Cox's account of Sisson, brief though it necessarily was, conveys just that impression. Sisson, if he took note of this review (and there is some reason to think that he did), would have smarted under such rebukes and yet in the end should have been gratified.

However, what is involved is something far-reaching. Cox in this piece seems to imply that all poets, not just those who have out-moded and cranky views, must abjure firmly held opinions and convictions, or else if they have such convictions must suppress them in, and for the sake of, their poems. So much is implied by a memorably insolent throw-away, early in the review: 'There appears to remain the relic of a belief that poetry consists in the making of remarkable statements . . .' Rather plainly, if Cox has heard the expression, 'a poetry of statement', he regards the expression, and the notion behind it, as a 'relic', designating a sort of poetry that has been conclusively superseded, for which in the modern world no place can be found. Curiously, at Cox's prompting or else independently, Sisson, as he moved on from *In The Trojan Ditch*, seems to have agreed with him; not only by implication in his later poems but explicitly, in certain pages of *PN Review*, a magazine that for a time in the 1970s he co-edited, Sisson seems to have agreed that 'poetry of statement' is a contradiction in terms. Holding such views, Cox predictably scouted Sisson's claims to have aimed at 'the plain style'. (Finely and justly he says, of Sisson's translations from Catullus, 'Rather than helping him attain plainness the exercise, a limbering up, appears to have enabled Sisson to derive long fluent movements from educated English conversation and to diversify blunt generalities with something of its modesty, artifice and banter.') And as predictably, he decides that the best things in the collection are the poems where Sisson is furthest from statement, such as the Virgilian 'In Insula Avalona', which Cox does not scruple to call, approvingly, 'romantic'. (However, not much in Cox's account is predictable; he applauds for instance 'A Reading of Vergil's Eclogues', a sustained performance by Sisson which has never yet attracted the surely admiring attention that it deserves.)

The document most often cited, to vindicate a prejudice against poetry of argument and ratiocination is a famous letter by Keats, in which he speaks of '*Negative Capability*, that is when man is capable of being in uncertainties, Mysteries, doubts, without any irritable reaching after fact and reason.' This is often cited by admirers of Geoffrey Hill, who certainly is very far from writing a poetry of statement in the plain style that such poetry demands. It is therefore unexpected that Cox should have assailed Hill's poetry very vehemently.[1] His attack (for that is what it is) did not appear in *Agenda*, where indeed it could not easily have been accommodated, for Cookson had promoted Hill as assiduously as Sisson. In its intemperance this piece is unlike any other by Cox, and it may well be felt that it overshoots its objective. From Hill's *For the Unfallen*, 1959 ('the writing is inflated and resonant in the imperial manner but of a thicker weave'), through his *King Log*, 1966 ('bombast . . . a boring exercise in a technique to be adapted later: the heaping up of phrases held together by nothing but tonality and vague association with a subject'), to *Tenebrae*, 1978 ('movement slowed to a processional drag . . . all inanimate, embalmed . . . like being beaten about the head with balloons') Cox's account of Hill's career certainly suffers from over-kill. (The only work he can admire, and that grudgingly, is in the prose 'canticles' of *Mercian Hymns*, 1971.) But it is important to recognize that this is not just a spurt of malice on Cox's part; his admiration for the spare and stripped-down language of Robert Creeley and Lorine Niedecker and Louis Zukofsky, or in Britain of Bunting and Tom Pickard, could not help but make him suspicious of Sisson's more elaborate diction, and wholly out of patience with

---

[1] *Montemora* 7 (New York, 1980), pp. 223–24.

the sumptuous indirections of Hill. Catholicity of taste is all very well, but certain ways of using language are incompatible with certain others. This is not often acknowledged; and if there is any respectable reason why no British publisher has been ready to collect Kenneth Cox's criticism into a book, it may well be his fierce repudiation of the well-regarded Geoffrey Hill. Meanwhile we perceive that what Cox most esteems in poetic language is not plainness but limpidity – as he says admiringly of Sisson's *Eclogues*, 'lines pure water'.

There is one place in the review of Sisson where Cox's suavity overbalances: 'The application of traditional forms to present purposes, dear to English habit, succeeds to the extent that it introduces into the model handed down some element not apparently at variance with it but actually different. Such being the process of language itself, the work of the poet is mainly conservative and selective.' It is hard to read the first of these sentences except as saying that the method being discussed succeeds when it succeeds. And the second sentence, by invoking 'the process of language itself', seems to imply that the 'conservative' and 'selective' writer who applies traditional forms to present purposes is the true poet, or else the best sort of poet. But this is not what Cox means, as we can see from the surely jeering interjection 'dear to English habit', even if we discount his admiration of American poets like Zukofsky and Niedecker who proceed quite otherwise. There seems no way of working out what he meant to say.

Cox's masterpiece in criticism, 'The Poetry of Hugh MacDiarmid', appeared not in *Agenda* but (in its perfected form) in Australia.[1] It is the most thorough-going vindication yet attempted of MacDiarmid's verse-writing as a whole. To launch such a massive rescue-operation, Cox has to occupy a position of extreme relativism about what is good in poetry, what is bad; for, as he plainly tells us, he is concerned with a body of poetry in which 'banalities and audacities become difficult to tell apart'. Accordingly, he is quite frank: 'Some will prefer appeal to a principle supposed universally valid. This may be possible but it cannot be taken for granted that universal principles exist, any that do will be difficult to discover and any discovered are likely to prove too vague to be much use.' (All very well; but by what principles, then, is Geoffrey Hill's practice found wanting? And equally, by what principles is Pound's *Hugh Selwyn Mauberley* found to be, in the essay on Bunting, 'poetry of the second order but

[1] *Scripsi* (Melbourne, 1982) Vol. 1, 3-4.

the finest quality'? In practice, no critic is as much of a relativist as he may pretend and fondly suppose.)

What Cox has particularly in his sights is an allegedly universal principle, ill-advisedly imported from the French and given respectability in a last despairing book by Lionel Trilling. For he goes on to say: 'The fashionable test for "authenticity" is no help either, for what it establishes is not the authentic, the sincere utterance of real people, but the ability to sound authentic and this is a verbal faculty whose relation to experience, if any, is retrograde and indirect.' This is a hard saying, but obviously true; and it makes nonsense of much resolutely anti-academic criticism of the 1960s and after. The point is very important as regards MacDiarmid, because he practises what Cox calls 'the method of synthetic composition', a method not peculiar to Scottish literature but characteristic of it, in which burlesque, parody, excerptings, refashionings of various kinds, figure largely. As Cox says, 'There is little point in examining such writing for verbal vestiges of firsthand knowledge: it is not that sort of thing.'

MacDiarmid's 'sort of thing' offended against more long-settled notions, dating back to the letters of Keats:

> In contradiction to a widely accepted opinion about the function of poetry MacDiarmid's may be said to have a palpable design on the reader. Its intention, if intention can be inferred from effect, is chiefly to exalt. To this end it uses a process of persuasion extending beyond all possibility of demur or misapprehension. Energy is provided by an ardent will to instruct and admonish: even when not engaged in polemic the writing tends to remain on one insistent tone and to exert a quasipedagogic force. So far from assuming the presence of a sympathetic audience it sets out to overcome the resistance of one it expects to find if not hostile at least ignorant indifferent or incredulous. It extends itself, emphasises, illustrates, reiterates, quotes. Values are quantitative: longwindedness for example becomes a merit (it may be renamed stamina) and excellence in general lies less in satisfying standards of workmanship, as in the crafts, than in breaking records and beating opponents, as in sport.

Here one sees the peculiar excellence of Cox as a critic, and it is an excellence that depends on his deferring, if necessary indefinitely, all value-judgements. He is incomparable simply as a *describer* of a poet's distinctive procedures; and his descriptions can be so accurate only because what he discerns is offered with the unstated qualification, 'for good or ill'. There can be no doubt that MacDiarmid's characteristic procedures are indeed what these sentences define.

On the other hand all but the most fervent admirers of the poet have singled out for approval those parts of his work where he is least characteristic, least himself. Because he is determined to see the poet *as a whole*, Cox cannot endorse such judgements, and so his account of MacDiarmid is strikingly revisionist. Those many readers for instance who have valued most the Lallans lyrics of *Sangschaw* and *Pennywheep*, written in the 1920s, have to be rapped over the knuckles:

> His second and third books are written in Scots, natural or syn-
> thetic, but their inspiration is German. A number of short poems
> see the earth as if from outer space and make high-flown far-
> fetched statements equating the terrestrial with the cosmic. Some
> of these poems have appeared in anthologies and become well
> known. The best have an eerie or a poignant beauty but many
> betray formula: a lilt, a word or two out of Jamieson, and away
> to the empyrean.

So too with *A Drunk Man Looks at the Thistle* (1926): 'It has been called a classic but it is not that. It is a long ill-ordered high-spirited unstable and apparently spontaneous effusion, by turns witty and senseless, *but above all things lively*: nothing like it since Byron.' The naming of Byron is particularly worth thinking about.

In place of these poems generally esteemed that Cox would like to discredit somewhat, he offers for approval two later poems more characteristic: 'On a Raised Beach' (1935), which has indeed found its admirers in the past; and 'Tam o' the Wilds and the Many-faced Mystery' (1934), a stanzaic poem nearly four hundred lines long which was omitted (such were the vagaries of MacDiarmid's self-editing) from both of the so-called *Collected Poems* published in the 1960s.

After giving a long and representative quotation from what MacDiarmid considered his *magnum opus* (or as much of it as he ever managed), *In Memoriam James Joyce* (1955), Cox sums up his essay in a coruscating last section:

> Whatever MacDiarmid wrote he wrote out of a largeness of mind,
> with a superabundance of matter, from the furthermost reach of
> his thought. Few men can have been less petty or less prudent.
> Inseparable from writing others would blush to see in print is
> poetry nobody else could have written of a kind not many would
> have dared to attempt . . .
>   He had a head for heights and was fascinated by the diversity
> of detail at the fringes. Brilliantly as his catalogues of particulars

are written they are not, like those of Joyce or Rabelais, games of a mind exulting in its virtuosity but Whitman-like acts of humility and wonder. The middle-ground he was ignorant of and uninterested in . . .

He had the facility and the fallibility of the journalist and no finesse at all.

There is only one of the older critics in English who delineates an author's characteristics thus impassively. It is the past master whose unmistakable cadences are at one point audaciously echoed: 'If not among the most intelligent of the poets he is among the least superstitious. His intellect was more capacious than acute, its range extremely wide, his knowledge of men not large, his emotional base rather narrow.' This is the note of Johnson; and those who take Johnson to be the most judicial of critics (or, as the modern vulgarism has it, the most *judgemental*) cannot have much frequented his *Lives of the English Poets*, where page after luminous page is devoted to just such sharp and exact delineations of what in one poet's work distinguishes him from all others.

If in the end one decides that Cox's essay is special pleading after all, the plea is of a sort that could be entered only by a critic of whom one might say, as Cox says of MacDiarmid, 'few men can have been less petty or less prudent'. To rebut his case, or turn the force of it, one is driven back behind theoretical principle into considering the history of our culture, into pondering for instance the casual admission that MacDiarmid 'had no use for the Mediterranean tradition'. We can come to a firm decision about MacDiarmid only when we have severally considered just how much use *we* have for that tradition. It is only the finest criticism that thus forces us back into re-examining our real or supposed inheritances.

Seamus Heaney's Station Island

'Station Island' is the title both of a poem and of the collection in which that poem appears (London 1984, New York 1985). The two are intricately related; we are not to understand, 'Station Island & Other Poems'. The volume is elaborately assembled. The title-poem, loosely strung on the narrative of a penitential pilgrimage to St Patrick's Purgatory (or 'Station Island') on Lough Derg in Donegal, occupies thirty-three pages in the middle of the book; it is prefaced by no less than twenty-six poems, constituting 'Part 1', and followed by twenty more sub-titled, 'Part 111: Sweeney Redivivus'. This last section is particularly significant because it relates *Station Island* to Heaney's translation (1984) of *Buile Suibhne*, an Irish epic (of sorts) composed some time between 1200 and 1500, known to Heaney in the bilingual edition of J. G. O'Keefe (1913).

The poem 'Station Island' is insistently Dantesque, in several ways but especially because it is structured, like much of *The Divine Comedy*, around dialogue in *oratio recta* between the poet-pilgrim and the ghosts of some recently dead. The attempt thus to connect this European classic with the indigenous *Buile Suibhne* suggests that among all Heaney's Anglo-Irish predecessors J. M. Synge rather than Yeats has been his model and mentor; for Synge, notably in his translations from Petrarch, was in the generation of the so-called Irish Literary Renaissance the one who saw most clearly that his task was to prove Ireland's claim to an honourable part in European civilization, rather than offering a beguiling or challenging alternative to that shared tradition. Heaney's ambition or presumption should have been very clear. He was not content to be some sort of neo-Georgian with an Irish accent, like Francis Ledwidge, though some British admirers were happy to take him on those terms. More pointedly, though he has been welcomed both in the USA and the UK in circles that are happy to call themselves 'post-modernist', his ambitions outstripped theirs also. He aimed, like Synge before him and like Joyce, who is given the last word at the end of 'Station Island', to contribute to international modernism from his special but not extraneous Irish standpoint. This dimension of his endeavour was seldom appreciated, even by those readers most devoted to him; and on several pages of *Station Island* we can see Heaney trying to throw off the reputation and the following that his earlier less exacting collections had brought him.

The Dantescan ambition, which had been foreshadowed in some pieces in his preceding collection *Field Work* (1979), was not altogether vindicated in 'Station Island', if only because, at least until Section 1X of that poem, Heaney's versification was too permissively various to bear the weight of meaning that the Dantesque authority demands. (Only in the last dozen lines of the poem is the pentameter, always present though continually denied, allowed to assert itself.) A better, more persuasive instance of how Dante's achievement challenged Heaney is in one of the prefatory poems from Part 1, 'Sandstone Keepsake':

> It is a kind of chalky russet
> solidified gourd, sedimentary
> and so reliably dense and bricky
> I often clasp it and throw it from hand to hand.
>
> It was ruddier with an underwater
> hint of contusion, when I lifted it,
> wading a shingle beach on Inishowen.
> Across the estuary light after light
>
> came on silently round the perimeter
> of the camp. A stone from Phlegethon,
> bloodied on the bed of hell's hot river?
> Evening frost and the salt water
>
> made my hand smoke, as if I'd plucked the heart
> that damned Guy de Montfort to the boiling flood –
> but not really, though I remembered
> his victim's heart in its casket, long venerated.
>
> Anyhow, there I was with the wet red stone
> in my hand, staring across at the watch-towers
> from my free state of image and allusion,
> swooped on, then dropped by trained binoculars:
>
> a silhouette not worth bothering about,
> out for the evening in scarf and waders
> and not about to set times wrong or right,
> stooping along, one of the venerators.

In this poem, where the licentiously variable metre does little harm since it is not required to carry any narrative impetus, the elaborate allusion to Dante (Guy de Montfort is in *Inferno* X11, 118-20) may seem to be dragged in by the ears. But it is not so, as we see in succeeding lines with 'my free state of image and allusion', and especially in the penultimate line which alludes to a famous poem by Robert Frost. The point is crucial: to the Irish poet, as to no conceivable English or American poet, Dante presents himself first and foremost as a poet who was politically partisan, who passed vengeful judgements which could not be appealed against. Heaney had been under continual pressure, from his Irish and sometimes his British readers, to declare himself for one side or the other of the murderous conflict that since 1969 overtly, and before that covertly, had riven apart his native Ulster. The *Station Island* volume shows, not for the first time, Heaney recognizing the legitimacy or at least the plausibility of this demand upon him, and confessing – now ashamedly, now defiantly – how impossible it was for him to meet it. This is the significance, sardonic and self-accusing, of 'my free state of image and allusion'.

In *Station Island* there are many, in truth rather too many, confessions like this of equivocation, of what can be mistaken for an aesthete's detachment. What is notable however is that Heaney, unlike for instance his English peer Geoffrey Hill, refuses to set up an equation in which one side cancels out the other, leaving us with an ironic zero. This is the significance of Sweeney, who represents a transcendence.

It must be allowed that *Sweeney Astray* or *Buile Suibhne* would seem to be, without the 'Sweeney Redivivus' section of *Station Island*, only a quaintly antique curio from the Gaelic past. In the context that Heaney has created for it, it becomes an Ovidian poem, a *metamorphosis*: the ancient Irish king, transformed by the curse of St Ronan into a bird, becomes, as Heaney hints quite heavily, a symbol of the poet whose accursed fate it is, as well as his salvation, to wing over and above the Irish factions locked in bloody and inconclusible conflict. Thus it is appropriate that in the 'Sweeney Redivivus' sequence we come across 'An Artist'.

> I love the thought of his anger.
> His obstinacy against the rock, his coercion,
> of the substance from green apples.
>
> The way he was a dog barking
> At the image of himself barking.
> And his hatred of his own embrace
> of working as the only thing that worked –
> the vulgarity of expecting ever

> gratitude or admiration, which
> would mean a stealing from him.
>
> The way his fortitude held and hardened
> because he did what he knew.
> His fortitude like a hurled *boule*
> travelling unpainted space
> behind the apple and behind the mountain.

If the last three lines leave us in no doubt that the name of this artist is Paul Cézanne, yet if we have read Section X11 of 'Station Island' it will be clear that the name might as well be James Joyce. It is important in fact that we *should* have read that passage before this one, for Heaney from the first time he appeared before the public has never lacked for 'gratitude or admiration'; and without the evidence of his searching inquisition by the shade of Joyce, we might well feel that his identification with artists neglected and misunderstood was something he came by too cheaply. It must be said, however, that another Irish name besides Joyce's which could have been supplied in this place was that of Austin Clarke; and it is disappointing that in Clarke's Irish generation the poet who most commands Heaney's allegiance is, unaccountably, Patrick Kavanagh.

The poet's metamorphosis into a bird is earnestly embraced as a destiny by the author of 'On the Road':

> In my hand
> like a wrested trophy,
> the empty round
> of the steering wheel.
>
> The trance of driving
> made all roads one:
> the seraph-haunted, Tuscan
> footpath, the green
>
> oak-alleys of the Dordogne
> or that track through corn
> where the rich young man
> asked his question –
>
> *Master, what must I*
> *do to be saved?*
> Or the road where the bird
> with an earth-red back

and a white and black
tail, like parquet
of flint and jet,
wheeled over me

in visitation.
Sell all you have
and give to the poor.
I was up and away

like a human soul
that plumes from the mouth
in undulant, tenor
black-letter Latin.

I was one for sorrow,
Noah's dove,
a panicked shadow
crossing the deerpath . . .

This, the last poem of Part 111 of *Station Island*, responds to the last poem of Part 1:

No birds came, but I waited

among briars and stones, or whispered
or broke the watery gossamers

if I moved a muscle.
'Come back to us,' they said, 'in harvest,

when we hide in the stooked corn,
when the gundogs can hardly retrieve

what's brought down.' And I saw myself
rising to move in that dissimulation,

top-knotted, masked in sheaves, noting
the fall of birds: a rich young man

leaving everything he had
for a migrant solitude.

What he leaves, what he gives to the poor, includes the short-sighted quasi-political certainties that they perhaps need, which he must do without and will withhold from them.

In between had come the twelve sections of the poem, 'Station Island', several of them in an approximation to *terza rima*; and if most of these are disappointing as regards versification, in diction and narrative impetus they just about give Heaney the right to put Dante by as firmly as he seems to do when he equates 'the seraph-haunted, Tuscan/footpath' with 'the green/ oak-alleys of Dordogne'. This is one modern poet who emerges from his prolonged encounter with Dante not daunted nor abashed; he pursues an alternative path – Ovidian, we might say, rather than Dantesque. It cannot be accidental that the poet who thus survives the Dantesque encounter is a Roman Catholic, whose verse recording the encounter is shot through with memories of his inherited Romanism and with allusions to Scripture.

It must be said that by 1987, it had become difficult for an English reader to invoke such illustrious perspectives as 'Ovidian' and 'Dantesque' in relation to Seamus Heaney, so nimble as he had shown himself in manipulating the poetry market and the poetry-reading circuit. He had shown himself lamentably ready to fall in with catchpenny enterprises in Britain like the Arvon Poetry Competitions or the Faber anthology that he edited with Ted Hughes, *The Rattle Bag* (1982). The mere title of that collection impudently proclaimed its lack of any rationale. In London, many anthologies of the 1980s have proffered themselves under titles not much less perfunctory, and poets of some repute have readily lent their names to such dubious and redundant compilations. In the apparently still lucrative British market for anthologies, the principal competitors (capping each other's bright ideas, trumping each other's tricks) have been Oxford University Press, Penguin Books, Faber and Faber. All three are publishing houses with something to be proud of in their past; all three have for some years now cynically played to the prejudices of an ill-educated or half-educated and trivializing public. The most distressing case is surely Faber, once T. S. Eliot's publishing house which, so long as he was involved, was without doubt the most respectable imprint for twentieth-century poetry. For Heaney and others to fall in with their publishers' manipulations seemed dependent on the assumption that poets, merely by declaring themselves such, were absolved from civic responsibility.

And yet Heaney, it should be plain, has never sought such absolution; as an Irishman writing in the first place for the Irish, his refusal to endorse unequivocally one or the other bigoted faction in his native Ulster has been, not a shucking off of responsibility, but (implausible as this must seem to the hard-liners on both sides) an admirably tenacious and costly assertion of just such responsibility. The poet has a civic duty, which Heaney has recognized, though Dante did not, to resist the seductive simplifications of the one party as of the other. Heaney, however, unlike such precursors as Clarke and Kavanagh, has had to reckon with three audiences: British and American as well as Irish. Probably no one could have behaved responsibly to these three different constituencies all at the same time. So it is not really surprising, though it is lamentable, that he has been less responsible in dealing with his British audience than with his notably fewer and less generous Irish readers. In Ireland, one would like to believe, he practises and exemplifies poetry as a one-man manufacturing industry; in England on the contrary he represents a *service* industry. And the service that he offers is (one thinks of Tom Moore) conspicuously consumer-friendly.

Afterword

From time to time in these pages mention has been made of 'modernism' and 'modernists'. And it may be objected that nowhere has modernism been defined. But I believe I may plead a historian's privilege: for so many years now has 'modernist' been the tag attached to Pound and Eliot, Yeats and Wallace Stevens, Joyce and Wyndham Lewis, that the grouping of them under that rubric may be taken as itself a historical fact, a convenience, an allowable short-cut. What we mean or may mean by thus characterizing them, or any one of them, is a legitimate question, but one for the critic or, if for the historian, for the historian of a much earlier period than 1960 to 1985. In what sense, if at all, can MacDiarmid or Austin Clarke or David Jones be called 'modernist'? That too is a legitimate question, but also, I have to think, a sterile one. Even with Bunting, in whose case the question cannot be avoided because of his documented association with Eliot and Pound and Yeats, consideration of his alleged modernism is likely to deflect attention from what is most distinctive, and distinctly valuable, in his achievement. Modernism in the arts was a historically bounded phenomenon of the early twentieth century; to invoke it in the second half of the century is to risk being distracted.

This is very far from saying that a responsible English-language poet in the 1980s can safely proceed as if Ezra Pound had never written. The artistic monuments remain, and remain potent; it is only the flags which once flew over them that come to seem in time tattered and grubby and irrelevant. 'Post-modernism' is the awkward formula now in use that tries, not very successfully, to acknowledge in this way how the modernist masters are at once sharply pertinent to our needs and yet distracting. We are surely right to think that taking up positions for and against 'modernism' is in 1985 an absurd anachronism; the trouble is, as usual, to take care that in emptying out that bath-water we do not also lose certain babies.

One baby that is in every danger of being sluiced away with the bath-water is the modernist conviction that poetry is only one of the arts, and that all the arts in some ways hang together. Another is the perception that artistic endeavour is international, multi-ethnic and therefore, in the case of the linguistic arts, multi-lingual.

Charles Tomlinson (b. 1927) is in his generation the British poet who has shown himself most alert to these dangers, and most alarmed by them. In his four Clark Lectures for Trinity College, Cambridge (*Poetry and Metamorphosis*, Cambridge, 1983), Tomlinson seemed to adumbrate nothing less than a cultural history of the twentieth century, and of the role of the United Kingdom in that history. He made it clear that the Britain he spoke for and spoke out of was one that most Britons were happy to think defunct: the Britain of Ford Madox Ford in 1913-15, which had been host to Wyndham Lewis's earliest paintings, to the sculpture of Henri Gaudier-Brzeska, and to Ezra Pound's first translations from the Chinese. This was a Britain (or, not to put too fine a point on it, a London) that it was convenient to think had been snuffed out on the battlefields of the Somme, though Tomlinson suggested that on the contrary it was given its quietus only in the 1920s by the depraved insouciance of 'Bloomsbury'. As he wrote the history, it went like this:

> The wave of energy throughout Europe and England, which made men like Pound believe they were living in a new Renaissance, was spent in England by the First World War. It had its renewals in Paris. It reached Russia (until group antagonisms and political suppression ended it there) in the work of Malevitch, Popova, Kliun, Tatlin and the constructivists: . . . The Revolution extended for a while in Russia what the war and Bloomsbury sapped in England. Gaudier dead; Lewis impoverished; forgotten as a painter since, for ten years from 1921 onwards, he never exhibited; Pound demoralized and, like D. H. Lawrence, abandoning the England on which he had centred his hopes for a new age; Pound in Italy swallowing Mussolini whole. These were the sad facts of the twenties.

This would never do for a Poet Laureate. Who was Kliun, who was Tatlin, who were the constructivists? And if poetry was what we were concerned with, why all these mostly foreign names of painters, sculptors, architects? Moreover, Tomlinson was wrong in detail: it was not until the 1930s that Pound was 'swallowing Mussolini whole', and if Lewis did not exhibit in the 1920s, it was because he did not want to. But clearly what gave offence (as it did) was Tomlinson's imputation that England at any rate – never mind about Britain – had failed its artists and betrayed them; he could not help but be black-balled by people who had invested in a more consoling and self-congratulating version of English cultural history through seventy years. One sees clearly why Tomlinson, though on paper he was a candidate for the Laureateship that went to Ted Hughes, could never have been a serious contender.

Tomlinson's account of what international modernism was, and of the allegedly inglorious part in it played by the English intelligentsia deserves to be taken seriously, *but not necessarily by readers of his poetry.* This needs to be insisted on. Whatever Tomlinson's views of modernism, they do not define the only nor perhaps the most profitable perspective down which to see his achievement. They are not part of an enabling mythology to which we must give at least provisional assent if we are to enter this poet's imaginative world. For Tomlinson, like all the poets in this book, has been writing through a period when modernism was for good or ill irretrievably past; not forgotten nor forgettable, but already historical.

This shows up very interestingly in his translations. Through his career Tomlinson can be seen to have assumed that verse-translating was a special, and yet not *very* special, aspect of what it meant to be a poet. True, he could appeal for vindication of this opinion to a figure so far from modern as John Dryden, who accordingly is the hero of his *Poetry and Metamorphosis*. But in the present century the exemplar of this view was unavoidably Ezra Pound. For it was Pound who most notably in the twentieth century had acted on the assumption that we can see to have been Dryden's also: that the distinction commonly thought so clear-cut, between writing poetry and translating it, for some poets is not clear-cut in the least. And this was one point that Tomlinson's Clark Lectures elegantly insisted on. Thus his verse-translations, which in 1983 his publisher valuably excerpted into a separate volume, cannot be properly regarded as a different transaction from what was going on in the collections he put before the public as 'original'. His versions of Tyutchev, of Machado, of Lucio Piccolo and others, bulked as large in his oeuvre as Dryden's versions of Virgil and Juvenal and Ovid in his – a protestation which sounds less ringingly than it should, since Dryden's verse-translations are still not taken account of in the college classrooms of the 1980s.

In his brief but instructive comments on the poets he had translated, Tomlinson could not in honesty avoid sounding the note that had given offence in *Poetry and Metamorphosis*. We read for instance that 'Ungaretti, pulling against the current of d'Annunzian heroics, attempted in his early work something similar to that reconstruction of the syllable and the short verse line such as one finds in Pound and Williams . . . Eduardo Sanguineti . . . implies that the anguish and religiosity of the later work is a touch willed and that there is reason to prefer Ungaretti's moment of setting out . . .' The implication that discrimination was not only possible but necessary – even inside the oeuvre of a single poet, and him moreover a poet in a foreign language – could not fail to set teeth on edge. It asked for the exercise of abilities that most readers, including fellow-poets, knew they did not command. (Some things cannot be helped!) But the important point is that in practice Tomlinson showed himself far from doctrinaire, as we see if we look at his versions from Lucio Piccolo (1901-69), baron of Calanovella, cousin to that other Sicilian aristocrat, Lampedusa, author of *The Leopard*. For Piccolo, as Tomlinson acknowledged, composed his verses not syllable by syllable nor line by line but as it were in *slabs*:

> What days those were! and little was enough to make
> story and fable flourish, and the lip
> was prompt, the ear attentive amid the suspense
> of faces. The word was a sprig of corn in the wind
> dense with grains that the air
> scattered to perplexed city, to somnolent village,
> to far-off cottages.
> The skein-winder of the hours
> reeled-round times of quiet expectation,
> cool returns to the vast divans of patterned flowers.
> St Elmo's fire spelled safety
> in the sea storm and the serene Bear
> came back to shine
> tiptoeing on the sea
> before the beacon-lights, before the dark
> irresolution of the further coastline.

This has nothing to do with Pound or William Carlos Williams. It is perhaps Virgilian; or else it is, what Tomlinson called it, baroque. At all events it showed, with its persistent enjambements, how far Tomlinson's modernism was from being programmatic. He had let the idiom of the foreign author dictate what English idiom he would use in translating him; and so in his translations, and for that matter in his own poems, he would as often write flowingly as in the terse and tensely modern style that he applauded in Pound and Williams. Lucio Piccolo perhaps never asked himself, nor thought to ask, whether he was a modernist. And Tomlinson, translating him in the 1960s, appropriately waived the question. If this is what it means to be 'post-modern', then Tomlinson too is a post-modernist.

In giving so much attention to Charles Tomlinson at this point, it is not my intention to cast him in a starring role, alone on the stage and taking his bows as the curtain comes down. With only a little more trouble I could have focused on some other poet to prompt the same reflections. There is for instance F. T. Prince (b. 1912). Prince, to the best of my knowledge, has never delivered himself of opinions about modernism and, since he appears to be a notably non-combative person, it is easy to believe he might be uncomfortable with the opinionated stridency of an Ezra Pound. Yet from as long ago as 1938, with his 'Epistle to a Patron', through the relatively famous war-poem 'Soldiers Bathing', to *Walks in Rome* as recently as 1987, Prince has quietly assumed the liberties, and reached for the ambitious objectives that we associate with modernism. Just as in 'Soldiers Bathing' the anecdotal subject honestly announced in the title requires of Prince cross-lighting from a Michelangelo cartoon and a painting by Pollaiuolo as well as the Crucifixion, so in his latest poem his walks about the Holy City (he is Roman Catholic) have to be made resonant by allusions to a Petrarch *canzone* as translated by Thomas Wyatt, and to paintings by Caravaggio. Here too is a post-modernist; a poet who assumes that modernist procedures and assumptions have been assimilated, no longer needing to be argued for nor raucously foregrounded.

Cases like Tomlinson's and Prince's – and there are many such, as I hope preceding pages have shown – demonstrate that, whereas indeed several generations of British opinion-makers may have 'copped out' more or less shamefully, that cop-out is not carried like a brand of Cain by subsequent generations of British poets. Yet just that seems to be assumed, notably by American and Antipodean commentators who have listened to speeches for the prosecution by Tomlinson and others. They have the excuse of widely publicized British opinion-makers who even today exult in making London, as has been said, 'headquarters of articulate Philistia'. Among such reactionaries no one, I am afraid it must be said, is so blameable as the late Philip Larkin. Reading him, his confederates and epigones, foreign observers have been persuaded that the British have comfortably opted out from twentieth-century endeavour in poetry; that British poetry has chosen to turn inwards, parochial, self-comforting and serviceable, content to address no public outside the tight little islands. But this image can be sustained only if we trust the commentators and publicists more than the poets, and only if we embrace a historical determinism less defensible than that of Marxists. An unprejudiced reading of British poetry since 1960 (including, oddly enough, the poetry of Philip Larkin himself) gives the lie to any such high-handed account. That at least is the conclusion I find myself forced to, after reviewing the evidence.

Index